The Future of Private Equity

The Future of Private Equity

Beyond the Mega Buyout

Mark Bishop

First published 2012 by
PALGRAVE MACMILLAN

Palgrave Macmillan in the UK is an imprint of Macmillan Publishers Limited, registered in England, company number 785998, of Houndmills, Basingstoke, Hampshire RG21 6XS.

Palgrave Macmillan in the US is a division of St Martin's Press LLC, 175 Fifth Avenue, New York, NY 10010.

Palgrave Macmillan is the global academic imprint of the above companies and has companies and representatives throughout the world.

Palgrave® and Macmillan® are registered trademarks in the United States, the United Kingdom, Europe and other countries.

ISBN 978–0–230–35493–7

This book is printed on paper suitable for recycling and made from fully managed and sustained forest sources. Logging, pulping and manufacturing processes are expected to conform to the environmental regulations of the country of origin.

A catalogue record for this book is available from the British Library.

A catalog record for this book is available from the Library of Congress.

10   9   8   7   6   5   4   3   2   1
21 20 19 18 17 16 15 14 13 12

Printed and bound in Great Britain by
CPI Antony Rowe, Chippenham and Eastbourne

Contents

Figures

Acknowledgements

There are a great many people I'd like to thank for helping make this book possible. The most important of these are, of course, those who gave freely of their time and risked their professional reputations – during a period in which the private equity industry was under widespread attack by politicians and the media – to talk to me. I am conscious that the private equity industry is, by instinct as well as by name, private, and without their trust and co-operation this book would not have been possible.

Most of the resulting interviews, edited and abridged, and with introductory comments representing my personal opinions and observations, are to be found in this book. Sadly, there were a number of on-the-record conversations that I was unable to include in the published manuscript due to space constraints. These included contributions from the following:

- Cate Ambrose, Executive Director of the Latin American Venture Capital Association (LAVCA)
- Katherine Woodthorpe, Chief Executive of the Australian Private Equity and Venture Capital Association (AVCAL)
- Kathy Jeramaz-Larsen, Executive Director of the International Limited Partners Association (ILPA)
- Mahendra Swarup, President of the Indian Venture Capital Association (IVCA)
- Mark Florman, Chief Executive of the British Private Equity and Venture Capital Association (BVCA)
- Rhoddy Swire, Founder and Senior Partner, Pantheon Ventures (UK) LLP
- Sam Robinson, Head of Global Investment, SVG Capital
- Sarah Alexander, President and Chief Executive Officer, Emerging Markets Private Equity Association (EMPEA)

I apologise for the omission of their interviews; their comments informed my thinking hugely, so their influence is to be found throughout these pages.

There were a number of others within and close to the industry who spoke to me on condition of anonymity, to whom I would also like to extend thanks. I'm obviously unable to name them, but they know who they are. Also unnamed, but central to making the project possible, were numerous personal assistants and PRs who harried and cajoled busy people for diary time and chased down data; I appreciate their polite persistence.

I also owe gratitude to Sarah Laborde at TypeOut and Cathy Bennett at Fingertips and their teams, who produced most of the transcripts, and to my partner, Sarah Yearsley, who undertook the first wave of transcription and proofread the remainder: a Herculean task.

I wrote this book while completing a part-time executive MBA at Cranfield School of Management, where Drs Paul Baines, Ruth Bender and Catarina Figuera and Professor Mark Jenkins helped me variously with introductions to publishers and advice on content and style, and Barry Wilkins inspired me to proceed with the project. I believe that Cranfield is an excellent school, and I enjoyed my time there.

Finally I'd like to thank three individuals whose wise guidance was central to making this book happen. The first is Lisa von Fircks, my editor at Palgrave Macmillan, who shared my vision for the publication and commissioned me to write it; the second is her colleague Beverley Copland for her guidance and counsel as I worked on it. The third is Robert Mason, my partner in a small business we run that helps management teams secure private equity backing for buyouts, buy-ins, growth and turnaround, The Management Buy-Out Centre LLP. Himself the founder of a respected European mid-market private equity firm and an adviser to family offices on making investments into the PE sector, Robert gave freely of his expertise and contacts both in advising me on whom to interview and what to ask them and in making introductions to interviewees.

Introduction

History may well define January 2012, the month in which I began writing this book, as the nadir of the private equity industry. It opened with the issuance by Newt Gingrich's political action committee, Winning Our Future, of a 28-minute, seven-second video titled 'When Mitt Romney Came to Town'. Intended to associate the US Presidential candidate and co-founder of Bain Capital with the excesses of Wall Street by showcasing the plight of small-town Americans who had lost their livelihoods when Bain-backed companies downsized or became bankrupt, the film accused the firm, and by implication private equity as a whole, of over-leveraging investee businesses, asset-stripping and having no regard for the human consequences of its actions.

Barely a week later, the bond markets decided that the largest-ever leveraged buyout in history, KKR's and TPG's acquisition of the Dallas-based electricity company originally known as TXU Corporation (subsequently re-named Energy Future Holdings Corporation), was nearly certain to default on its $45 billion debt pile – more than 100 per cent of the $43.2 billion 2007 acquisition price. The two private equity behemoths had, in effect, placed a one-way bet on the premise that energy prices would continue to rise; in fact, demand was sapped by the Great Recession and the supply of domestically produced natural gas expanded with increased output from the USA's Marcellus shale fields.

Almost simultaneously, the founding partners of Carlyle Group walked into a storm of their own creation by proposing a flotation of the 28-year-old US buyout-to-financial-services firm on terms described by the *New York Times* as 'the most shareholder-unfriendly corporate governance structure in corporate history'. Provisions stipulated, among other things, that:

- the management team can elect the board of directors for as long as it and its affiliates own at least 10 per cent of the company;
- there will be no remuneration or nomination committees;

1

- there will be no annual shareholder meetings;
- the company can repurchase publicly held shares if they constitute less than 10 per cent of the firm's issued stock;
- shareholders are effectively unable to sue board directors for misconduct.

The Initial Public Offering was driven by the founders' desire to generate liquidity in the general partnership to facilitate succession planning and to fund the firm's continuing diversification away from private equity. While the aims may have been legitimate, the means appeared to contradict the group's stated mission, which commits partners to 'inspire the confidence and loyalty of [...] investors', 'demonstrate principled industry leadership' and 'be responsible and respected members of the global community'.

Meanwhile, in mainland Europe, intensifying fears over an impending Eurozone collapse, indications that the continent was slipping back into recession and the scrabble by banks to meet the European Banking Authority's requirement to increase their core tier one capital ratios to 9 per cent by the end of June conspired to produce a perfect storm of de-leverage. Not only did banks become reluctant to issue and roll over senior debt, but a number of mainland European banks with substantial exposure to private equity became forced sellers.

In my native UK, the 'good versus bad capitalism' debate opened by the leader of the opposition, Ed Miliband, at his party's conference the previous September was re-ignited by media coverage of the Romney video, the allegations in which echoed Miliband's criticisms of the conduct in the UK of another US buyout firm, Blackstone Capital Partners.

Blackstone is believed to have extracted close to £1 billion in value from care home provider Southern Cross Healthcare by disposing of the freeholds to its 750 properties through a sale-and-leaseback operation, prior to floating the operating company. In an uncanny parallel with the TXU deal, the US private equity firm signed up the healthcare provider to leases that tied it to stretching rents that would increase by 2.5 per cent per year, without apparent consideration of the risk that income from resident patients might not keep pace. In the UK, where many care home residents are funded by local authorities, public spending cuts caused Southern Cross to haemorrhage customers, with occupancy rates collapsing from 92 to 84 per cent, leaving the company unable to meet rental obligations. For much of the first half of 2011 it had seemed probable that vulnerable people, many of them in the final months or weeks of their lives, would be evicted, although eventually the government steered an orderly reversion of the properties to their landlords, who now either operate the homes independently or have let them to other operators at rents that reflect current economic conditions.

So private equity began 2012 facing attacks on both sides of the Atlantic from critics seeking to bracket it with investment banking as, to borrow a phrase used by then UK Prime Minister Ted Heath to describe Tiny Rowland's free-wheeling conduct as CEO of Lonrho, 'the unacceptable face of capitalism' and threatened by liquidity challenges in one of its most lucrative markets. It also faced a generational shift in capital flows.

While there is no consensus about when the industry was born – some say it traces its roots back to the Medici bank's partnership model in the 15th century, some to the 19th-century model under which Swedish banking families such as the Wallenbergs backed buy-in managements to provide succession for family businesses and others to the growth of the leveraged buyout under Kohlberg, Kravis and Roberts in the USA in the 1970s – there seems to be widespread industry consensus that half of the money ever committed to private equity was raised in the years 2002–2008. And that massive capital inflow ended, abruptly, with the arrival of the global financial crisis of 2008.

Today, the industry is no longer able to attract capital on anything like the scale of KKR's $17.64 billion 2006 Fund, thought to be the largest-ever private equity fundraise. In Europe, where mid-size buyouts are more commonplace, it's the firms specialising in that type of transaction that have been worst hit. Unable to raise new capital, some are suspected by investors of delaying portfolio realisations in order to continue to collect management fees and in the hope that funding conditions will improve. They are widely known as 'zombie funds'.

There are a number of reasons why developed-world buyout firms are finding it hard to raise capital, other than the obvious global economic shock and its aftermath. These funds put money to work principally in sizeable, highly leveraged buyouts. With hindsight, I argue that the returns generated by these investments were artificially enhanced by a happy coincidence of economic conditions that are unlikely to return for some years, and that – as TXU and Southern Cross, and many of the firms mentioned in the Romney film learned to their cost – these gains were won at the expense of a high *beta*, or volatility, a subject I will return to later in this book.

Finally, at least for the individual investment professionals senior enough to be entitled to share in the capital uplift generated by private equity fund managers, the furore over Mitt Romney's bid for the Republican nomination re-ignited debate about one of the most controversial aspects of the industry's remuneration policies: namely, that the overwhelming proportion of the incomes of the best-paid, highest-profile practitioners comes in the form of capital gains, which are taxed in most countries at lower rates than salaries – in Romney's case, at around 15 per cent, the US capital gains rate.

For readers not familiar with the fundamentals of how private equity firms are structured and individuals are remunerated, here's a brief summary. Most private equity firms are limited, or limited liability, partnerships. Two classes of partner are recognised: limited and general. Limited partners ('LPs') are the investors, typically pension funds, university endowments, sovereign wealth funds or wealthy family offices; the general partner ('GP') is the fund manager. The fund manager receives at least two forms of recompense.

First, it takes an annual management fee, which is intended to cover the running costs of the firm, including salaries for employees. Typically this is 2 per cent of the funds under management, with the mega-buyout firms typically charging a lower percentage as they are able to exploit economies of scale, and many firms tapering charges during the second five years of a typical fund's ten-year life, during which it is managing and exiting portfolio companies, rather than acquiring new ones. In recent times there has been a trend towards greater transparency, with general partners providing budgets to justify their outgoings, and greater push-back against GPs earning additional fees on transactions or for monitoring portfolio companies.

But it's the second part of the package that is controversial. Traditionally most, if not all, employees actively engaged in the management of a fund receive a share of the uplift in capital value achieved for investors (known as the carried interest or, colloquially, 'the carry'). This is traditionally set at 20 per cent of the uplift, above an agreed hurdle rate (often an internal rate of return of 8 per cent). Coincidentally, Bain Capital, Mitt Romney's firm, is rumoured to have commanded until recently an industry-leading 30 per cent.

Given that many funds, and especially those specialising in highly leveraged, large deals, hold relatively small portfolios and hence employ surprisingly few investment professionals, a large gain can be distributed among a small number of people, leading them to become very wealthy. KKR co-founder Henry Kravis, for instance, was estimated to be worth $3.7 billion by *Forbes* magazine in September 2011.

With President Obama already threatening to introduce a 'Buffett Rule' that would address legendary investor Warren Buffett's discomfort at the observation that, in common with most of the USA's wealthiest citizens, he pays tax at a lower rate than his secretary, the media seized on whether carry should be taxed as ordinary income, as opposed to capital gains.

There is no doubt that private equity faces many challenges. But it is far too early to proclaim the death of the industry. On the contrary, in emerging markets it is growing fast, and is attracting record amounts of investment. Asia alone is estimated to have accounted for 22 per cent of the capital raised globally in 2011, according to analysts at Prequin, almost outstripping for the first time Europe's 23 per cent share; just three years earlier, the Far East won just 9 per cent of inflows to the asset class. Indeed, just as TXU started looking terminal in early 2012, KKR was rumoured to be working on the largest-ever Asia fund, expected to total up to $6 billion in commitments. Similarly, single-country funds in China and India continue to prosper, and even African private equity, an investment formerly the preserve of development finance institutions (DFIs) such as the World Bank's International Finance Corporation, the UK's CDC and France's Proparco, now has sufficient track record of attractive returns to be attracting private sector capital.

And even within developed markets there are niches within private equity that have proved far more resilient than the mega buyout, in which capable fund managers are achieving very attractive capital uplifts against a backdrop of economic uncertainty and in a low interest-rate environment in which most other asset classes are failing to achieve their long-run average returns.

While there is much to criticise about the excesses of the mega-buyout boom of the Noughties, I make no apologies for taking an overall supportive approach to the industry. Where private equity creates genuine, lasting value in portfolio businesses through the provision of expertise and active shareholder involvement not experienced by publicly quoted firms, I believe that society benefits. Furthermore, the lion's share of the returns generated by the industry accrue to the many, rather than the few: private equity has long been the best-performing asset class invested in by pension funds and university endowments that have enabled many Americans of modest means to obtain degrees they would otherwise have been unable to afford and funded pioneering research that has benefited the world as a whole. And in countries that lack developed public markets or commercial banking sectors, economic growth can be stalled by a lack of capital; the best private equity firms not only provide the motive power of development but also bring with them higher corporate, social and environmental governance standards.

So it is against a complicated but fascinating backdrop that I began committing words to screen. I am privileged to have an opportunity to write about the future of an industry at a crossroads, its previous business model arguably unfit for purpose in an age of de-leveraging, but with new paradigms being explored, and some flourishing, in both developed and emerging economies.

Most of the chapters in this book are based on one-on-one interviews with private equity professionals. Taken together, they represent every continent on the planet, bar Antarctica. Some hold senior positions in established private equity firms, while others have founded their own; they range from well-known *éminences grises* who came to prominence two decades or more ago to a new generation of challengers, many of whose names are relatively unknown outside the industry but who, I believe, represent the best of the newcomers now driving the industry's future. Still more are analysts or advisers, or run professional associations.

There are a handful of people who spoke, some or all the time, on condition of anonymity and a number who kindly gave their time for interviews which informed my thinking but which I was unfortunately unable to accommodate in these pages. I have referred to their insights *en passant* where relevant. But it is heartening, for an industry that is often accused of a lack of transparency, that only two of my requests for interviews with GP (fund manager) representatives were declined, with one being excusable due to genuine mitigating circumstances.

Section I
An Industry at a Crossroads

1
Introduction

On the grounds that those who fail to learn lessons from history are determined to repeat it, I planned to begin my quest for insights about the future of private equity by interviewing people who have been active and successful in the industry for many years and have therefore seen it operate across several economic cycles.

But first I thought it productive to define the asset class, and to explore whether the definition has changed over time. Technically, I suppose that 'private equity' ought to mean equity in any company that is not publicly traded or owned by the state. However, in practice it excludes closely held private businesses, such as owner-managed ones and those rare beasts, private companies held for extended periods or in perpetuity by collective investment vehicles, such as Warren Buffett's Berkshire Hathaway. So any satisfactory definition should include the fact that these are collective, professionally managed investments in private companies, held temporarily with the intention of profitable divestment.

In practice, all firms that are referred to broadly as private equity tend also to adhere to the LP/GP (limited and general partner) model. However, there can be variations to this paradigm. First, either the general partner – the asset manager – or the limited partner (the source of capital) may be publicly quoted. As previously observed, Carlyle Group and KKR are among the first-generation US buyout firms that have part-floated their general partnerships in recent years. Motivations can include a desire for older partners to achieve liquidity at retirement, a requirement for additional capital to be injected at the GP rather than LP level to fund diversification, and making it possible to offer incoming investment professionals liquid equity incentivisation.

But it's when the limited partner is a quoted entity that, for me, things start to get interesting, because the model overcomes one of the most often repeated assertions about private equity: namely, that it is a high-performing asset class from which people on average incomes are excluded. The criticism is misleading in that, as I mentioned in the Introduction, most limited partners are institutions investing pension money or sovereign wealth on behalf of individuals of modest means or university endowments that support students from disadvantaged backgrounds and fund important research. But there's a kernel of truth in that people of average means are unable to make direct investments into most private equity funds – except, of course, those that are publicly quoted.

In the USA, such funds are typically structured as Business Development Corporations (BDCs). These pass through income and gains free from corporation tax, much like a limited partnership, except that they are able to issue shares. In the UK, which is also the centre of the private equity industry for mainland Europe, quoted private equity is a mix of conventional public limited companies such as 3i, which operates separately listed conventional and infrastructure funds, and investment trusts (for instance, HgCapital, Electra and Dunedin). Both these and the US BDCs tend to manage smaller capital pools than many conventional private equity firms, suggesting that the big limited partners that can meet the minimum investment size of the closed-end funds and operate with investment horizons that do not require instant liquidity prefer to steer clear of such funds.

Second, there are private equity firms that invest limited partners' money in other private equity funds, known as funds of funds. There are three attractions to this approach: first, by aggregating small investors' stakes, they can enable people who would otherwise not afford to do so to participate in funds that impose high minimum-investment thresholds; second, by investing in a number of funds rather than one, they offer diversification; and third, fund-of-fund managers are well placed to acquire knowledge about the track records of general partners and hence should be able to steer money towards the better-performing ones and away from the laggards. The drawback, of course, is that they introduce a second tier of general partner, and with it, a second management fee and share of carry. The hope is that by directing capital to the better underlying GPs, fund-of-fund GPs generate returns that compare favourably with the market, even after these additional fees.

Major investors can employ people or engage advisers with expertise in identifying the better GPs that perform similar roles to fund-of-fund managers. So the fund-of-fund approach tends to be popular with investors who wish to diversify away from their core geography, such as US investors wanting to build modest stakes in Europe, or USA or European LPs wishing to invest in Asia.

However, it would seem that the investors who stand to gain the most from the expertise and diversification offered by fund-of-fund managers are small-scale private investors, who also require a listed structure. So it is unsurprising that there are a number of quoted funds of funds. Two of the most interesting are London-based: Pantheon International Participations and SVG Capital.

In practice, the latter began life largely as a quoted vehicle for those wishing to invest in the mid- to large-cap European buyout firm Permira, although it is diversifying away from that firm over time. Both are run by high-profile, respected individuals who have been in the industry for a long time, who kindly granted me interviews for this book.

There's a final aspect to defining the industry: namely, to distinguish between it and venture capital. Until 1978, when Jerome Kohlberg, Henry Kravis and George Roberts raised the world's first dedicated leveraged buyout fund (a mere $32 million), the two investment classes were barely differentiated, with many firms that we now recognise as private equity specialists having their roots in venture capital but also providing growth capital to later-stage businesses and acquiring control stakes or achieving outright buyouts when offered suitable opportunities, in the early days using little or no debt.

Today, if anything, the situation has reversed. The British Venture Capital Association (BVCA) – the membership of which consists predominantly of private equity firms, but whose name reflects the profession's venture heritage – provides the following definition on its website of the difference between private equity and venture capital:

> Often the source of confusion, in Europe venture capital is a specific component of the private equity industry and refers to when funds used to invest in companies in the seed, [...] start-up [...] and early stages of development. In turn, private equity denotes management buyouts and buy-ins.
>
> In general venture capital funds invest in companies at an early stage in their development when they often have little or no track record and are cash-hungry. In contrast, private equity funds invest in more mature companies with the aim to eliminate inefficiencies and drive growth.

It seems to me that the key differentiator between private equity and venture capital is that firms invested in by the former are, or have until recently been, profitable, whereas those backed by the latter have not yet reached that milestone, and require injections of working capital to fund growth.

As we will see later in this book, some of the most innovative practitioners in private equity, particularly in emerging markets, are beginning to blur this distinction – to good effect. But the overall focus of the work will be the future of private equity, meaning buyouts and buy-ins of established businesses.

2

Jon Moulton, Chairman, Better Capital LLP

My first interview is with a man well known to followers of UK private equity: Jon Moulton. Often controversial, he is in many ways the conscience of the industry, willing to take a public stand in criticising his peers when he thinks they are going astray. In the boom prior to 2008, he was one of the few practitioners openly to criticise the levels of debt others were taking on, telling Maggie Lee of *The Independent* in 2006:

> Over the last six years it's been easy to raise debt. This flood of fresh capital into the market has enabled buyers to pay more for companies. While you can make a lot of money in the buyout market just by watching the debt multiple ascend, there'll come a point when portfolio companies will find it tough to repay the interest on their loans; and at that point we'll see liquidations and distressed companies.

Always one to translate opportunity into action, Moulton positioned his then firm, Alchemy, to make money from this distressed debt, launching a £300 million fund for the purpose. Unfortunately his partners wanted to pursue other strategies, so he quit and founded Better Capital, a London-based, publicly quoted turnaround private equity (PE) firm. At the time of writing it is one of the very few listed PE vehicles to trade at a premium to net asset value – a sign, perhaps, of the market's confidence in Moulton.

Better Capital's website includes a high-hearted A-to-Z of private equity that typifies the man's take-no-prisoners, straight-talking approach. It includes such gems as:

> B is for ... Business plan. Expansive and unrealistic document
> O is for ... Over-leverage. The natural state of megafund portfolio companies. Recently the nation too
> J is for ... Jersey [the Channel Islands tax haven]. Where many VC [venture capital] funds are domiciled. Because they like the weather.

Moulton's career in many respects mirrors the development of the industry in the UK and USA. A chartered accountant, he entered the profession in 1980 with Citicorp Ventures in New York, a venture capital firm transitioning into buyouts. The following year he returned to the UK to run Citicorp's similar UK business. Four years later he and Nick Ferguson launched Schroder Ventures, which is generally believed to have raised the UK's first-ever institutional buyout fund. While the firm initially concentrated on ventures and small buyouts, over time it raised larger funds and, after a difficult period, was bought out from Schroders and became the mid- to large-cap European buyout house Permira – presaging two notable trends, namely buyouts and re-brandings of firms linked to other financial sector parents and the growth in fund size.

After Schroder Ventures, Moulton worked alongside another controversialist, Sir Ronald Cohen, at Apax, prior to striking out on his own, founding Alchemy in 1997. There he achieved prominence with the general public for the first time with his prescient if ultimately unsuccessful bid to buy Rover cars. Given Moulton's background, I felt his interview would make a great start to this book, since he can provide an excellent context for where the industry now stands, based on how it has evolved, and from that base, offer projections of where it is going.

* * *

MB: What have been the principal changes to the private equity industry since you came into it?

JM: It was an absolutely miserable pin-head of a business when I came into it. 1981 was essentially the launch of what became the BVCA [British Venture Capital Association]. There were about 20 people and you knew everybody. Now you have not much chance of even knowing a tiny fragment of the industry. The industry doesn't really meet so you don't really know your competition. You don't work with each other or stand lunch. The scale of the industry has fantastically increased.

The second thing is the really serious growth and concentration on large buyout, mega buyouts and large-/mid-market deals. That's where 80 or perhaps 85 per cent of the money goes now. The industry has become very much brand-name, large-ticket with very different dynamics.

Third, whereas people used to be hands-on, doing things themselves, in a large firm you can have an office of 20 investment professionals that does a deal most years so most of the team realistically are working on deals that never happen, flogging their way through an auction process and a relatively small proportion of the firm is involved with portfolio companies, portfolio issues, changing management or whatever. It's quite a different world from the days when I started, when we used to work in the early or even late 1980s on roughly three deals per investment professional per annum.

MB: That ratio doesn't exist much any more, does it?

JM: No. Now we are as active as any other company going and we are doing about one per person per annum whereas for the large firms, I think it's more like 0.1.

MB: Is the two-plus-20 model broken or at risk? There is a school of thought that says that if the 2 per cent [annual management fee, intended to cover the running costs of the firm] enables you to have surplus investment professionals, it is too high.

JM: You don't need them. The observed fact though is that mega-funds have been very successful [in attracting capital]: investors seem to be prepared to go with brand names. You've also watched the larger managers morph into semi-quoted vehicles, the Blackstones, the KKRs of this world, where the two-plus-20 model is really quite odd because there's quite a lot of the fees and carry being shared with shareholders who clearly don't add value to companies. The economics are being shared with a lot of people who don't actually have anything to do with the deals.

MB: You're talking here about the flotation of the GP, rather than the LP? Because using publicly quoted liquidity as you have done for raising funds for limited partners is surely a different matter; there's a democratisation argument that says it reduces the minimum entry point to private equity and a practical one for institutional shareholders that it gives them a market price for their holdings at any point in time and the possibility of liquidity whenever they need it.

JM: Yes, I think quoted LPs are fine, they're good. At Better Capital we are essentially a distributing, funding, quoted format. The fees are low. There's no options schemes, no long-term incentive plans, nothing. We report at least the detail of any private firm, probably more. We provide all the legal protections you get in a private fund plus the very simple one. Buy 51 per cent of a public company and you can do what you want! Much more powerful than no-fault clauses. Institutions like it.

MB: Returning to the issue of publicly listed general partners, you could argue that in a conventional firm the shareholders deserve a return on their equity because you need their capital in order to operate the firm, but in private equity, where the investment is coming from the limited partners, you don't need it. It is just a liquidity event for the original partners.

JM: It's just a way for the general partner to flog part of his interest and trouser some more money. And as for the morphing of these large firms which have grown, and in some cases have always had, their advisory sides, hedge fund activities, generalised investment management – it's interesting how they are tending to become conglomerates in the financial world themselves. History shows that the private equity arms of the big banks and insurance companies pretty well universally became independent. We are actually seeing a reversal of that process.

MB: Is there a school of thought that says that these mega-funds were very successful in the past because of market conditions and leverage levels, but they may not be going forward, and that's why they are now diversifying away from private equity?

JM: Maybe. What you have seen is really quite different epochs. The right thing to do in 2004 was to buy any asset with whatever you had to pay to get it. Lever it up to the armpits and flog it by 2007. That was a great business model. That generated a very large percentage of the record of the industry because that was the period when rising prices, very high levels of leverage and scale really applied to the industry.

We had this fantastic wall of money invested in 2005–2008, where not far off half the total of all the money that has ever been put to work by private equity was invested in three years. The businesses are largely still sitting in GPs' portfolios. If interest rates had been high, the results would have been catastrophic. So the industry has been through some interesting times. People were predicting 50 per cent failure rates in 2008. It hasn't happened because interest rates have been kept low because it would have taken the sovereigns down. So returns in the mega world definitely have come down.

Much of the return now is tied up in relatively theoretical valuations of the portfolio, which range in practice from quite conservative to laughably optimistic. In recent quarters, public markets have been very volatile. The mega-funds are a lot more highly geared than public markets, so their volatility should be higher. But quoted private equity firms seldom reflect that in their NAVs [net asset valuations].

MB: I guess that's why so much quoted private equity is valued a discount to NAV – the good guys are tarred with the same brush as the bad, and people are wary of the underlying valuations.

JM: Yes, in 2008 you were seeing people valuing the mega-funds and their quoted stuff on methodologies such as their own estimates of year four's profits multiplied by the median price earnings ratio of the S&P [Standard & Poor's 500] for the last 15 years. That was roughly the methodology that Blackstone were using. There isn't the return, so the mega-funds realistically now haven't got a compelling return argument. It's a bit of diversification for investors, and it's very convenient for investors because they can put a big lump of money away in one go.

MB: Because of the changes in the economy it's unlikely anyone can replicate what happened in 2005–2007, but funds that are specialised and transform the inherent value of a business are perhaps going to be the ones dealing with the better returns in the current environment.

JM: Yes. They are limited in size, but they are people who do really specialist bits of private equity. They may do nothing but asset managers, or in the USA you get funds that do nothing but communications equipment. Things like that. They provide an opportunity at least and sometimes the reality of very superior returns. That's not the general reality of the industry, though. The general reality of the industry is auction process, large buyout, commodity financings, equal access to excellent management. Big funds can really attract very high-quality people because lots of money is swilling around – big companies, powerful positions, you can get very good people into those roles. It's hard to get a competitive edge because this stuff is all pretty well public domain.

MB: If you were launching a new fund now, not as a direct competitor to Better Capital but to find a new niche, what segment would you look for in the private equity market that can create superior returns?

JM: It depends on the geography. If I'm in India, the economy is growing very quickly – while you can have some spectacular failings you can also have some very big wins – so in that sort of environment I would look at ventures and development capital. In the UK, which is currently experiencing a long period of low growth, I favour poking away at distress and turnaround rather than trying to back anything that relies on explosive growth.

Again all these statements are of a general nature. There are exceptions, so you look at retail. High Street retail is horrible in the UK at the moment. We've seen endless trouble with retailers. But internet retailing is going well. So there are always bits that are working. People made good money at Dunkirk clearing the beaches, so there's always some angle. But angles are smaller in a low-growth economy.

MB: The picture you are painting is that the opportunities in the future are about picking attractive niches, which may be quite small. Clearly the private equity industry has grown a lot in the past 30 years. Has it become too big – and will it now contract?

JM: I think the answer probably is that it's grown somewhere close to its reasonable limits. It's very hard to say what its limits should be. You need a period of two or three years of success or failure to attract money into the area or force it away. The structures which I've always believed to be really quite inefficient in the industry allow people to fail slowly; people don't quit the market in great quantity. What have we lost? Forstmann Little. That went completely, vanished without trace; it was a large firm. That's about it. So firms of scale that die away are going to be quite small in number.

MB: There are firms, which some call 'zombies' or 'the walking dead', that have portfolios to manage but have been unable to raise new funds. Will they die eventually? There are quite a few of them.

JM: There are going to be more of those. Alchemy hasn't been able to raise any fresh equity. It may well be a casualty. Others? There are a lot of mid-market firms struggling to make a difference. Call it 85, perhaps 90, mid-market private equity firms operating in London. They are doing between them at the moment only about 40 or 50 deals a year. There's got to be a thinning-out of that group. It's very sad.

MB: It might take the life of a fund, though, because many of them haven't yet put to work all the capital committed in the boom [estimated to be $924.9 billion of undrawn commitments from 2006–2008 alone by Altius Associates, as at 31 December 2011].

JM: If you get half-way through the fund and you haven't done very well, the logical course of action is to invest the rest very slowly and let it drag out for a couple of years' extension. You've got maybe seven years to sort it out. Not many industries give you that luxury.

MB: I guess once a firm has the investors' cash, there's not much they can do about it.

JM: The number of firms actually ever closed down by investors in the UK is I think, two.

MB: There's another growth area of private equity that's not so visible in the UK, which is the growth of the industry in the developing world. That's been quite spectacular, hasn't it? Much of the money raised this year has gone to South America and Asia.

JM: You would expect it. Western economies are mostly growing little, if at all, and the BRIC [Brazil, Russia, India, China] and other so-called emerging economies are hurtling past them. If you are looking for growth and prosperity, Singapore is wonderful compared to the Western world: economy under control, orderly, nice set of legals, a great place to do private equity. Compare that with trying to do a deal in the Eurozone without any real certainty of what currency they're going to be denominated in within three years' time, and it's pretty obvious what you want to do.

MB: What about the counter-argument that says debt is harder to obtain and the risk is greater, due to lack of transparency in some developing markets?

JM: Yes, there's no question that some of the emerging markets are bloody risky places: you've got corruption, weak rule of law. Russia is an obvious example, where private equity is purely for the brave or the well protected. I'll never forget being offered a job in Russia which featured weekly commutes from Moscow and a bodyguard. Do I really need a bodyguard? And is one enough?

MB: In some of those places, there's the feeling that if you co-invest with those who have influence or are close to the seat of power, or have them among your LPs, you are more likely to be OK ...

JM: Yes, you can definitely make money. On the other hand, it's difficult for institutions, as some of this stuff is on the ragged edge of honest. Some of it's not the ragged edge. Some of it's the wrong side. The rule of law is quite important to be able to invest properly in places. Some places don't have it, but others do, and many of those places that don't have it are progressively acquiring it. There are very few places turning themselves into the Wild West, most of them become more civilised as their economies become more sophisticated. So a large chunk of the world offers better prospects medium to long term than the UK and the Western world.

MB: Have you thought about setting up a fund specialising in emerging markets?

JM: I have one objection to it. The wife. She would kill me! I am too old. I've done quite a bit in the emerging markets, and if I was a younger lad now, then no question, I wouldn't be in London.

MB: Singapore?

JM: Yes, it's my favourite. It's easy, the language works. They are dead straight, straighter than London. One of the things that has happened in the industry is a definite loss of old-fashioned straightforwardness and integrity. Competition has forced people to pursue unethical practices. Investment bankers producing projections that nobody believes in. It's now endemic in the industry. We've got the accountants producing vendor due diligence reports which, quite frankly, could be signed by Enid Blyton for the amount of validation that's gone into some of them. We work on turnaround, so we see all the bad stuff.

MB: A fair number of US firms, particularly the big ones, have gone into India and China in a large way, and yet UK firms haven't to the same degree. Why not?

JM: UK-led firms really haven't prospered greatly internationally. Permira was doing, but it had a bad patch a couple of years ago and that's stopped it in its tracks. CVC has done pretty well. Have other UK firms done well internationally? Doughty Hanson really hasn't prospered outside the UK. Anybody else? Cinven did, but not for long.

MB: It's strange, isn't it? There's so much expertise in private equity in the UK, you'd think that we'd be exporting those skills.

JM: The same thing has happened to a lot of our financial services industry – UK-centred investment banks don't exist any more.

MB: At least there are plenty of deals going through London that are involving companies in other countries.

JM: The UK remains a very vibrant, substantial, financial services centre. It probably will unless we allow Europe to kill it, which we might. The Alternative Investment Fund Management Directive – an incomprehensible piece of junk without any actual objectives – it's hilarious to read, but it's going to be very painful to operate with. Increased regulations are a force that drives toward bigger firms because the regulatory overheads are the same whether you manage £200 million or £20 billion. There's some poor sod who's got to read all that stuff all day. The big firms are quite keen on regulation.

MB: Is there a school of thought that says that high regulatory standards are a form of reassurance to limited partners?

JM: No. There's no demand for regulation among limited partners, particularly of the kind of stuff that's actually in the IFM [Alternative Investment Fund Managers Directive]. Hardly anybody knows what's in it. If you've got a few days you are prepared to waste, then try reading it. What do investors want? They'd like reporting. They'd like honesty, no backhanders. What else do they need? Not a lot really! Let them go and have a look at the detail of the IFM. See if they can make any sense out of requirements for third-party custodians, third-party valuations. Is it cost-effective? No! Auditing the valuations of private equity firms is the job for an astrologer.

MB: Could it actually force some firms out of the UK?

JM: Yes. It certainly will, and the EU too.

MB: So that leaves you with alternatives such as the Channel Islands?

JM: They are in an odd and, at the moment, reasonably favoured position, as is Switzerland. Whether that remains so is anybody's guess. What it does is it makes the asset-class less attractive. It's a cost.

MB: I guess another factor affecting returns is the debt market. There's a lot less leverage available, and on very different terms from before.

JM: Since the crisis there have been very brief glimpses of reasonable leverage, but then it vanishes. The banks have gradually been forced to admit the reality of their balance sheets.

MB: That's one of the weirdest things, isn't it? There's talk about extra regulation in areas like private equity and hedge funds, and yet huge banks, even ones part-owned by the state, have balance sheets that are works of fiction, sometimes on a spectacular scale, and the people working in them admit it.

JM: I've had conversations with numerous bankers over the last couple of years which make you pretty much giggle when you look at the tier 1 capital. Barclays, HBOS and RBS have three different definitions of it.

MB: Quoted companies here and in the USA are subject to the same borrowing constraints and are hoarding cash because they worry about whether they can roll over debts and whether there could be another financial crisis on the horizon. So in a sense is it a level playing field, but with the valuations of target companies coming down to make up for the lack of leverage?

JM: While deals have been done with remarkably 100 per cent equity, it takes very aggressive assumptions to believe that the excess costs inevitably associated with both the transactions and the management of private equity can be overcome. A typical private equity transaction has execution costs in the order of 6 to 8 per cent, in and out.

MB: You've got to add a lot of value to overcome that kind of inertia over a typical hold period. There is a suggestion that holds will take longer, and many of the deals that were done in the boom are not going to be exited any time soon.

JM: Exit periods are just steadily drifting out at the moment. Long holding periods seem to be more likely than not. The average fund is actually something round about 14 years now, and not ten anyway by the extensions. We will see more of that.

MB: That is bad for the IRR [internal rate of return] because they are not going to get any higher valuation on the exit, they are just going to take longer to get there.

JM: Yes, but don't forget those transaction costs are better spread over a longer period. If you can actually get a company to do well for seven years, throwing off cash, then hold it for seven years. If, on the other hand, you are just hanging on for grim death and collecting the management fees, then it's not good for the investors. It's only when they are exposed to the hard reality that some firms will realise that the returns need the fees to be 1 per cent and not 2.

MB: Given the reduced leverage and extended hold periods, combined with the excess staffing and difficulties in raising new funds, I am surprised there aren't GPs already differentiating themselves by running much leaner structures and lower fees.

JM: I'm surprised that nobody has; the opportunity for somebody to enter as a low-cost mega-fund is all too obvious. Sooner or later somebody will. It might be a new entrant. It might very well turn out to be somebody from the Far East who thinks that actually making a couple of million quid a year is quite enough to keep him going. If you raise a $5 billion fund at 1 per cent, you've got $50 million a year. You can run a quite reasonable business out of that, maybe on even half that figure. The mega-funds are taking out, as you'll have seen from the studies, 80-odd per cent of their revenues in management fees, rather than carried interest.

MB: That ratio seems the wrong way round, from the perspective of aligning the fund manager's interests with investors'.

JM: Very much so.

MB: What would happen if somebody good offered to run a fund for no management fees at all, and make their return solely from carried interest?

JM: It would work, as long as they managed the overheads for the first few years.

MB: Any working capital needed in the early years would effectively be the general partner's investment in the fund because it would be what they would sacrifice in order to get the carry.

JM: One of the things investors are gradually waking up to is the best thing they can do is to get people like me to put a good chunk of money into the fund on exactly the same terms as them. Very often it hasn't been done like that. It has been deemed an investment from rolling up management fees, money borrowed from the fund, all this kind of stuff.

MB: It's not a real investment then, is it? Real investment on the same terms as the LPs makes a lot of sense.

JM: Our own firm is putting in nearly 10 per cent of the capital in our fund.

MB: I can see that this is possible for a small, specialist fund such as yours. [Better Capital's first fund was £210 million.] But what about the mega-funds: surely it's hard for the partners to raise a meaningful percentage of the fund from their own resources?

JM: Actually, large funds don't find it so hard, or at least they didn't. The banks, in order to get the leverage loan business, were offering limited recourse or no-recourse loans to the staff of mega-funds to invest into their own funds.

MB: That's an interesting conflict of interest, isn't it?

JM: Yes. But it happened.

MB: That touches on the question of whether the bad reputation that the public now bestows on private equity is largely the fault of the banks, because in making the big loans, it could be argued that bankers were acting irresponsibly by being driven by commission that was paid, as the money went out of the door, rather than being based on than the actual returns made by the banks, which were contingent on those loans actually being honoured.

JM: It's a bloody reality. They are driven absolutely by ludicrous, fat, short-term remuneration packages, and that's not much to do with the banks, it's more to do with the people. It was all about deals done. Nobody ever asked whether it came out the other end or not. It's an integrity issue, and people really were just living for the day and screw the future. Unfortunately that applied to countries as well as the banks.

MB: There's an interesting philosophical point, and I would be interested in your view on this. There's integrity which can mean acting in a way that is more principled than the law requires you to and that is against your economic interests. Then there is acting as an economically efficient animal, allocating capital and resources in the most effective way, within the law. They can be in conflict.

JM: I am personally more in favour of the former than the pure market argument. The pure market argument involves handing out very large amounts of misery to people who don't deserve it. Good economic results leave society with extremity of distribution of wealth. The situation now, where a mid-ranking banker earns perhaps five times the salary of a Chief Executive of a manufacturing concern of size, is very silly.

MB: It's illogical, isn't it, but there are reasons why that happened. An integrity approach would suggest they should voluntarily forfeit some of that salary, whereas a market argument would say that pay is too high because profits are too high, because there are too few big banks for there to be real competition. Mergers and acquisition activity in the banking sector that was allowed perhaps, with hindsight, shouldn't have been.

JM: There's no question that the structures of the industry are behind this. To some extent the same things are emerging in private equity. The very large firms at the moment really don't represent a competitive threat. There have been one or two twitches towards it in the USA – you'll have seen the litigation that's going on there. The banks, on the other hand, the returns that are available for the individuals in the banks regardless of what the returns are for the shareholders, because actually nobody really knows what that number is, including the shareholders, imply that there isn't adequate competition in the marketplace.

MB: So there needs to be more competition?

JM: Yes, which is why the banks are screaming like smoked pigs over being threatened with being broken up. On the very narrowest of definitions, banks cost us a third of our drop in the GDP [gross domestic product] in the financial crisis. On a broader definition, probably two-thirds. So the cost to society of having the banks like this is enormous. So you have a governmental issue of scale. Government has to create a situation where the banking sector is not such a threat to the economy. It has a tremendous impact on the economy, and it's a threat. It'll happen again because it hasn't been sorted.

MB: I wonder whether, not just this government but governments generally, are unnecessarily scared about the banking industry because the bankers say, look we're very mobile, we can get on a plane to Switzerland or Singapore, wherever?

JM: That's the wrong answer. The Singaporeans run their banks pretty well. You don't want 20 per cent of the economy in the banking sector if it means that your economy goes completely tits up every ten years.

MB: For that we either need to shrink them or we need to grow everything else.

JM: Preferably the latter. Although we won't grow the latter until we get the state smaller. And deal with our debts. There's only three things you can do with debt: service it, inflate it, default. I expect to see some combination of these things.

MB: With most of the UK's debts in long-term and in our own currency, presumably inflation will feature in the solution for Britain. Which means the current low-interest rate environment we're in now won't persist for ever.

JM: Until this current period, base rates in the UK have been below 4 per cent for just 13 months out of the last 25 years. When you consider that there's a mountain of very highly leveraged, aggressively financed, overpaid deals done in the past few years, actually the number of failures is really very small – low interest rates have rescued the industry. So just think how it would look at 4 per cent, let alone 8.

MB: A good time to be running a turnaround fund!

JM: We wouldn't be able to handle it. The numbers now are quite remarkable. If the base rates went back to 5 per cent, it's perfectly reasonable to assume the deal-flow will increase by a factor of 10.

MB: Returning to the issue of the country's fiscal position, there have been calls to revisit the taxation of general partners in private equity. What are your thoughts on that?

JM: The reality is private equity has been lowly taxed. Some high-profile people in the industry have been incredibly tax-averse. Paying much more than 10 per cent is unnecessary and can be done without anything that involves offshore status or anything, just using the current partnership law in the UK. It's called 'basis shifting'. It's remarkable how many members of the industry have resorted to avoiding paying tax on management fees and their head office is at Luxembourg or some other location so that they can evade tax completely. It's not a very graceful thing to see.

I personally have paid full income tax, capital gains tax and stayed a UK resident throughout my life. I have a house in Guernsey, so everyone assumes I live there but I really don't. The industry needs to be more straightforward about paying a reasonable level of tax. A simple tax regime for private equity that resulted in people paying tax at something like the entrepreneurs' rate would increase the amount of tax to a more equitable rate.

MB: While we're on the topic of tax, should the system be used to redress the anomaly under which interest is a tax-deductible expense for firms but dividends aren't? It might reduce the current bias in favour of high leverage.

JM: There's no question, one of the big benefits of the industry is a very simple one. The investors in the industry, pension funds, don't pay tax. If they receive interest income, there's no tax. The interest deduction in the companies is a reduction of tax base, so private equity fundamentally get benefits from the pension funds' deduction, and people have been able to make money simply out of that arbitrage. That's a major component of the returns of the industry.

At the level of individual firms, there's definitely an argument for limiting interest deductions. The Germans do it. At the extremities there's people funding deals with high-rate PIK [payment-in-kind] or PIC [Pay-If-you-Can] loans to get the interest deductions and wipe out all the tax. Some of that's been backed off with the recent tax changes, but a simple structure which might limit interest deductions to perhaps a third of pre-interest profits would substantially deal with the issue and result in a fairly sensible position.

Over-leveraging companies is not a bad idea. At the limits, over-low rates means you don't invest in capital, company can't take any risk, can't survive any adverse [trading conditions], you've got an insecure set of foundations under your companies. That's not fair on the staff, customers or society in general.

3
Nick Ferguson, Chairman, SVG Capital

In Chapter 1 I opined that fund-of-fund managers are a great source of insights on private equity trends, because their roles necessarily entail talking to a wide range of both general and limited partners. Where their investment remits are international, as most are, they are also well placed to give a global perspective.

Among the most experienced is Nick Ferguson. Having founded Schroder Ventures with Jon Moulton, he remained with the firm post-buyout, re-branding it Permira, subsequently creating the FTSE 250 firm SVG Capital, which he chaired until the end of 2012. SVG is a fascinating hybrid, in that it traditionally comprised four principal types of activity and investment:

- limited partner positions in Permira's funds, which are principally mid- to large-cap European buyouts;
- some small LP positions in other private equity funds;
- SVG Advisors, a private equity fund manager that offers a number of unlisted funds of funds;
- SVG Investment Managers, a fund manager specialising in public equities.

The balance sheet therefore comprises the managers' valuations of the holdings in Permira's and third parties' funds and the directors' valuation of the two SVG fund management businesses. The financial crisis hit Permira harder than many, wiping out at one point 90 per cent of SVG's market capitalisation.

Another event took place in those dark days that is worth taking a little time to understand, because SVG was far from alone in being affected, and its impact on the future of the industry has been sizeable. When a limited partner commits money to a fund, it does not have to write out a cheque for that amount on day one; rather, the committed capital is drawn down by the general partner as and when it is required to fund transactions. Likewise, when a private equity firm sells an underlying asset, it generally returns cash to investors immediately, not when the fund is wound up. Normally, portfolio investors in private equity can project likely cash calls and realisations and invest in such a way that they can be reasonably confident of meeting commitments without having to hold a lot of cash, an asset class associated with poor returns.

In the global financial crisis, GPs found it hard to achieve exits at sensible valuations, so LPs' cash inflows from realisations dried up; meanwhile, some portfolio companies required further investment to remain solvent in those exceptional times, and fund managers rightly recognised a once-in-a-generation buying opportunity, so cash calls continued unabated. Some LPs therefore faced a dilemma: sell assets at a heavy discount to honour commitments, or breach them – something that triggers punitive clauses in partnership agreements.

Some of the biggest LPs in the world, including the likes of Harvard's endowment fund, were affected; those that held highly liquid assets such as public equities generally sold down some of their holdings, although fund policies restricting the proportion of investments that could be directed to private equity led to another interesting development: pressure on GPs to write down the values of portfolio companies in proportion to the catastrophic collapse in quoted equities.

GPs were understandably reluctant to do this, since the case for accepting the inflexible liquidity of private equity is that, in the long run, it out-performs public equities. Marking down investments to highly volatile public markets, which in many cases was not warranted by the performance of portfolio businesses and gave an unrealistically sombre reflection of likely exit values in normal circumstances, would paint an unnecessarily negative picture of their funds' performances, hampering their ability to raise new ones.

The second option available to cash-starved LPs was to sell their holdings in existing funds. Known as the secondaries market, this consists of a mix of auctions, informal transactions between limited partners and a range of specialist private equity firms that buy secondary positions (an interview with the founder of the largest of which, Coller Capital, is included in this book). The third, which SVG took, was to negotiate a reduction in its commitments in return for financial penalties. Since then, as you would expect, the firm has been diversifying away from Permira.

As well as investing in other funds, SVG is now pursuing opportunities to co-invest alongside private equity firms. This is another growing trend among LPs. In an uncertain world, why make large, risky capital commitments as much as a decade into the future when good managers are finding it increasingly hard to raise new funds but still spot good deals, for which they then seek investors on a per-project basis? Co-investment also opens the door to investing on different terms to those open to a 'vanilla' limited partner, for instance by providing lower-risk mezzanine finance (subordinated debt or preferred equity) – crucial to funding some transactions in an era in which senior debt is less readily available.

Finally, SVG is also returning cash to investors and buying back shares in an attempt to reduce the discount to NAV at which its shares have traded since the crisis. At the time of writing, this stood at approximately 40 per cent – around the market norm. In the boom, it was not unusual for quoted private equity firms to trade at a premium of 20 or 30 per cent.

Since SVG is a quoted firm and Ferguson a director (its Chairman) until the end of 2012, I was conscious that he would be unable to be specific about the future strategy of his firm; but there was nothing to stop him expressing personal opinions about trends at an industry level, to date and going forward.

*   *   *

MB: What have been the principal changes to the private equity industry since you entered it?

NF: It's bigger. There are far more general partners and investors involved in it. It's far more documented, in the sense that there's a lot more data now about performance and trends. It's also far more international. The idea of a buyout in China would have seemed off the wall in 1984.

MB: Which of these changes have been positive, and which negative?

NF: They're all a bit of both. If an industry gets bigger, it gets more competitive. But it only grows if people are willing to put money into it, and they only do that if it generates the returns. The good overall results are why investors either stay in at their current scale or increase their allocations; I don't see that changing. I chair a big private fund manager for a series of families, and we're just about to up our private equity, not because of me but because, looking back over the last seven years through the dip, it's done so well – everything except the big leveraged buyouts.

This growth means that there is far more competition for deals. Everybody knows how to do the financial structures, especially at the big end. You're far more reliant on finding growth businesses, and there'll always be an exception to the rule where you can find something because you have a connection and the process is non-competitive. Permira has done several good deals where that's been the case. But more and more of the deals are priced to a tee. It's far harder at the big end to find things where you can really make massive changes to the company. There are always exceptions: Boots is one.

The people in the large buyout groups are predominantly financially oriented; they are investment banker types, so it's all about pricing models. So I think it's far harder to make returns now. It's much more interesting lower down the scale. But there is a lot of competition there too. When we started in India in '92, there was nobody else you could talk to, and now there's hundreds of people claiming to be private equity groups.

I think the other important change that's come through is that you're getting a second generation. People like Ronnie Cohen and I, who were involved at the beginning are sort of out of it. We're part-timers now. Not all: [KKR co-founder] Henry Kravis still goes to work every day, though whether he's investing or buying Monets I don't know; certainly Leon Black [founder of US buyout and turnaround firm Apollo Global Management] goes to work every day.

You've also now got quite a lot of spin-outs: people who've come out of the larger firms for good or bad reasons and want to set up on their own. They now have a depth of knowledge in particular fields. One we invested in the other day is absolutely focused on oil and gas service companies on the Norwegian continental shelf, and they know everything about it, so they've got specialisation and they've proved it works.

There's also a trend to have more people deployed in particular regions or countries. The days of people flying into a country and doing a deal and flying out again are over. You've got to really know what's going on. That's another great change, and that opens up possibilities.

If you look at the industry by funds under management, it's dominated by a dozen companies. I think that will change. Unlike most industries, autos or chemicals, where you need vast capital investment to compete and it's low-margin, this is a wonderful industry in the sense that if you have a good record and you have a good team, investors will listen to your story. Once you raise a fund, you've got your income guaranteed for at least five or six years. So I see growth coming from people who prove themselves in certain areas in larger groups spinning out and focusing their own teams on that. I think it's great. We'll happily encourage it.

MB: So on the one hand these specialist firms may be able to source better-priced deals because there's less competition for them and the pricing is less driven by financial structures and models, and on the other, they should have sector or geographic experience that enables them to add more value to portfolio companies?

NF: That's what the WEF [World Economic Forum] study [*The Global Economic Impact of Private Equity Report 2009*] concluded, and I think the advantage will grow over time. I was an active member of the supervisory panel for that report. What impressed me most from all the academic work that was done was the analysis of whether private equity was a better form of management and governance.

Obviously I've been involved in private equity for years, but I've also been involved in public companies in that SVG Capital, which I chair, is listed, I'm deputy chairman of BSkyB and was a non-exec with Schroders. So I've seen both, and I believe that the coincidence of interest between the private equity firm and a portfolio business's management team can be a very powerful force. I say 'can be' because sometimes personalities make it a bad thing; sometimes the private equity guys aren't competent and are disrespected by the management. But if it works properly, it can be very powerful because, unlike a public company where directors get sent pieces of paper and then go to the board meeting then move on to your other things and come back six weeks later and pick up where they were, these guys are talking and sharing advice daily.

The WEF concluded on the whole that private equity companies are better run and governed. I believe that. I think it's true. Not all. There's some rottenly managed private equity companies. There's some great ones. There's some rottenly managed public companies and some great ones. But overall I think it's probably one of the key contributors to the industry's success.

MB: There's also an argument that over the past couple of decades the average period for which shares in a publicly quoted company are held has dropped dramatically, so one of the interesting characteristics of the public markets today is that most publicly quoted companies don't have active and engaged owners, they just have short-term investors because there are hedge funds trading in and out of them, lending shares to one another or shorting the company. Even fund managers are holding stocks for increasingly short periods of time, so there isn't really anyone there to say, 'This management is underperforming, let's get them out. We're going to spend some time and effort in sorting this out because we're still going to be an owner in two years' time, when the pay-off will come'.

NF: Absolutely. I believe the average shareholding period on the London markets is about 11 months. And investors are very short-term-oriented. When I go and see investors in the public companies that I am involved in, the questions are all short-term, whereas if you are going to run a company decently you've got to think three or four years out, what investments to make and what are you doing to win market share. That's the way it is, that's the way those guys are measured, so I don't complain about it. But the private equity people can take a longer view.

MB: At the same time, comparing public and private equity, the latter tends to put a lot more debt onto the balance sheets of businesses, especially the big buyouts. Doesn't that add to volatility and risk?

NF: Was there too much debt in private equity? The evidence is no. I mean by that, that if you take on too much debt, you can't service it and you go bust, whether you're an individual who has his mortgage foreclosed on or a country like Greece that can't sell its bonds or you're a company that's completely overstretched. It's very interesting that the whole corporate sector came through the recession very well, and private equity-backed firms particularly suffered very few insolvencies. Everybody points to EMI, but how many others were there? You'd think there'd be dozens of them, but people really have to scratch their heads for examples. We didn't have any in our portfolio that literally went bust. I have to admit I was quite amazed, but it shows you the resilience of the model.

So, was there too much debt? No. Could fewer people have lost their jobs because of the cutbacks firms had to make to cater for the extraordinary drop in demand that we had? Possibly. Having said that, do I think that it's wise to go back to the same levels of debt? Not unless you've got really strong nerves!

MB: I've also heard it said that private equity is a better saviour of firms in distress than public markets, because when times are really tough it is nigh-on impossible to re-capitalise a quoted firm as shareholders worry about throwing good money after bad, and even if it's possible to get a rights issue away, it takes time to do so, whereas there are private equity firms such as Better Capital and Endless that are turnaround specialists and can act quickly and pick up firms where there's a liquidity problem.

NF: Yes, people getting into trouble has been a source of deals for as long as I can remember, whether it's the company itself, firms being forced to sell off subsidiaries to raise cash or family owners in trouble.

MB: You said earlier that the industry has grown because it has been successful, so has been able to attract more investment. But the recent trend for big buyouts is that they haven't done that well, and there are many firms – even really good ones – that are now finding it hard or impossible to raise new funds. Does this mean that private equity may have peaked, at least in developed markets? And will it get smaller?

NF: For the time being, yes. A few years back, Henry Kravitz came out with a famous and, in retrospect, unwise statement about it being the golden age of private equity. What I think he meant was that it had never been so easy to raise money, and that certainly was the peak and it's far harder now, even for very good managers.

The reason is that a lot of investors just sit on their hands. It's so easy not to take a decision. With a big pension fund, you don't know where the world's going, you know the guy's going to take a year and a half raising his fund, so what the hell's the point of saying yes now? So people are going round markets at the moment to find other people saying, 'It's really interesting, come back and see us and we'll keep it under review.' They are not getting sales. That's a function of where the world is and the markets are at the moment, which is gloomy and difficult. My own view, for what it's worth, is we're going to have quite strong inflation over the next 15 years as a result of all this money being pumped in, and historically, if you look at all the financial crises since 1600, governments have chosen inflation as a way to bail out their debts and I don't believe it's going to be any different.

MB: So the current problem is cyclical rather than structural?

NF: Yes, I firmly believe that we are going to enter an inflationary period, and on the whole private equity does well in such times because you get a de-leveraging effect [inflation erodes the real value of debt over time], and earnings growth, if you've got a positive margin, will be fine. So I think people will come back to it.

I also think more and more funds [LPs] are seeing that the private equity part of their portfolio has done damn well over the last six to seven years, a period that includes the dip. That rules out the really brilliant deals done a year or two ago, since the crisis. So it's been not bad at all. It's been much better than most sectors. I know it'll come back; private equity will always be there.

It does mean the average size of funds at the top end will go down in the next few years. Good! That was part of the problem. There's clearly too much money around. I don't know what the overhang is today, but there's still several years' dry powder [funds committed to private equity firms but not yet drawn down] there for acquisitions. It's interesting to watch the supply of raised and committed uncalled funds versus the deal usage. It's pretty bloody high at the moment [industry sources suggest as much as $1 trillion globally], so why do we need loads more funds? That's not an argument you'd get from people who've just run out of their last one and have to fundraise.

I think what the sector will be is much more dynamic, and this is something that is really important. It's not like many industries, where you get a reduction in the number of players. Curiously 30 per cent of all hedge funds disappear each year, but in private equity practically none disappears because you've got this ten-year thing. I think you will get a much more active and creative portfolio approach, with people like Sam [Robinson, who managers SVG's Asia fund of funds] and others all looking for the bright people with the special knowledge and less interested in the great big funds.

A lot of people will want to go on investing in the big funds, the big pension funds and so on, although the CalPERS [California Public Employees' Retirement System, the world's largest public pension fund] bribery thing will have scared some of them. [This refers to allegations that members of the pension fund board, including then CEO Fred Buenrostro, received bribes from an intermediary between the fund and some large private equity firms, known as a placement agent.]

So the balance for LPs is now between supporting the new niche firms and still investing in the best of the established guys. I'll give you an example. Golden Gate is an extremely good American buyout group. They had a team that were doing just retail investments. They recently spun out and we supported them, but we still fund Golden Gate, they're still terrific.

MB: The underlying logic must be that with these more focused funds there's at least the prospect of getting better returns.

NF: Correct. There's the belief that for your large, traditional, dominant groups, life's going to be harder. Whether it proves right or not, God only knows. I'm just observing a trend.

MB: Yes, although if you're right about inflation, highly leveraged big deals could be very good indeed, because the debt's going to be eroded quite quickly …

NF: Could be, but if we have another crisis, it could be quite hairy!

MB: I guess so. What about the developing world, because I guess one of the other characteristics of LP fundraises is how much of the money is flowing into funds in emerging markets?

NF: If you ask these surveys that are done on big investors in private equity, it's always emerging markets will increase, but I haven't seen it prove itself yet. We've seen some stunning deals come out, but it's still anecdotal stuff, individual deals. I haven't seen much data on how the industry as a whole has really done in developing markets. Maybe I'm out of date.

MB: I know what you mean. It's a quality of earnings question, isn't it? Many of those funds can point to some exits that they've got that have been very successful, but very few have run a fund for a full cycle and returned money a couple of times in order to prove it wasn't a fluke.

NF: That's really a question for Sam [Robinson].

MB: Fund of funds is interesting. It's an area you are in and traditionally have been in, and I guess people would say in volatile times fund of funds is a great way to mitigate risk.

NF: When you say 'traditionally', we've only been in it since 2001, when we started this business here; ironically it was a whim. I thought that by having a quoted vehicle like this we'd attract more individuals who wanted liquidity, but actually we're owned almost entirely by institutions. So it didn't work; or rather, it worked, but not as I'd intended.

MB: It surprises me that money isn't now flowing into funds of funds, especially quoted ones, because they combine liquidity and diversification, which I would have thought is an attractive proposition in times when global macro-economics are volatile and maybe being concentrated in a single fund or territory or being locked into a ten-year fund could have some risk attached.

NF: Also, the fund-of-funds business serves a purpose, which is providing access to private equity for those investors who are not big enough to support their own staff or retain advisers to analyse funds, get into the funds (because they have minimums, even today) or get a spread. Those are the three things – knowledge, scale for entry and spread – that we offer. So CalPERS and GM Pension Fund are not investors with us, whereas for loads of other pension funds and foundations and endowments and individuals it's a super way of accessing private equity.

MB: I think the idea of encouraging private individuals to invest in quoted private equity is an interesting one, because it answers the criticism that it is an investment class for the wealthy. In the USA it's a moot point, because most public sector workers' pension funds have money in private equity, but in the UK it's much less common.

NF: Yes, the minimum entry point in our case is just a couple of quid, the price of one share. And at the moment you can buy in at a 40 per cent discount to NAV too.

MB: That's an interesting point, isn't it, the discount to NAV. There seems to be quite a trend of quoted private equity being valued at a discount to NAV lately, which perhaps implies people don't trust their balance sheets.

NF: No, it's that there's a fear, some of it real, that when the market's going up private equity will outperform and when it's going down it'll under-perform, because of leverage. There's also a perception that in private equity firms the asset base is illiquid. True you can sell secondaries, but companies are hard to move and so people just get worried. And I should say that it's not just private equity that is discounted or under-valued. Even Apple has bought back its own shares, and it's the biggest company in the world. It's not just us. But the private equity moves tend to get exaggerated.

The smart guys tend to buy when people are frightened. And they're frightened about private equity at the moment because they're frightened that the world of private equity appears to be one of those extreme things – which data suggest is not true. Witness in 2008 how few companies went bust. I've talked to politicians about this, and they don't want to hear, it's not about the real stuff, it's good anti-capitalist fodder. Private equity sounds nasty. But the evidence is that private equity creates jobs, runs companies better and most sensible people appreciate that. Frankly, I loathed Gordon Brown, but one of his few redeeming features was that he understood that it worked. So I don't care what Miliband says. With luck he will never be imposed on us anyway.

I doubt the quoted private equity sector is going to grow much in the short term. I don't see a huge latent demand for more and more, that's part of the discount issue – if you can buy into an existing fund at a discount, why would you want to get into a new one at par? Most of our life, we've traded at a premium, but if you look at the graph, it takes several years to get back up. When that happens, you might get one or two others listing.

Looking at the industry generally, I think the LP structure and the carry is pretty well established. People like it, they feel it works, it's easy to understand, it's perpetual. So I don't think it will change much. I think much more change will be from within that structure. I'm always amazed that, given all this difficulty of raising funds, you never hear anyone suggesting that they sell on a 15 per cent carry instead of 20. It's unbelievably rigid.

There's no movement on pricing, except on the margin. Deal fees have gone, deal-by-deal carry has gone. There are still one or two out there punting 30 per cent carries, but not for very long. I think I'm right in saying that Bain Capital, which had done very well, had a 30 per cent carry but had such a rotten last fund they've given that up. So at the margin there are pricing improvements, and various of the other terms that make life better for the LP have been strengthened. The core, the biggest earner, which is the carry, has hardly shifted.

4
John Hess, Chief Executive Officer, Altius Associates Ltd

In Chapter 3 Nick Ferguson mentioned advisory firms that help limited partners direct capital to funds that match their priorities. Such businesses largely target mid-size investors that are big enough to retain such firms but not so large that they can justify hiring in-house analysts. They also help sizeable private equity investors allocate capital to geographically non-core territories (for instance, large US investors that invest the bulk of their money in North America using in-house expertise might rely on a third party for their European and Asian diversification).

Given these advisers' privileged insights to the thinking of both limited and general partners – not least their knowledge of where money is being allocated and why, and what returns it generates there – I felt this first, background section of my book would be incomplete without an interview with a respected elder statesman from that profession.

That's how I came to be speaking with John Hess, founder of UK-, US- and Singapore-based Altius Associates, a boutique private equity advisory firm. We met in his London office, which is in an attractive period building opposite Buckingham Palace Gardens.

Hess, born in the USA in 1947 but resident in the UK, began his career with private equity as a placement agent with Continental Bank, acting for general partners wishing to raise funds. As both Hess and Jon Moulton have observed, UK private equity in the early days was a cottage industry in which everyone knew everyone, so it comes as no surprise that Hess's career dovetails with those of my first two interviewees, since he raised much of the capital for Schroder Ventures' funds in that first decade. Subsequently, he co-founded an independent placement agency, Helix Associates, in 1993, and Altius in 1998. The following year he moved full-time to the advisory firm, which he has led ever since. Clients typically allocate around $25 million a year to the asset class over a four-year period to ensure sufficient diversification by manager and fund vintage. In 2008 Altius launched a fund-of-funds arm, offering both private equity and real assets (infrastructure, energy, timber, natural resources) vehicles; the typical minimum entry point is $5 million, although smaller commitments are accepted on a case-by-case basis.

Prior to our meeting, Hess and I exchanged emails. Our correspondence began with his observation that:

> I might start off by saying: 'Investing in private companies is most likely the world's second oldest profession. Like the oldest, it has become mature and highly sophisticated and has stubbornly survived and will continue to survive attempts to control and regulate it.'

Although our interview did not in fact begin with those words, it became clear that Hess is a firm believer in the hypothesis that the developed private equity market – including the mega-buyout firms – will survive and in time prosper again, and is more cautious than many about the flows of capital into emerging markets and alternative assets.

I suspect this is borne in part of the fact that he has seen private equity transition through several economic and regulatory cycles. But it may also owe a lot to the fact that an adviser's reputation and business model are predicated on successfully steering clients towards funds that can be reasonably certain to generate positive returns relative to the market, which requires an acute awareness of past returns and risk adjustment, which may in turn point to an understandable preference for established funds and markets rather than less well-proven ones that make bolder promises but with little track record.

* * *

MB: Given the slowing of investment into new funds over the past few years, I would imagine that things are not what they were in the advisory sector?

JH: That's true. We're OK, because we're smaller [Altius employs 35 people in three offices], have a very low cost base and are quite conservative, but I think some of the firms that expanded are having it tough. Being in the business, we knew that at some point, if things didn't keep growing, the shit was going to hit the fan, you know. And the shit'll hit the fan anyway, but if you've got a little protection, it's OK. That's what's happening in our end of the business.

MB: How have you been affected by the pay-to-play scandals in the USA [advisers and placement agents bribing public pension fund directors or making contributions to politicians' party funds in order to secure investment]?

JH: I think and hope we have a good reputation in the marketplace. We pride ourselves on never doing anything funny. We just won't do it, and if we think someone who wants to hire us is a bit odd, we'll walk. It's just not worth taking the risk. We've had that happen a couple of times. The USA can be a bloody corrupt place: the state pension funds, no matter what anybody tells you . . . They try to regulate against it and do all sorts of things that prohibit this and prohibit that, but at the end of the day, you know, it happens anyway.

One that has been in the public domain was a group called Markstone Capital, run by Elliott Broidy in Los Angeles. [Broidy pleaded guilty of paying almost $1 million in bribes to New York State officials, their friends and families, to secure $250 million of investment from the New York State Common Retirement Fund.] We went through a terrible time with that with one of our clients. It's the nastiest situation I've ever been in, in terms of pressure from him, our client and others. I had to take the whole thing off of the portfolio manager and do it myself because it was getting so nasty, but we stuck to our guns. We didn't buckle and he has been convicted, but this happens more often than it should.

MB: Do you think the current downturn in private equity is cyclical or structural?

JH: I believe we're at the bottom of a private equity cycle and that we're already seeing some of the signs that are obvious markers of the bottom of the cycle. The reluctance of banks to lend money. Prices coming down. The overhang being eaten gradually. Commitments being cancelled. Institutions negotiating the hell out of terms successfully. These are all things that happen at the bottom of a cycle.

MB: And what about the macro-economics?

JH: We're going to be in a low-interest-rate environment for a couple more years at least. The banks are going to be hammered for a couple more years. When banks recover, they recover very fast, though. Banks in the USA have repaid all the TARP [Troubled Asset Relief Program] money. They recover very fast. They just don't want to get stuck with crap again.

From the private equity standpoint, the most worrying thing in the short term is the economic downturn and the risk of a true recession. Consumers aren't spending any money. If the consumers in the developed world don't spend, then we're in trouble.

MB: When you're thinking about allocating funds to private equity firms – whether that's in your fund of funds or advising clients – do you tend to take that into account when thinking about sectors? For example, retail is probably quite a risky area to be in at the moment in the UK, whereas it may be safer to back funds that invest in firms providing infrastructure to the government or medical services or devices that play to an ageing population?

JH: Not as much as you might think, because the best general partners have tended to be generalist and have developed general areas of specialist expertise across a range of industries that don't fall into neat overall specialisations. That said, there are some now that are specialising more. The energy sector is one where there are now some really strong specialised firms. Retailing's another. We at Altius tend not to over-emphasise the groups that specialise. We like the diversified general, certainly in the buyout space: guys who know how to put a good deal together and can do it in different industries.

MB: So does your analysis suggest that generalists perform better?

JH: It's more that they've been doing it longer so have better track records of great performance. We've done some research in that area and have found serial out-performance by certain GPs, which you don't find in the listed mutual fund market. It's significant in private equity. It stands to reason. Sellers of companies are going to want to go to the folks that are the most successful for obvious reasons, because they're usually the better payers for businesses. And the management will want that bump too. So good performance can be self-perpetuating.

MB: What else do you look for?

JH: Other areas that we spend a lot of time looking at are strategy and strategy drift. Are they doing, and are they going to do, the same thing that they've done before? There are some classic examples of that coming unstuck, Hicks Muse being the classic. They were a buy-and-build specialist, and they'd done extremely well doing that. Then they decided they liked telecoms and did eight PIPEs [Private Investments in Public Equities], I think, and then seven went belly-up and pretty much killed the firm.

Alignment of interest among the team and with the investor is quite important. That's taken on a lot of weight because of ILPA [the Institutional Limited Partners' Association, which represents the interests of the big LPs]. As a result of their influence, many US funds are doing things now [on the governance front] that European funds have been doing for 20 years.

Within the GP group, we like to see a balanced team. We like to see good senior middle management, because if there's a gap there that's usually where things get into trouble. If we sense a one-man show, we'll walk, Guy Hands being the classic example.

We also do not commit to buyout firms that have linkages with larger organisations. We've never done Barclays, for example, because of the connection to the bank, though now they've bought themselves out, so things have worked out OK. DLJ merging with Credit Suisse was another example. DLJ was probably the best-performing US buyout fund ever. The merger happened, which was totally outside their control, and the team just went. So captives are off our list.

We then look at experience, the investment strategy how they source deals. We have a very advanced way of doing that. At the very start of the process we do a very detailed peer-group analysis, rating it into three separate groups of the ones we like best, medium and not as much, and we try to select from the top group. The analytical process is designed not to overweigh too heavily any of the factors. [Hess later sends me the template. It is proprietary, so I have not reproduced it here; I would describe it as a four-page balanced scorecard-type exercise which evaluates the management team, investment strategy and market, performance and alignment of interests under a number of weighted criteria to arrive at an overall quality score. Interestingly, performance, which I had expected to see heavily weighted, represents only 30 per cent of the total, perhaps because some of the other criteria could be seen as near proxies for it.]

So although we look at what's happening in the marketplace, our investment recommendations and philosophy are much more based on a bottom-up approach to analysis with the view that what one really wants to find is the consistent serial outperforming fund manager that tends to do well over a long period of time and over a lot of different economic cycles. A classic example is TA Associates.

MB: TA has delivered 30-odd per cent IRRs for, what, 20 or 30 years?

JH: They came up with an approach that works. They hire in young pre-business school people – a lot of them – and they give them each a 'phone book and a telephone and get them to call owner–managers to talk about whether they might be interested in selling the company or growing it then exiting. Many of them need growth capital and expertise, which TA can provide – and that's where they generate their leads. Others have since copied the model – Summit, for instance – but it still works. And they're typically not driven by debt, they're growth companies, so it's pretty resilient.

There are some people around who spend more time than us looking at the top-down macro approach. We don't ignore it, but it's not the main consideration, and it usually is a risk factor and not a return factor. There's a huge myth in private equity investing that is perpetuated even today as we speak, that high-growth markets equate to high-return private equity markets. Total myth.

MB: I've seen data on public markets that suggests that the opposite is true. In high-growth markets, the expected growth is factored into the price of businesses, whereas in mature ones the value is mainly in observable performance and the balance sheet, and in growth markets the potential future earnings enhancement may be insufficiently discounted because there's an inflow of capital chasing those equities, so actually what you're doing is increasing the risk more than you're increasing the return.

JH: We're very strong believers in the portfolio approach to private equity and diversification across sectors and geographies. We don't tell investors not to put money in emerging markets, we just say, 'You should beware of the risk-return characteristics of these places.' In China, for instance, you may need a 40 per cent IRR to compensate for the political risk, whereas you'd be happy with half that figure in a developed market. If you look at it that way, then your portfolio composition begins to take some good shape and you end up having a much stronger or larger concentration in the developed markets anyway.

I've been doing this long enough, so I've seen the cyclicality. What's happening today is nothing quite like anything that has come before, but in the early '90s developed country private equity also went dead, following the Resolution Trust crisis in the USA. [Resolution Trust was the vehicle created by the US government to deal with the insolvencies of hundreds of mutually owned small banks and lenders following the savings and loan crisis of the late 1980s.] Same sort of crisis we're having today – not as bad possibly – and any sort of private long-term illiquid investing was dead.

At the same time people discovered something that would offer the same returns, but was liquid – emerging markets. So they all piled into that, without thinking too much about the risk characteristics. In that situation I think it was useful to look at the macro-economic dynamics because you could you could see that what had to happen to maintain these things was never going to be achievable. So a lot of people put money big-time into Asia, India and East Asia. And if you look back at the ten-year returns and compare them to the developed world for that cycle, they were way below: half or worse.

The jury's out on the current cycle, but we believe that certain markets like India are way over-invested and are over-fundraised; there's a bubble. Probably certain places in Asia are the same. We think China's dangerous as hell.

The African markets are beginning to develop, which is great. It really is very positive, the number of really strong investors like Actis, for example, who've gone in. They've taken no nonsense over social responsibility and governance, and things are happening. Good news for the continent and for investors, but it's still pretty small. And that can be an issue with our clients – certainly the larger ones – let alone the bigger state pension funds. It doesn't make any sense for them to make just a $20 million investment in anything. It could have a zillion per cent IRR. It's not going to move the needle very much.

Some people, including some of my colleagues, argue that it makes sense to make a small investment in a frontier market to learn about it. I disagree with them on this; I'm not a believer in this argument that you need to invest to get an education. There are cheaper ways to do it.

MB: How else?

JH: I think it was the Stanford Endowment team that moved to China for six months to observe and learn . . . that's probably cheaper than putting in your own money.

MB: Unless the China bulls are right, in which case staying un-invested in that market could be an expensive decision.

JH: There's no doubt that the developed West is in relative decline and the East in long-term growth. The West has been in decline for 50 years, but there's also no doubt in my mind that the decline is and will continue to be much more gradual than you read about in a lot of the papers. This is not the end of America in, say, 2018. So while there are some things that the developed world needs to worry about, there's also a massive economic imbalance right now. These things tend to equalise over time, and I can't see how this time is going to be any different.

China has some really big problems. Really big problems. Huge elements of the population are still among the poorest people in the world. How long will they be accepting of that fact? Production costs and labour costs are going up. Production will start to move. They've got a massive natural resource issue that is a lot nearer-term than people think. We actually met with the guy who's the head of the minerals research department in Beijing, and he was telling us how they source their iron ore and coal and so on. At the moment they rely on a couple of markets, like Brazil and India, both of which will stop exporting in ten years or fewer because they need the resources themselves. Then what will China do?

If I were predicting something, it would be that the imbalances will sort themselves out. Maybe it's because I'm American, but I don't think America's quite as dead as a lot of people say it is. Certainly in the technological area. Just look at medical technology for one.

If you look at where the money's actually made in private equity, the best returns have been made in two areas: early stage venture/growth – the TA/Summit model – and leveraged buyouts. I don't believe that these emerging economies are going to come up with some other model that's going to make a lot of private equity money. I just don't see where it's going to come from. As I said, private company investing is the second oldest profession. There's nothing that hasn't been tried before.

The elements for a successful buyout business don't exist in China. Early-stage investing might exist, and maybe there are some opportunities in the growth space, but on top of that you have a massive sovereign risk issue that may negate any other advantages. In India there's no buyout opportunity. There's a growth opportunity. Very little early-stage opportunity, I would say. There's technology, but I believe the Indians tend to be followers rather than technical entrepreneurs.

As for Brazil... I've never been able to figure it out. I've put my own money into it in two other cycles and lost both times, so I'm a bit gunshot. My younger colleagues tell me I'm just being silly. I don't know the market well enough there at the moment to say whether I would believe it to have the right characteristics or not. They have some very large companies. There have been buyouts done in that market before that might have been successful if they hadn't borrowed dollars. If they'd financed them in their own currency it might have worked.

MB: And what about Europe?

JH: I think it will come right. Even the Eurozone will work itself out. It has to.

MB: You mentioned TA as an example of a great US firm: what about Europe?

JH: We think CVC is the best of the European lot. The strategy isn't complex: they're a buyout firm, they just invest very well. They've got good people, they're very disciplined and they do good deals.

MB: Some people say that the buyout market will take a long time to deliver again the returns it did in the past because debt is so much harder to come by and almost all the deals are on-market, so fully priced, plus big companies are already pretty well run so it's hard to add value.

JH: Yes, but they can structure the transaction in a way that maximises the value of the equity.

MB: How can they do that better than others?

JH: It's a mixture of expertise and firepower. And they know how to work their companies. They know how to get rid of excess costs without killing the company, when and how to change strategies. Having the independent third-party view come in and say, 'You'd probably be better off if you did this.' Or bringing in a consultant to help the purchasing unit find savings. All the stuff adds up. It does make a difference

Some people ask why can't the shareholders of quoted companies do this and achieve the same results. They very rarely do. There are some that do, and they're the stars, but they're rare. Everybody has their theory, but I think it's just that in a quoted company you don't have a small group of motivated long-term shareholders who are really pushing for a return. If a quoted business is heading for the rocks, its shareholders are more likely to sell their shares and buy them back at a lower price in a year's time than they are to actually help fix the problem.

I believe that the folks who've gone into the private equity general partnerships in the past 15 years that have been successful and grown are very, very smart people. They're ambitious, and they want to make money. And the industry has a model that makes practitioners and managements very wealthy if they do well, so there's an alignment of interests. It's pretty powerful, and it's not just about the CEO, like it is in most quoted companies.

OK, buyouts loaded up companies with more debt than the public markets. But quoted companies could have gone down that route too if they'd wanted. And default rates are still very low, partially because debt covenants were almost non-existent. Debt has been re-negotiated, and the banks really are on the back foot.

MB: Is there a moral argument that loading up companies with debt is a bad thing?

JH: My view is that it's a market, and if both parties go into it with their eyes open, that's OK. Whereas lying to pension funds about your CDO [collateralized debt obligation] structures, that's bad. The regulators drive me nuts, because private equity folks don't lie. They have no incentive to mislead anyone, because it's a cash-to-cash business.

But it's having a major effect on new deals obviously, and I'm told by my financing friends that all of the debt arranging is sequential now. It's linear. You have to go one, two, three for the different tranches before you can get a deal. Mezzanine is taking a far greater role in getting deals structured than it did in the boom days, because hardly anybody needed it when you had the high-yield [bond] market and banks were willing to provide covenant-free senior debt. So what's happening now is the mezz players are stepping in.

MB: It seems to me now is a good time to be running or investing in a mezzanine fund.

JH: It is a very good time, yes, because you can get some pretty good terms. Those deals may be restructured down the road, but it may be a way down the road.

Also, it hasn't really happened yet, but there's a lot of cash around, and there's a lot of liquidity for obvious reasons. Nobody's doing anything with it. At some point it wouldn't surprise me to see some of the larger liquidity positions begin to provide finance directly rather than through banks. It wouldn't surprise me. Sovereign wealth funds. Others. What else are they going to do with their money? It's very hard to put as much money to work in private equity on the equity side as they would like to. They can't get it all to work.

MB: By providing the debt side of the equation they can enable more of the dry powder on the equity side to be put to work.

JH: And some of the pension funds have AA ratings, and there are all sorts of things you can think about how that could be useful. And I know some of the larger pension funds have gone to their favourite managers – GPs – who they have very close relationships with and have suggested ways of working together that haven't been done before because they can take advantage of the current environment.

MB: So they'd be direct participants in funds as LPs, and they'd also be indirect participants as mezzanine or debt providers?

JH: They're talking about it. I don't know if anybody's done it yet, but I know they're looking at things like that. They might do it through a co-investment or a direct investment, rather than through the fund, because the large LPs want to do more direct co-investing. This has taken on a huge head of steam now. It's a fee reduction thing mostly, but it also has other implications, and they're getting much more involved in the deals because it's a special environment right now.

And of course, some of the large buyout firms have moved into a different business. They're not really buyout firms any more, they're emerging investment banks: the Blackstones, KKRs and Carlyles. As a result, they're looking to their major institutional investors to help support other parts of their business as well as the principal equity investing part. The large investors that have a lot of liquidity are saying, 'Well maybe we can do something here because, Christ, we're not earning any money anywhere else.' Nobody has said, 'I want to decrease my private market exposure these days.' Teacher Retirement System of Texas has been pioneering some of this. CalPERS is considering it too. They're the ones who are looking at it, because they have the muscle.

MB: If there's more co-investment and more mezzanine in buyout structures, presumably there will be downward pressure on the returns delivered for LPs?

JH: This brings me on to another interesting point. A lot of people still say, 'Well, unless I can see 20 per cent plus, net, net to me, I'm not interested.' How much have they been getting on their quoted portfolio in recent years? And what are their expectations for equities over the next ten years?

Our view has always been that if private equity can outperform the public markets by 500 basis points plus, it is going to give you a bump to your overall portfolio if you have 5 per cent or more invested. That's what you should be aiming for, and if that means your private equity portfolio is delivering 18 per cent or 13 per cent, then that's all right if the public markets are doing 13 per cent or 8 per cent or are falling. What's the problem? I sometimes boil it down to my own modest portfolio. The only place I'm making any return on at the moment is private equity. And it's probably about 12 per cent. I'm happy with that. [Hess subsequently sends me some illustrative IRR figures showing that Altius clients' portfolios have typically out-performed quoted benchmarks by between 600 and 1200 basis points.]

MB: Is there also a case for saying that over the longer term private equity returns could rebound, because deals are being done now at low multiples that could see decent valuation uplifts and possibly be refinanced down the line?

JH: It depends on how long will we be bumping along at the bottom of the trough. One thing that definitely has to happen before we start to see what's really going to happen is that the un-invested capital committed to private equity in the golden years has to shrink down to probably 100-ish. [Hess later sends me a spreadsheet suggesting that the un-invested capital from funds raised between 2006 and 2008 alone totalled $924.9 billion at the end of 2011.] When that happens, everyone will get a much better idea of what contraction there's going to be and what's a normal investment pace going to look like. How far away are we from that? I don't know. Some commitments will be cancelled, because a lot of LPs just are saying no. There's a lot of bargaining power with the LPs at the moment.

MB: Talking about the LPs and their bargaining power, do you think the two-and-20 model is going to be under threat?

JH: No, because this is the model that the industry has grown up with. It's a model that the best-performing practitioners are standing by. They appear to be able to raise capital based on this model. Plus, two has already come down to one or one and a half for the really big firms. Firms can drop their prices, but they won't get any money unless their performance is really good. If their performance is really good they'll get money even if they maintain their prices and maybe make some small adjustments like on the transaction fees, but they'll be able to maintain their management fees and carry.

MB: So why are firms finding it so hard to raise new funds?

JH: Partly because LPs are scared of economic and political events. But there's also a structural problem. Roughly 200 institutions account for 80 per cent of all private equity commitments: mainly very large American and a couple of European pension funds. The 20 or so largest American pension funds and endowments account for a bit chunk of that. They're now in an over-committed phase because of the fall in the value of their overall portfolios [the proportion of the carried value of their investments in private equity is above target], and they are reluctant to sell holdings to adjust for that, so they're waiting for a bit of a run-off and more distributions to be made to get it back to where it ought to be. They don't want their private equity to be at 15 per cent of their portfolios, they want it at 8, and that has to happen before they will commit large amounts of money. Clients that might have committed $500 million or $750 million to a single fund are now doing $200 million, and that's having a big effect on the bigger funds.

It isn't helped by the accounting profession making everybody mark to market now, which is nonsense. If you go out tomorrow and try to sell your portfolio at market, you're not going to be able to do it, are you? It's totally meaningless to an investor. Particularly if you have no intention of doing anything with that portfolio until it matures.

MB: It seems to me it creates particular problems with funds of funds, and especially for quoted private equity, because there's a huge lag between the portfolio valuations and market reaction. Especially as most are trading at discounts to NAV.

JH: I'm surprised people aren't trying to buy them. The independent ones, anyway. If I were a sovereign wealth fund, I'd be making bids. If you want to build up assets quickly, even if you only get them at par, it's still a lot cheaper than setting up your own programme.

MB: Do you expect the number of funds to reduce?

JH: Yes, over the next five years there will be a contraction in the number of managers, advisers and fund of funds. Those who want to survive will find ways to do it, but not everyone will want to. We're starting to see that happen now. Some groups are just going away. They're deciding not to raise further funds.

Private equity has grown into an industry that has spawned publications, accounting firms, brokers and an ecosystem of specialist lawyers, advisers and consultants. Fifteen years ago, very few of those were there, so it's turned into a massive industry. It reminds me of US commercial real estate in the '70s and '80s, when it was discovered by institutional investors. All of a sudden it became an established asset class and spawned all sorts of other things that went along with it.

Private equity technically isn't an asset class on its own, but it's treated that way today, and a lot of people make their living from it, so there's a tremendous support that will keep it going. But like any other industry that becomes a bit more mature and established, there has to be some rationalisation and consolidation in the bad times, and some of the bad firms have to go away; and there may be some new entrants, there may not.

The major threat to capital flows in the developed world, I believe, is over-regulation, which we're starting to see. The IFM thing is part of it, but lawyers are smart too and they've already figured out ways to get around all this crap, and the limited partners are just going to say, 'Yes, fuck it, I'm not going to pay any attention to it, I'm just going to do what I want', and you can see it's what's going to happen.

I think Solvency II [a European Union Directive specifying the capital ratios of insurance companies] is a threat. Insurance companies have been big investors in private equity in Europe and were increasing, and this puts a dampener on things, although the German accountants, for example, have already come up with ways to structure it as a bond. The Americans have come up with FACTA [the Foreign Account Tax Compliance Act], a requirement on non-US insurers that have to warrant they have no accounts with Americans who are trying to evade tax. A lot of European companies are refusing to sign it and will just not invest in the US any more. Then there's Basel III, which will limit banks' ability to make commitments to funds and to do their own investments. And there have been a whole bunch of announcements in the USA at the state level banning placement agents and all sorts of other crazy stuff. LPs say they don't need protecting, that they know what they're doing.

One of the impacts of this in the medium term may be to divert some capital flows away from developed markets into the developing markets. It almost certainly will divert GPs offshore from places like London. Eventually it will dawn on everyone that, 'My God, we're losing jobs, market share, taxes, whatever by doing this, we're going to have to change this.' So it isn't irreversible. But it is increasing compliance costs. We're a little firm, but our compliance cost has tripled in the last three years.

I believe another major trend will be on the investor side, which is the market power of the sovereign wealth funds. They're becoming massive and their appetite is huge, and as CIC [the China Investment Corporation] has proved, they're able to do things for almost nothing in the marketplace. The problem is that they have too much money to put into the market and a lot of GPs don't want to be overburdened with it.

MB: Some surveys suggest there's a negative correlation between fund size and performance.

JH: I also think there can be problems when a firm increases its fund size too quickly. It's one of the things we look at when we're evaluating a fund. One of the lessons that everyone has learned from the boom times is that you really do need to have discipline on size, and it moves investors into a different business if they increase their fund size too much. I think that's what happened to a number of the ones that have been having trouble in Europe.

MB: What is your view on secondaries?

JH: The business is going to be pretty good for a while, because there are a lot of forced sellers of funds. They are a good opportunity if you can get the right price.

MB: Is there anything else you foresee in terms of trends?

JH: No, except that I hope the public and politicians and regulators come to recognise how little fraud and dishonesty there has been in the GP community. It's tiny when you compare it to the stuff that's gone on in hedge funds, investment banking and other parts of the financial world, and yet private equity gets tarred with a really bad brush.

5
Jeremy Coller, Partner and Chief Investment Officer, Coller Capital

Among the many brickbats thrown at private equity is the accusation that it is a monoculture: a profession populated by straight white men from privileged backgrounds, educated at fee-paying schools followed by Ivy League universities or Oxbridge, holding accountancy qualifications or MBAs, who find their way into the industry via investment banking or, occasionally, consulting.

As with most stereotypes, it is both unfair – not one of the figures I interviewed for this book to my knowledge ticks all of the above boxes – and yet not entirely without foundation. In particular, I was struck by the extent to which firms seem to recruit 'quants' – people with maths and science backgrounds – as opposed to 'poets' – those with arts and humanities training.

At first, this tendency may seem unsurprising: after all, the ability correctly to value a business and optimally to structure the funding of its acquisition are at the heart of the industry, and these are plainly quantitative skills. And yet, for a profession that now recognises that much of the return lies with operational enhancement and value creation – disciplines that require, in addition to hard skills such as cost control, capabilities in softer areas such as marketing and people management – it is interesting that few of those who have achieved prominence in private equity are what is stereotypically, but from an anatomical viewpoint incorrectly, termed left-brained.

So my next interviewee, Jeremy Coller, stands out from the crowd for three reasons. First, he has a Master's degree in philosophy from that stereotypically liberal British university Sussex, where by coincidence I gained a Bachelor's degree a little over two decades ago; second, he is a published author – not of a dry tome about an aspect of finance or management, but rather of an entertaining and well-written whistle-stop tour of the world's greatest pioneers, the magnificently titled *The Lives, Loves and Deaths of Splendidly Unreasonable Inventors*. But the third, and perhaps most surprising factor, is that Coller stands at the top of the one sector within the industry in which, on the face of it, quantitative skills are at the greatest premium and qualitative ones of little import: the secondaries market.

My previous interviewee, John Hess, observed that this market looks set to be buoyant for the foreseeable. I agree, but would first like to provide some clarity around definitions. There are three types of secondary transaction in private equity:

- GP to GP mergers and acquisitions activity: this is where one general partner acquires a portfolio business for a fund that it manages, from a fund
managed by another general partner. Sometimes GP to GP transactions take
place because the seller's fund is in the final stages of its realisation phase and
there is pressure from investors to realise and distribute cash; at other times
they occur because the business has evolved in ways that mean it would
more effectively be managed by a different kind of private equity firm, with
other capabilities and assets – such as a growth business that now requires
access to substantial acquisition capital, which the original investor cannot
provide, or a leveraged buyout that hits financial difficulties and has to be
rescued by a turnaround fund.
- LP to LP secondary: here, one limited partner sells its interest in a particular fund, or more often a portfolio of positions in a number of funds, to
another investor. Sometimes, such sales take place informally or are facil-
itated by a GP between the existing LPs in a single fund; alternatively,
interests are auctioned, in which case they often pass to LPs new to those
funds, and there are also general partners that run funds that specialise
in acquiring secondary interests – of which Coller Capital, the firm that
bears my next interviewee's name and which he founded in 1990, is global
leader.
- 'Direct' secondary: a limited partner acquires a GP-like interest in a portfolio
of investee businesses. This can happen under a number of circumstances,
the most common being when a financial institution or corporate venturer
has built up such investments, often through the vehicle of a 'captive' private equity firm (one linked to a financial or, occasionally, corporate parent)
and wishes to exit the market for strategic or financial reasons, but it can
also mean a tail-end investment (acquiring the assets of a private equity
fund that has reached the end of its life without divesting all its assets), or a
structured secondary, in which a limited partner that is unwilling or unable
to meet future cash calls from a GP in effect shares its LP position in a fund
with an incoming investor in return for the latter providing the additional
capital.

Of the three types of transaction I've outlined, the second two constitute the secondaries market that Hess was talking about and that Coller's firm specialises in.

Typically, the value of private equity investments follows a J-curve: in the early days capital is eroded by management fees, and portfolio companies re-invest and re-invent themselves; also, the most disappointing investments tend to become apparent in the first few years. So the value of even a well-managed portfolio can be under water after two to four years from fundraise, a phenomenon that scares nervous investors and represents an opportunity for secondary buyers.

Prior to 1990, Coller managed pension funds for ICI, in which role he bought ten secondary positions – a pioneering approach at the time. In 1990 he decided to launch a fund-of-funds business, supplemented by co-investments. However, the start of the first Gulf War means that investors were shying away from private equity. 'So I changed my strategy', says Coller. 'If everyone hates private equity, why not buy it?'

Unsurprisingly it took him a long time – four years – to attract capital from LPs to acquire assets that most LPs wanted to be out of. But with the support of what he terms 'visionary' backers, such as the State of Michigan, Abu Dhabi Investment Authority and Guardian Royal Exchange, Coller eventually scraped together $50 million and began buying.

There wasn't a formal secondaries market back then, especially in Europe, just occasional transactions between fellow LPs within the same fund when one wanted to downweight a holding and the other was looking to build. So in building the portfolio, Coller had to communicate the concept to potential sellers who, in some cases, did not even realise that selling to a third party was an option.

Today the market is much more sophisticated, with many secondaries changing hands at auction. Rather than paying full prices for commoditised assets in competitive processes, Coller's London- and New York-based firm now concentrates on doing deals where extensive due diligence is required or where the transaction structure is complex owing to the nature of the portfolio or situation or because the seller's requirements are non-standard. In such situations Coller could be seen to be leveraging his depth of knowledge of the financial metrics of secondaries – or relying on the soft skills that, as an atypical private equity boss, he brings to the table. Whatever the formula, it appears to be successful, with the firm now having approximately $8 billion under management.

I met Coller in the firm's offices just north of London's Oxford Street. He was accompanied by Chris McDermott, Head of Markets and Planning, who is responsible for brand marketing, investor proposition and business planning.

McDermott opened the interview as Coller was taking a call from a prospective investor. (The firm was raising a new fund at the time, expected to be around €4.5 to 5 billion.)

*   *   *

MB: How do you decide which positions to acquire, and what to offer for them?

CMcD: First and foremost, the decision is about the quality of the assets and their manager. A secondaries firm is looking at future exit scenarios – their quanta and timing – and allocating a net present value to those scenarios. It is therefore a matter of judging the final value and timing of exits, bearing in mind the quality and reliability of the GPs involved, and then putting a corresponding price on the assets.

MB: Where do you sit on the risk-return spectrum, and in terms of stage? And what is the link between these factors and pricing?

CMcD: You can buy funds that are very young and only have a few assets – early-stage secondaries. This has more in common with fund-of-funds investing – in other words, it's closer to blind pool investing [committing capital to a fund 'on trust' with few if any constraints on how it will be invested]. Alternatively, you can buy into something at the other end of the spectrum, where the fund is already well beyond its investment period and is realising assets.

Most of the stuff we buy – and in fact the majority of the market – is somewhere in the middle. Funds will typically be some years into their investment periods, with some cash still to be deployed and with some of their earliest investments already realised. There will be assets sitting in the fund and a proportion of an investor's original commitment still to be funded. What we ask ourselves is what value we put on the assets already sitting in the fund, and what value we believe the GP will get from the un-invested capital.

The price we offer is a combination of the value of assets and the putative value of un-funded commitments, minus any liquidity discount. With the un-invested portion of a fund, we might think, 'Such-and-such is a good GP, but the market is looking very difficult for the next couple of years, so perhaps they'll only get 1.4 times on the yet-to-be-invested capital.' Or we might say, 'This is a great time to be buying in the market – lots of disruption. We think they'll make 1.7 times or two times on the un-invested capital.'

At the height of the bubble, some people were buying fund positions at a premium to net asset value. That hasn't happened except when the market was at its frothiest. When buying at a premium becomes widespread in the market, you can bet a correction is near!

MB: Is there a relationship between the discount or premium to NAV applicable in the secondaries market and that experienced by quoted private equity?

CMcD: There is a connection, yes. It's not exact, but you can see the correlation by comparing where quoted private equity vehicles are trading with average prices paid in secondaries auctions.

Secondary market prices have varied enormously in the last few years – just as prices in the quoted markets have. At the bottom of the market, following the Lehman Brothers crash, we saw secondaries market discounts to NAV of up to 40 per cent for well-known buyout funds. By the same token, the average discount to NAV for UK-listed PE funds (excluding 3i) widened from 15 per cent at the start of 2008 to 52 per cent by year-end. At the present time, secondaries market discounts for buyout funds are in the teens.

Since there are no third-party liquidity providers in the PE secondaries market – simply buyers and sellers – bid-ask spreads are in practice reflected in two ways: in discounts (or occasionally premiums) to NAV, and in deal volumes.

What happened after the market crash was very interesting. Most people assumed there would be a rush to the exit by private equity investors, and that this would result in massive transaction volumes. It didn't happen. The reason is that PE portfolios are reported quarterly in arrears – at best. In the 18 months following Lehman Brothers, asset values round the world fell off a cliff – which meant that the *value* of PE assets (which is clearly related to that of quoted equities) fell far faster than their *valuations*. Would-be purchasers were looking to tomorrow's value, putative sellers at yesterday's valuations. Discounts to NAV reached 60 per cent, and deal volumes became very thin.

In time, though, the declining valuations of private equity and the rebounding values of public equities came more into line, and investors keen to re-shape their portfolios in the wake of the crash said: 'Right, we can sell at these prices.' These tactical sellers were then joined by strategic sellers – banks facing regulatory and liquidity pressures, for example – and today's secondaries market is consequently at record volumes.

MB: Where do you expect pricing to go from here?

CMcD: We think pricing has been as high as it is going to go in the near future, and we expect to see further softening as demand outstrips supply of secondaries capital.

MB: How homogeneous is the secondaries market in terms of pricing, process and so on?

CMcD: When people talk about market prices, they are usually quoting auction prices for 'plain vanilla' transactions – a sale by a pension plan to tidy up its portfolio, perhaps. The seller goes to an auctioneer with a set of assets. The auctioneer invites many buyers to the party, because the assets are usually well-known funds, managed by well-known GPs. The buyers buy on price. The assets are transferred. End of story.

Many of the investments Coller Capital makes are not at all like that. We tend to operate where the needs of the seller are more exacting, structures are more complex, and the assets less well known to the market. The many banks selling in the European market in 2012 were a good case in point. For example, we bought a 70 per cent stake in a £480 million ($750 million) portfolio from Lloyds Bank [the former Bank of Scotland Integrated Finance business], where the bank was invested in both the debt and the equity of the portfolio companies, and the investments were all different: different capital structures; different ownership percentages; different time horizons – different dynamics entirely. Add to that the bank's own concerns and issues, and you can see that we were a long way from the kind of straightforward sale I mentioned earlier.

MB: Those assets must be much more difficult to value.

CMcD: The valuation process is the same, and in fact we are able to access even more information in these situations than we can for fund positions, but less of that information tends to be in the right format. In other words, the valuation of direct assets is a very in-depth process, but harder work for us! The acquisition and transfer processes are also more complicated – assets like these can come with all sorts of 'rights of first refusal', tag-along rights, and so on. It's hugely more complicated.

MB: I suppose you need to enter into an understanding with the potential seller early on to make it worthwhile spending so much time valuing the assets?

CMcD: Yes. One of the big questions for sellers in these situations is whether they are confident in the ability of potential buyers to close a transaction. It's easy for an investor to spend months going through a long, painful process, only to find out in the end that the putative buyer is not capable of putting all the pieces together: that is, of coming up with a sensible price, plus a workable structure.

There are relatively few firms able to do that. It's also a matter of reputation and track record. With Coller Capital, people know that if we say we can do it, we actually can. And, that if we say we will do it, we actually will. That's very valuable to them – and to us.

MB: So who are your competitors for these complex deals – other secondaries funds and sovereign wealth funds?

CMcD: When sovereign wealth funds buy in our market, it is usually the plain vanilla stuff: they're often invested in the funds in question and they've often got a lower cost of capital. The type of complex deal we have just been talking about needs very specialist skills. We've been doing it for 20 years, and we're still learning every day.

Even among secondary firms, by no means all of them try to tackle the really complex deals. Size is an issue, too. For some transactions you need to be able to deploy large numbers of people and hundreds of millions of dollars in one go. For instance, on the Lloyds Bank transaction we deployed a team of 20 people at one point – all experts, all crunching through the information to meet the bank's deadline. You can't do that if you're a small secondaries fund or a sovereign wealth fund – you just don't have the people or the skills.

MB: You mentioned Lloyds, but presumably some Eurozone banks are facing an even greater challenge in improving their tier 1 ratios? I imagine this is providing quite an opportunity for you.

CMcD: Absolutely. European banks are facing many issues all at the same time – pretty much a perfect storm. First, institutions now wholly or partly in public ownership have been instructed by governments to sell assets. Second, all Europe's banks had to get their tier 1 capital up to 9 per cent by the middle of 2012. Third, many have uncomfortable amounts of Eurozone sovereign debt on their balance sheets.

So they've needed to shore up their tier 1 capital – but they don't want to raise new equity with public markets so feverish. Restricting dividends and cutting back on lending are also both problematic – in terms of shareholder and government relations respectively. They don't have many options apart from selling assets. In late 2011 banking analysts put out three separate estimates of the de-leveraging required. The estimates came in at between $2 and $3 trillion. [Our interview took place at a time when Coller Capital's proposed acquisition of private equity assets from French bank Crédit Agricole, which was expected to improve its tier 1 rating by around €900 million, was awaiting regulatory approval, and the firm was linked in the specialist media with further asset purchases from European banks.]

MB: Is the Eurozone de-leveraging a one-time opportunity for you?

CMcD: The opportunity is far broader and deeper than that. The fall-out from the crisis will be multi-faceted and play out over years. In the USA, for example, the banks are dealing with the Volcker Rule, which limits the percentage they can own of a private fund and the amount of a bank's capital that can be in private funds in aggregate – to 3 per cent in both cases.

There are also numerous hedge funds that invested in private equity during the bubble. They have ended up with so called 'side pockets' of illiquid assets. Now investors want redemptions, and those assets need to be sold. We've already bought some of them – and there's more to come.

European insurance companies, who are again big investors in private equity, are also facing new capital adequacy and risk-management requirements – in the shape of the EU's Solvency II framework. Individual investors will make their own judgements about what this means for their PE programmes, but private equity assets will undoubtedly come to market as a result.

And the focus of the EU has now turned to pension plans. Until now, pension plans have been active, but tactical, sellers of private equity – disposing of assets for 'portfolio management' reasons when they saw pricing as sufficiently attractive. However, the EU is considering imposing a Solvency II-type framework on Europe's pension funds too. Although the industry will try to resist this change, it could well happen in some form. If it *does*, regulatory pressures may convert pension plans into motivated, strategic sellers, like the banks. All in all, we've got years of deal-flow to come.

MB: So it's a pretty good time to be sat where you are?

CMcD: Yes, it's going to be a very interesting market. We've probably already seen the peak of pricing; an imbalance of demand and supply for secondaries capital is likely to develop because of the market's huge need for liquidity. In the last 18 months, the amount of available secondaries capital has reduced significantly – to only about two-thirds of what it was a couple of years ago. Typically, you'd expect to have about 18 to 24 months' worth of capital available in the market. Today the volume of 'dry powder' has shrunk to about 15 to 18 months' worth. Given that private equity fundraising is now slower than it used to be, the capital available for secondaries may get shorter still.

MB: I suppose the caveat would be that the private equity asset class as a whole also has to perform in order for you to succeed?

CMcD: True. A good perspective on the prospects for private equity generally can be found in our Global Private Equity Barometer – a six-monthly survey we have run since 2004 – which looks at investors' attitudes to the asset class. Our latest [December 2011] shows that, although investors see a lot of challenges for private equity in the next few years, they think it has weathered the storm pretty well and their medium-term return expectations are good. [A third of LPs expect returns of 16 per cent or more over the next three to five years, and half of LPs expect between 11 and 15 per cent.]

Areas of private equity perceived as riskier are out of favour – large buyouts and venture capital, in particular – but funds with a small- and mid-market focus are viewed positively in both Europe and the USA. Emerging markets are seen as holding great promise for private equity, although there are also concerns about over-heating in the short term.

MB: How do the returns on your secondaries funds compare with primary private equity?

CMcD: Secondaries funds have so far proved to offer a very good risk-return profile. A secondaries fund is never going to shoot the lights out in the way that a successful venture fund can, but when it comes to good returns for a reasonable level of risk, secondaries funds have proved a good place to be.

MB: The Barometer also mentioned that around half of LPs believe their portfolios contain zombie funds [realisation-phase funds with general partners unlikely to be able to raise new money, whose managers may be motivated to exit portfolio businesses slowly to continue earning annual management fees]. Only 6 per cent believe they will be able to resolve these 'zombie fund' situations in most or all cases. Are these a potential source of direct secondaries deal-flow for you?

CMcD: Yes. They have been relatively rare in the past, though the fall-out from the crash may make them more common over the next few years. A typical solution might involve creating a liquidity option for the LPs in a fund, while resetting the terms for its manager. Investors can then exit the fund or maintain their participation on the reset terms. The aim is to provide an exit route for LPs that want it and to realign the interests of the investors with those of the manager for those that choose to stay the course.

We have fixed a number of zombie funds in this way, but it's never a simple process. First of all, because of what has gone before with the GP, a fund's investors have got to be willing to 'forgive and forget' to some extent. Secondly, the GP has also got to want to do it. And thirdly – and most importantly from our point of view – we have to be convinced that the GP can drive value from the remainder of the fund, if we provide the re-incentivisation.

Of course, it's also possible for investors to *replace* the manager of a private equity fund, but that requires quite a high degree of motivation and coordination from the fund's investors – and their nature does not suit them to collective action. The Limited Partner community is heterogeneous and international – from sovereign wealth funds in Asia to high-net-worth individuals in the Americas – and individual LPs have only a small percentage interest in any one fund. They therefore have relatively little in common as organisations.

JC: By the way, you also see these two types of transaction – where an incumbent manager does or does not continue to manage the assets – in the secondaries market for 'directs' [private equity assets, usually invested in by a bank or corporate, and not held within a fund structure]. They equate broadly to the management buy-in and the management buyout. Where there is no appropriate incumbent manager for a portfolio of directs, we would put a new one in place – the buy-in scenario. But where there is a strong management team already looking after the assets, we would facilitate a spin-out from the parent organisation – which is akin to a management buyout.

A classic example of the latter would be our NatWest transaction. As part of its defence against a hostile takeover bid from Royal Bank of Scotland, NatWest decided to focus on its core banking business and sell its private equity portfolio – which comprised 292 private companies, the vast majority on its balance sheet.

We went to them and said, 'Do you really want to negotiate with 292 different sets of lawyers, or would you prefer to deal with just one?' We did a portfolio transaction and helped the in-house team, NatWest Equity Partners, to spin-out as Bridgepoint.

MB: Returning to zombie funds for a moment, one of the arguments in favour of private equity is that the alignment of interests between investors, fund managers and portfolio company managers creates superior returns. Doesn't the existence of so many zombie funds challenge this? After all, the primary metric of success is IRR, and unless the values of underlying portfolios continue to grow, a GP that holds on any longer than is strictly necessary to achieve exits is not only taking out a couple of per cent from the committed capital each year but is also reducing the IRR by extending the time period.

CMcD: In general, private equity's built-in alignment is a very powerful feature of the asset class, especially when compared with the 'agency problem' inherent in the public company model. However, in the rare instances when PE's famous alignment slips – and zombie funds are still very much the exception, not the rule – it does create problems. Two other features of the PE model are pertinent and helpful in these situations: first, a fund's advisory committee, a group representing the body of LPs (usually composed of large, experienced investors), which can act as a sounding-board for the wider LP body; and second, the fact that every PE fund has a built-in expiry date, which puts a limit on investors' potential downside.

MB: The Barometer shows that four-fifths of LPs expect fund terms to become more favourable. Does this suggest that PE's current fee structure is unsustainable?

CMcD: The model has changed in LPs' favour in recent years as a result of a generally more assertive LP community and the efforts of the ILPA. Their message to the LP community has been: 'Look, we can't exercise power very easily in individual funds, but together we can specify best standards for the industry.' It's work in progress, of course – and always will be – but ILPA has been quite successful in changing the standard terms and conditions offered by PE funds.

MB: What sort of changes are we talking about?

CMcD: Where the guidelines have made most difference is in the area of transaction fees and a GP's eligibility for carried interest. Buyout funds have traditionally charged their funds and portfolio companies a variety of transaction-related fees on top of their headline management fees. Until recently, these fees added substantially to the costs and, especially in mega-buyout funds, to the rewards of the GP. ILPA recommended that any such fees should flow to the LPs rather than the GP.

The other area is carried interest. There are two main models for determining a GP's eligibility for carried interest: deal-by-deal and whole-fund 'carry'. The difference between them is a question of where the performance hurdle lies. In the first case the hurdle is attached to individual deals; in the second, it applies at the fund level only. Whole-fund carry is clearly better aligned with the interests of investors, because LPs want to invest in profitable funds, not just some profitable deals. It is true that funds stipulating deal-by-deal carry also contain claw-back provisions that entitle the LPs to take back the carry on individual deals if the whole fund does not reach its hurdle, but the truth is that it's hard to claw back carry that has already been paid and on which the GP team has already paid tax.

Limited Partners have not yet managed to get rid of transaction fees and deal-by-deal carry completely, but they have made considerable progress and will probably eventually consign them to the history book.

MB: The geographical spread of private equity has been changing fast. The past year and a half has seen the big firms finding it hard to raise new capital for developed-world mega buyouts, but some large funds are being raised – often by the same firms – for Asia. How does this impact secondaries?

CMcD: The secondary market lags the primary market by a few years; you need the latter to be sufficiently developed within a region in order to create fund positions for secondaries to buy. Currently, PE activity in emerging markets is relatively small, but as the primary market develops we will in due course buy more positions in local funds.

We have two other kinds of interaction with investors in growth markets, though. First, there are many investors in Asia, for example, that have international PE portfolios. We acquire US or European assets from them, in just the same way we do from LPs based in the West. Secondly, many emerging markets investors are also Limited Partners in Coller's own funds.

MB: How do you see things panning out over the next decade?

JC: In a decade's time, what private equity does for society will be more self-evident. In mainland Europe, where private equity is newer, they are only just beginning to see its benefits, whereas these are rather clearer from a UK perspective. The debate about Bain Capital's activities, which have been portrayed very negatively by Mitt Romney's opponents, has muddied the water in the USA. Whatever you think about the rights and wrongs of that case, it is hardly objective to view an industry through the lens of a single firm.

MB: This is an interesting time for private equity. When Romney went for the nomination before, in 1994, his background may have contributed to him losing the nomination; this time, perhaps the case for private equity was better expressed; and maybe the other change is that the moral case against *public* equity is stronger now than it was back then.

JC: Perhaps, but the truth is that private equity has a massive role to play in society. I believe private equity ownership directly benefits companies, and pension funds and other private equity investors agree [93 per cent of LPs in a recent Barometer said that private equity investment made for healthier companies]. It's hard to see anyone saying the same for hedge funds, say.

What has been little understood is that private equity has created a means for the man in the street to benefit from the wealth creation of private companies. Because the largest group of investors in the asset class are pension funds, private equity's beneficiaries include current and future pensioners – in their millions.

MB: I wonder whether that argument plays out better in the USA, where most public sector workers are members of the big state pension funds?

JC: Perhaps. I think the problem in the UK is going to be the decline of defined benefit pensions in favour of defined contribution schemes. Private equity investments are suitable for defined benefit and sovereign wealth funds, but less suitable for defined contribution pension plans because members in principle need to be able to request liquidity at any time, in order to move their money around.

There are ways round it; the Peruvians and Chileans have defined contribution schemes, but with a choice of three investment strategies – aggressive, moderate or conservative: i.e., 80–100 per cent equity, 40–50 per cent equities or 0–10 per cent equities. This enables them to combine the best of an aggressive and a long-term approach, allowing them the benefits of defined benefits, as it were.

MB: I wonder whether defined benefit schemes in the USA could go the same way as the UK ones? After all, many of the individual states are border-line bankrupt, and unfunded public sector pension liabilities are a big part of that.

JC: Clearly we don't know how the pension market will evolve in the USA, but were defined benefit schemes to fade away, that would clearly be a cause for concern for private equity.

MB: Do you think the current challenges in raising new funds will lead to a reduction in the number of firms?

JC: In ten years' time I think there will be just as many private equity groups, but the industry will be a lot healthier because there will be a shake-out in the meantime. We will lose GPs that haven't performed, and others will be created as we enter the up phase of another cycle. That should be very good for the industry.

MB: Where will the newcomers come from?

JC: They'll come mainly from the existing groups. Many private equity groups raised big funds in the boom and hired very good people from investment banking or elsewhere. Not all those groups have performed. There's a famous saying: 'An army of sheep led by a lion is better than an army of lions led by a sheep.' Some of the under-performing groups have turned out to be led by sheep...but the lions are trained and ready to go. Younger private equity professionals who have spent the last few years learning the industry will establish the firms that will succeed in the next cycle.

Section II
Developed Markets

6
Introduction

While the four interviewees in the first section of this book don't speak as one on all matters – in particular, they diverge about the prospects for private equity in emerging markets – it's striking how much they have in common. In particular, it seems that the enormous funds raised for highly leveraged large buyouts in the boom were a by-product of the liquidity bubble in the middle of the last decade, that they are judged to have benefited those running them more than the investors, and that, due to the substantial amount of 'dry powder' remaining in the system, challenges to the business model in a low-debt, low-growth environment and diversification by the managers, it will be some time before similar-sized funds are raised again – if they ever are.

But it is too early to proclaim the death of the mega buyout; and even if it were, it would not equate to the demise of private equity. On the contrary, even as LPs grapple with zombie funds and worry about the wall of debt that the big buyouts completed at the peak of the market will have to refinance over the next three years, the most striking statistics in Coller Capital's Benchmark report are those relating to the proportion of investors that plan to increase their allocation to certain types of private equity. While around 30 per cent expect to decrease their exposure to large buyouts (funds targeting transactions of $1 million plus), the same proportion intend increasing their investment in mid-market buyouts ($200–999 million), while slightly more will raise their stakes in small (sub-$200 million) buyouts and a little over 20 per cent hope to put more money to work in growth/expansion capital.

Academics have debated for years whether the relationship between risk and return is linear: that is, whether increasing market or financial risk (the latter driven principally by the relationship between debt and equity funding) genuinely increases long-run returns, or merely appears to do so in a rising market. They term the volatility of an individual investment relative to the market 'beta', and label genuine over-performance in excess of the relationship between risk and return 'alpha'. It is beyond the scope of this book to determine whether private equity, in general or for specific funds at particular points in time, delivers *alpha* returns: many research papers have been written on the topic, all of which are open to criticism, and the findings of which are sometimes contradictory. But it is probably fair to observe that the mega-buyout funds, which typically use the most debt in the capital structures of investee businesses, typically deliver some of the best returns in the good times and under-perform in the worst and that, whether through the typically greater use of leverage or the greater shareholder input and alignment of interests between management and investors, private equity as a whole would appear to have generated superior returns than the public markets for much of its life.

Thus it is unsurprising to see that, at a time when most developed economies face a decade of austerity and de-leveraging, investors are seeking to rebalance their capital towards the less leveraged niches in private equity, but that they remain committed to the sector, with Coller Capital's Barometer, for instance, finding that 59 per cent of LPs intend to maintain their current level of allocation, while 24 per cent plan to raise it and only 17 per cent to retrench.

In this second section of my book I focus on five private equity firms active in developed markets and operating in the niches within the industry that I expect to attract capital and deliver market-beating returns in the current macro-economic environment. They vary substantially in scale, geography and age, from a firm founded in 2005 with £400 million under management and focused solely on the UK to a 45-year-old group that has been pursuing its current strategy for perhaps 30 years, spans the USA, Europe and Asia and has $6 billion in its charge. Each has a distinct business model and has assembled resources, primarily people, with skills and backgrounds that differ from those typically found in the big buyout houses, in order to make its strategy implementable.

Hearteningly, at a time when private equity has faced criticism for asset-stripping investee businesses and causing them to shed jobs, the approaches they have developed focus on either saving jobs or actively creating them, and their principals are more willing than many in the industry to make the social case for what they do, including sharing data about employment and returns, some of which I've included in the relevant chapters. There can be no doubt that these are firms that generate net employment and fiscal returns for the countries in which they operate, as well as for their investors – something that is not convincingly, if at all, demonstrated by academic studies of large buyouts.

It lies outside my brief to engage in a philosophical debate about the purpose of capitalism and the extent to which it has a moral duty to enrich society as a whole, or at least to minimise or pay for any harm that it causes. But I think it is fair to observe that since, in a democracy, the principal role of government is to maximise the welfare of its citizens in order to perpetuate itself through re-election, prudent businesses should seek to avoid imposing significant externalities on society and, where possible, should benefit the communities within which they operate, since the alternative may be to provoke politicians into introducing regulatory constraints.

In the case of private equity, we have already heard that compliance costs are rocketing, that financial sector solvency rules, mark-to-market accounting policies and the decline of defined benefit pensions could choke its supply of capital, that US tax-avoidance rules may make it hard for European firms to invest in the USA and that questions are again being asked about the tax deductibility of interest payments, the tax treatment of carried interest and the use of tax havens by GPs. Indeed, on the carry point, it seems likely that the controversy over Mitt Romney's finances means that, should Barack Obama be re-elected, the threatened Buffett Rule will find its way onto the statutes, raising the US tax take on investment income to 30 per cent.

Faced with these challenges, it seems to me that the industry has three options: keep a low profile and hope its critics go away; shout loud and proud about the good stuff (and, despite the media furore, there's plenty of that) without fundamentally re-evaluating what it does; or stop doing the controversial stuff and do more of the good. Fortuitously, for the present at least, I suspect that the good stuff done by the firms in this section of the book, and others like them that I was unable to find the space and time to include, will prove to generate returns for investors, and possibly also GP teams, that exceed those from the more controversial types of transaction.

I am not suggesting that the industry will, or should, move away from large buyouts, but rather that the toxic combination of high valuations and debt to equity ratios, covenant-lite senior debt, pay-in-kind and pay-if-you-can (PIK or PIC) loans and sale-and-leaseback arrangements predicated on relentless revenue growth seen before mid-2008 are unlikely to return for many years, and hence the industry will of necessity leave behind it much of what has courted criticism. In the meantime, its interests and those of society are broadly aligned by focusing on turnarounds, growth investment and small buyouts – the areas covered in the next five chapters.

7

Ajit Nedungadi, Managing Director, TA Associates L.P.

While the debate about whether private equity as a whole achieves the elusive goal of genuine 'alpha' – superior risk-adjusted returns over the long run – there is little doubt that there are individual firms that do. At the top of that list is a manager already mentioned by one of my interviewees, John Hess: namely, TA Associates.

I would venture to suggest of all the private equity GPs in the world today, TA is perhaps the one most widely admired by practitioners in other firms, famously delivering an IRR of around 30 per cent pretty consistently for the past 30 years, a multiple of around three times invested capital, without heavy reliance on debt.

Founded in 1968, TA started out as what its originators termed a 'balanced venture' firm, meaning that it invested a couple of hundred thousand dollars at a time from an initial $6 million fund into a mixture of early-stage (pre-profit) enterprises and profitable, high-growth businesses.

By the early 1980s the firm had largely ditched the early-stage part of the strategy, having observed a negative correlation between risk and return, but retained a focus on growth. It targets firms that are growing at a minimum of 15 per cent a year, with a typical annual revenue increase of 25 to 30 per cent.

Of course, investing in high-growth businesses is not in itself a recipe for superior returns; generally the cost of buying in is high, since any discounted cash-flow valuation has to allow for the expectation that the growth will continue, and risk can be considerable, because there is always the possibility that it may not. There is also a suspicion that such firms may be heavily reliant on entrepreneurial founders, and that allowing them to crystallise any of the value they have created can reduce or remove the incentive for them to continue to deliver value enhancement under a financial owner.

Over the past three decades, TA has diversified geographically from its Boston base, first to California, then, a decade ago, to Europe, and in the past five years to India and Hong Kong. It has developed a model that it applies across all those geographies and that would appear to go a long way towards mitigating the potential downsides of its chosen investment strategy. I see six facets to the firm's approach:

1. Deep sector focus. While TA is open to investing in any businesses that meet its growth and scale criteria, it has built up significant experience in certain verticals, and actively seeks out opportunities in those sectors. Currently these are: technology, financial services (especially asset management), healthcare, certain business services (for instance, financial technology) and some consumer markets, such as for-profit education.
2. Asset-light businesses. With a handful of exceptions, TA prefers to invest in businesses that require little investment in fixed assets, on the basis that while such firms may be less suitable for highly leveraged transactions (see below), the capital investment required to achieve further growth is generally modest. As a result, perhaps surprisingly, more than 90 per cent of the capital that TA spends to acquire equity in portfolio businesses provides one-time liquidity to existing shareholders, rather than going into the firms by means of new share issues.
3. Low leverage. A typical TA deal involves anywhere between zero and three times EBITDA [earnings before interest, taxation, depreciation and amortisation] leverage, compared with four to six times in a typical buyout.
4. Off-market deals. Every TA office employs a number of largely pre-MBA associates who are tasked with identifying and contacting predominantly privately owned, high-growth businesses in its preferred sectors, then visiting those that express an interest. The firm estimates that it contacts 10,000 firms a year and visits between 1500 and 1700 of these in order to make typically 15 new investments.
5. The management proposition. Taken together with the bottom-up approach to deal origination, this is probably the key to TA's success. The firm pitches itself as a value-adding investor that can also provide liquidity for owner–managers wishing to offer minority shareholders an exit or take some money off the table for themselves at a time when they either do not want to sell to a trade buyer because there is still a lot of growth ahead or do not want to IPO [make an initial public offering] because of the costs and distractions to management that it entails. The value-add is pretty extensive, encompassing areas such as strategy, M&A, recruitment to strengthen the senior management team and preparing the firm for IPO or trade sale. It is a delicate balance, allowing an entrepreneurial founder to continue to run the business while at the same time making the firm less reliant on that individual.
6. Understanding and aligning motivations. TA describes itself as 'control-agnostic', meaning that it is happy with both minority and majority positions, without and with effective control, and indeed most of its investments

are minority stakes. It rejects the notion that a founder who realises a proportion of the value of his or her business via a sale to TA is unlikely to be
motivated to enhance the value of the remaining holding, on the grounds
that anyone taking such a view would prefer to sell the entirety of the company. Instead it structures deals in such a way that managements are aligned
with itself, especially in the area of downside protection, for instance by
investing by means of a senior instrument that sits ahead of the founder's
remaining equity.

Given that TA began in the USA but Europe now accounts for around a third
of its assets under management, I decided that the best subject for this interview would be Ajit Nedungadi, the US-born Managing Director, who began
his career with TA in the firm's Boston head office in 1999, before moving to
London three years later to set up its European operation. I met him in the
firm's Knightsbridge office.

*   *   *

MB: I understand that TA is built around a number of sector specialisms.
But how were those sectors chosen? Why, for instance, asset management
rather than restaurants?

AN: It's partly about the way the firm has evolved and the expertise we've
picked up along the way, and partly about the financial characteristics.
Our heritage as a venture investor means we've always had an interest
in the tech sector and started out by looking for boot-strap businesses.
We still like tech and companies that are asset-light and which don't need
a lot of capital to get them going. We moved into asset management
and speciality healthcare in the '80s because they shared those characteristics, they rely on intellectual property and you can scale them up
quickly.

MB: I'm interested that you prefer asset-light businesses, whereas many private equity firms like sectors that have lots of assets, as they can either
borrow against them or do sale-and-leasebacks.

AN: It's another defining characteristic of our approach that, because we're
investing in high-growth companies, we tend to use a lot less leverage.
A third of our transactions are unlevered, and where there's leverage it's
seldom more than four times, compared with four to six times for most
private equity firms. And maybe two-thirds of our transactions in recent
years have been minority investments.

MB: What is the rationale behind minority deals? Surely if you're investing
in a high-growth business, it's better to own all of it than part?

AN: We prefer to invest in high-quality, profitable, high-growth businesses.
They're generally not up for sale and you can call them all you want, but

if they're not interested in selling their company, they're not interested in selling their company because they see there's an attraction to staying invested. So the product that we therefore came up with over the years, and is a real speciality of ours, is to provide equity release to individuals in the context of a minority investment in the company, getting on the board and being involved in the business in a very strategic way, but not trying to get control.

MB: A lot of private equity firms are wary of that kind of proposition, perhaps because they worry about the motivations of the entrepreneur post-transaction and the level of control they'd have.

AN: We don't worry that it reduces motivation because if you were losing motivation you'd sell the whole business. Our view is we'd rather buy 30 per cent of a company that's not up for sale if it meets all our other characteristics, even if it means we're not in control, than 100 per cent of a company that is up for sale because there's much more of an information asymmetry and much more of a knowledge gap when the vendor is selling up entirely.

MB: And how about the eventual exit? If an entrepreneur doesn't want to sell 100 per cent when TA becomes a shareholder, what about five years down the road?

AN: We have the usual drag-and-tag provisions and minority protections, but it's our view that if you're relying on them, something has probably gone badly wrong.

How do we know they're going to sell? We have very seldom run into that problem. These are not GDP growers, stable businesses that fathers are going to hand to their sons. These are dynamic, aggressive, fast-growing businesses in sectors where the founders often know much better than we do when they should be selling the company to maximise value. All things are not perfect, so there are situations where we need to exercise our influence and where maybe we would prefer to be in control because we think the business is not going the right way, but that's the trade-off we make.

It's all a question of how you like your risk. In a highly levered control deal you own the business and can do whatever you want. But it's levered, and typically the first dollar of loss would be the investor's. But in our deals the first dollar of loss is not ours, and there's a lot of value in that.

MB: Even within the growth private equity sector, your approach seems to be different in that most growth deals are about acquiring new shares in return for putting cash onto the balance sheet to fund further expansion.

AN: I'd say 95 per cent of our capital goes to buy secondary shares, not to put up primary capital. These are companies that generally don't need money, and if they do, they can generally borrow it from the bank. So it's like showing up and offering me financial modelling services. You could come and you could pitch me a hundred times, I'm just not interested. I can do it myself. These companies don't need our cash for development. The very best business models can grow without the use of capital, so trying to force feed our capital into the capital structure would be viewed as unnecessary dilution.

So we try to provide entrepreneurs who own amazing businesses that they wouldn't ordinarily sell the opportunity to crystallise some of the value that they've created, because most of them have very undiversified portfolios. They've got a lot of their wealth tied up in this one asset, and so the ability to take some chips off the table and then continue to own and run the company is very powerful. Our industry is about judgement. The judgement is whether this gentleman or this woman is likely to change their approach if they got 30 million, 50 million, 100 million. It's a judgement call on the individual and the situation.

MB: It has occurred to me that there may be some entrepreneurs who achieve higher growth post-transaction, because they are no longer betting much of their net worth each time they make a major strategy decision.

AN: We see that; some cautious managers become more aggressive. Diversifying your portfolio is very powerful, and that's an interesting value-add that we deliver. We often say, 'Look, you're thinking about the world in terms of three alternatives. You could do nothing, maybe you take monthly dividends, but you do nothing with the ownership of the business. And by default that's what you're doing every day.

'The second option is try to go public. Going public has its appeal at the right time in the right market. We know what the markets are like these days. The markets are not always perfect, there are good times and bad times and more importantly they come with a lot of headaches, a lot of overhead, a lot of energy invested.

'The third is to sell the entire company to a strategic or financial buyer, but the point there is that there is still opportunity available, so why do it?'

So what we like to say is that we're giving owners a fourth alternative, which is that they get the liquidity of a sale or an IPO without the negatives of being a 100 per cent sale or the negatives of having to do an IPO. We try to be competitive on price, and we present ourselves as a serious, interested investor who will spend a lot of time dedicated to trying to make the business even better.

MB: I guess if a founder wants to take some money off the table or there are some minority shareholders itching for an exit but the founder wants to stay in, the more you can emphasise the value-adding aspects of TA's proposition the less critical the price per share for the minority holding becomes? Is that one reason for TA's attractive returns?

AN: Possibly; it's not just a zero-sum game. It's really that we're offering a different type of deal, making the transaction look and feel different. We're not just competing purely on price; we're changing the dimensions of the game, which is a much more interesting way to compete.

MB: We've talked about the strategy and process for identifying investment opportunities and the proposition to managements. How about the post-investment process? How do you add value?

AN: We don't overwhelm the owners. So, for example, we tend not to stuff the board with our people; we take one or two seats at most. We generally stick with the same people that did the deal, we don't put in a post-acquisition or operational team, so the individual partner that did the deal lives and works and breathes and dies with that decision.

Our overall theme is to encourage managers to raise their ambitions. One way we do that is to help them hire good senior people. That takes a lot of work; we're interviewing people all the time. Another is M&A. As part of our outbound strategy we find investments for ourselves, but we also find smaller companies that don't fit us but could fit our portfolio companies, so we introduce them. There are a lot of acquisitions that have been introduced by TA that way over the years. And finally, because of our sector focus, we tend to know the industry well too, so we're pretty focused on strategy.

MB: Has your approach to value creation changed over time?

AN: We've become more aggressive about helping companies to make acquisitions. We've become more cognisant of international growth opportunities, given that we are ourselves now so much more international. We've become that much more ambitious in terms of hiring world-class management into companies, which is never easy. And we have entered some new sectors, such as financial technology, for-profit education and mobile telephony, which have given us more skills and connections that we can share with portfolio businesses.

MB: What other changes have taken place since you joined, in 1999?

AN: The evolution has been linear and geographic. The real big step-change in the last 20 years was to go into Europe, because that really has taken our business to a different level. When I joined TA, we were strictly a US business. As our fund sizes have got bigger, we've been casting our net ever wider to do deals. We started covering Europe on a grassroots basis, then decided to open up the office in London, and it's now about a third of the firm, maybe more, and we did the same thing in Mumbai and more recently in Hong Kong.

MB: How about the continents TA isn't in? I suppose being a US firm, the obvious one is South America.

AN: It's unlikely we'll be opening up in Brazil any time soon. It's just a question of focus. We'll maybe get there at some point, but not right now.

MB: Or Africa?

AN: It's too emerging. I think private equity is very, very nascent today in Africa. I just can't see how long it would even take. Maybe not in my career lifetime in this business.

MB: Its big disadvantage compared with India and China is that it is a continent comprising a lot of countries that together equal a billion people and a meaningful amount of GDP, rather than one big nation. It's not a single market.

AN: Exactly.

MB: Is the TA approach any different in India and China from in the USA and Europe?

AN: Not really; the key point is that while growth private equity is a niche in developed markets, it's mainstream in emerging ones. They are very competitive markets, so it helps to be able to say to entrepreneurs that we are not just doing this in, say, India, but that it is what we've always done, which happens to have the benefit of being the truth, versus some of the big buyout firms that go into those markets trying to do minority deals. In India you can often take processes in a much more entrepreneurial way. Vendors don't run strict, disciplined auctions because they basically want people to get excited and enthusiastic; they allow people to develop at their own pace.

MB: And how about in Europe? I see you run the entire European operation out of London. Have you considered opening offices elsewhere on the Continent?

AN: We like the idea of not trying to force too many offices, because what happens is, if you have an Italian, Spanish or German office, they're going to feel the pressure to do a deal in that country whether it's good or bad, whereas if you're sitting in London and you've got a pan-European team you can pick any country where you find a company that fits our target profile and go and try to make it happen. That's pretty powerful. We have native speakers of nine languages here in London – a brilliant mix, including Germans, French, Scandinavians and Spanish.

MB: Do you notice any differences in returns by continent?

AN: I think Europe has been at least as good for us in the past ten years as the USA, if not better. I think India will be interesting because we don't have enough evidence there so far. It's a huge market, very, very competitive and expensive. And for Asia it's very early days.

MB: I notice that TA invests from a single, global capital pool. Recently there has been a trend for US GPs to raise regional or even national funds, presumably because some LPs want to target their capital towards particular geographies. Does this trend make it hard to raise global funds?

AN: I think that raising different funds just creates all kinds of screwy internal dynamics within the organisation, because not everyone accesses the same pool of capital or participates in the same carry … it's just very complicated. And our view is that we'd rather raise a big global fund than try to raise many regional funds. Some people have raised European funds. We might potentially do it, but I don't see it any time soon.

MB: I wonder whether separate pools make it harder to internationalise portfolio businesses. For instance, a US business may want to work with a growth private equity investor that can help it get into Europe. But if the firm's European fund is separately managed and its team incentivised separately, would they be as focused on helping them set up in Europe or identify European acquisition opportunities?

AN: I think in any sensible set-up you would have to ensure that they weren't totally independent, that there was still some cross-pollination. My concern is more that by having separate pools you put undue pressure on yourself. This business is not one where you can predict where your deals are going to come from that easily, whereas if you have a global fund, any part of the world can make the numbers in any given year.

MB: Talking about making the numbers, looking back to the boom years in the middle of the past decade, were you ever tempted to get into the big buyout space?

AN: Not really, we avoided it, not just here in Europe but also in the USA. We just didn't get into the mega-buyout world. We don't like doing those things. We're not well set up to do those things. It's not what we're focused on. We're growth investors. You can't do mega-buyout growth.

It's critical not to style-drift in this business. And it's important to stay true to your theme and have a simplistic message you can go to your limited partners with for investment and to investee companies to explain what you do. It makes a big difference.

MB: Given your focus on growth, do you find it frustrating to hear the industry as a whole being criticised for over-use of debt, asset-stripping and the destruction of employment?

AN: There's a bit of that. Anyone with any level of sophistication understands that is not what we do, but subtlety is not necessarily helpful to politicians.

MB: Do you think the buyout guys have learned the lessons of the past few years?

AN: Private equity is just too big an industry, it has too big a presence and is too profitable to conduct itself as though it doesn't exist, as though people will just ignore it. The Republican candidate nomination process undoubtedly only increased the public interest in the sector. The lesson the industry has learned is that you have to be proactive and strategic in the way in which you respond to criticism. All this stuff, I think, the industry has only really started to get to grips with in the last ten years, whereas the business has been around for a good 30 years.

MB: How do you see things playing out for them?

AN: I think the number of GPs will come down, that's for sure. I think the industry's going to shrink in terms of number of participants. It will take a long time, because it's very hard to kill a private equity firm because of the committed funds structure of the business, but I think there's no question, if you talk to the limited partners, that they want the number of GPs to come down, so that's the first thing that'll happen. Whether that's a decline of 20 per cent or 30 per cent or 40 per cent I don't know, but it'll come down. It's a very good thing for the industry.

The trend of building large multi-asset class management firms out of private equity will slow down for a while. Meanwhile we'll continue to see more specialisation. More going east, right or wrong. I think people are paying way too high prices, but it is what it is.

MB: I guess it depends on whether those economies continue to grow at the rates they've achieved over the past few years. A lot of deals are based on present values that require continuing economic growth at 7, 8, even 9 per cent...

AN: The problem is, even if it doesn't continue, it has a long way to go before it becomes as bad as here [the UK].

MB: I suppose it depends on the extent to which developed and emerging markets are interlinked.

AN: A lot of the interesting investment opportunities in India and China are not dependent on export. They're about domestic consumption.

MB: Do you see the de-leveraging in developed economies as a challenge to your business model?

AN: It could impact on growth, which isn't great, but not on our core proposition. The companies we're looking to invest in don't rely greatly on bank financing, and nor is it critical to how we structure transactions. And when there's less of one form of capital in any market, there's more opportunity for the other forms of capital.

MB: So where do you think TA will be in five to ten years' time?

AN: I think we will be ever so much more global, so we'll have significant operations in India and Asia. I don't know how many people we will have added in the US...I think we'll have added a lot of people outside of the USA, which is interesting. We will probably have picked up one or two more verticals, one or two more industries and sub-industries that we go after. But I think we'll largely still be doing what we're doing. I think our strategy is what it is. It's a good strategy. It works. I think we'll just continue it.

8

Steve Klinsky, Managing Director, Founder and Chief Executive Officer, New Mountain Capital

The fundamentals of growth private equity – identify highly scalable businesses in attractive sectors and acquire stakes without heavy leverage – may be universal, but there are many variations in execution. Perhaps the most interesting of these is the approach taken by New York-based New Mountain Capital, whose founder, Steve Klinsky, is my next interviewee.

A quick perusal of the firm's website highlights a few unique characteristics:

- The investment focus is on achieving control stakes in market-leading firms in what it terms 'defensive growth' industries, which the firm defines as 'sectors that should succeed in both good and bad economies, but which are also large and growthful enough to achieve very high valuations and returns at exit';
- The firm aims to be the most knowledgeable investor in each of these sectors, an approach that includes working with executives-in-residence and securing exclusive retainer agreements with brokers and consultants in those industries;
- The firm has never acquired a business as a result of a sealed-bid auction, instead preferring to identify and approach off-market acquisition targets;
- Minimal use is made of debt; in fact, as at February 2012, 14 of its 23 private equity investments used no third-party debt in their acquisition funding structures and the firm made the proud claim that 'New Mountain has never had a bankruptcy or missed a debt payment on any Fund investment since the Firm began. New Mountain's founder/CEO has not had a bankruptcy or missed debt payment on any fund investment made with New Mountain or his previous partnership for over 20 years.'

Dig a little deeper and you'll find something else that some other private equity firms are beginning to do, but in which New Mountain is a pioneer:

every year the firm publishes a social dashboard that compares employment levels in its portfolio companies as at 31 December, compared with the acquisition dates, separating out net movements in the constant companies with those added by acquisitions; it also reports on average salaries, compared with national statistics, and levels of research and development spending by its investees.

Reviewing the 2011 figures, it is hard to escape the conclusion that if all GPs reported this way, the private equity industry, or at least the portion of it that is not engaged in highly leveraged buyouts, would pretty quickly move from being bracketed with investment banking as an object of public scorn to the beneficiaries of widespread support. Key statistics included:

- A net increase in employment levels of 52 per cent, or more than 10,000 positions, since New Mountain invested. Of these jobs, around 56 per cent came from organic growth, the rest from acquisitions.
- The median salary level, $59,357, was 127 per cent above the national equivalent. The mean figure, $70,107, was 83 per cent above the US average.
- In 2011 alone, the portfolio businesses invested $441.4 million in R&D, software development and capital expenditure.

And yet, far from being some kind of social enterprise that creates well-paid jobs in firms that invest for the long term at the expense of investor returns, New Mountain has been among the highest-performing mid-market private equity firms in the USA since its inception in 2000 – including in the period of, and subsequent to, the global financial crisis of 2008.

So are there aspects of New Mountain's approach that other private equity firms could learn from, and which point towards an alternative model for the industry? Or is there something intangible about the founder and the team he has pulled together that makes it incapable of replication?

Intriguingly, in one small regard New Mountain has followed the lead of the big US buyout firms by diversifying into the management of other asset classes – in its case, public equities and corporate debt instruments. Could this also be a sensible option for smaller, more specialised, mid-market firms and their investors?

Founder Steve Klinsky spoke to me in his New York office, which is located on Seventh Avenue, just a handful of blocks north of Times Square. We began by exploring how he got into private equity. It turns out his parents had sold the family's Michigan-based chain of womenswear retail stores shortly before he went to graduate school. While he was there, KKR completed what many regard as the first true leveraged buyout, the 1979 acquisition of Houdaille Industries. Klinsky wrote a thesis on the subject, with the intention of using the technique to buy into a business with his father. In fact, he followed a different path, joining Goldman Sachs in 1981 and co-founding its buyout group before being head-hunted by Forstmann Little in 1984, making full partner two years later. After a 'great period' with the firm in the 1990s, during which time he was the most senior partner outside of the Forstmann family, Klinsky left in 1999, before founding New Mountain the following year.

*   *   *

MB: Why did you name the firm New Mountain?

SK: We are located in Manhattan: there are no mountains outside my window. The name New Mountain comes from the idea of building new mountains in the industries where we invest, and the way we try to build our own firm with some institutional permanence.

MB: What approach have you taken to building these 'new mountains'?

SK: Our strategy from the beginning, which has not changed, is not to count on a bull or bear market, inflation or deflation, but rather to buy what we call 'defensive growth' businesses; that is to say that we focus on industries that grow whether the macro-economy is good or bad, and we use debt very conservatively, and then work to really build the businesses.

We are a generalist firm but proactively pick specific sectors ahead of time and build deep specialisations in those industries, but keep freshening the list up every year in other defensive growth niches and never get stuck in one niche and keep identifying defensive company targets and building relationships with them.

MB: Some might call the phrase 'defensive growth' a tautology, in the sense that there are defensive industries that never really decline but also tend not to grow very rapidly, and growth industries that can also be highly volatile. Are you saying there are some industries that combine the two qualities?

SK: Yes, we strongly believe that. But you have to hunt for them. It is one of the things we do formally, as a process. If I may, I'll give you a couple of examples.

The first company we ever bought was a university system for working adults called Strayer. It had been around for 100 years, the average student was 33 years old, the sort of person who had dropped out of college, who was working but had never finished their courses. Strayer gave them a very high-quality way to finish their courses and get promoted at work. When the economy is good and people have jobs, they go back to finish their courses while they are still working. And if they lose their jobs, it is a great time to finish their courses to get ready for their next jobs. So it was both high-growth and very acyclical. We were able to grow it from one city to seven states, and we built the online programme. We grew the value from $400 million in value to about $1.8 billion entirely debt-free.

More recently, we recently bought Stroz Friedberg, a business that was started by the head of the FBI cybercrime unit and the lead US cybercrime prosecutor in Manhattan. When some of the world's best-known digital businesses experience security breaches or attacks, they call up this business to advise them. Cybersecurity for corporations and the collection of data for related lawsuits is an area that we think has the wind at its back for some years to come. It could grow very rapidly, but is not tied to auto sales or home sales next month. It is, we think, a defensive growth space.

MB: According to your website, you identified and acquired Stroz Friedberg after a 'multi-year, proactive "deep dive" ' into the sector. I'm interested in understanding the processes you use to identify both the defensive growth sectors and the individual businesses to invest in.

SK: It is hard to find good companies to invest in and that is why we only buy three or four businesses a year, even though we now have 55 investment professionals at the firm. Every year we have everybody in the firm nominate their two or three best ideas for what defensive growth sectors we should be specially staffing up for the year ahead. Everybody writes their ideas down in a memo. We take the names off the memos because we think that good ideas are age independent, we then have a whole series of firm votes and debates and discussions and narrow it down to a specific list. So it is top down.

The thing that has never changed is this focus on defensive growth, high free cash, high barrier to entry industries. We don't want to have EBITD [earnings before interest, taxation and depreciation] and then spend all that EBITD on capex [capital expenditure] and working capital and use up all the cash, and we are very focused on sustainability.

Where people's nominations come from very often is based on their experiences and backgrounds, in that they are working every day throughout the year looking at a range of different companies. Our team members are involved with operating our businesses, and have a range of experiences. Some are CEOs, some are management consultants, some are private equity people. And so people's nominations come from all sorts of ways but it ends up in a unified, firm-wide identification process.

MB: You mention the range of experiences that your people have. It sounds to me like they do not all fit the typical profile of a private equity professional.

SK: New Mountain people have come from a wide range of spaces. We have continuously built the team by bringing in people from additional areas of knowledge; some as employees, others as independent contractors or consultants. We have a category of people in our team that we call Senior Advisers, which we might call Operating Partners. One of them, to give you an example, is Raj Gupta, who was CEO of Rohm and Haas Chemical

Company. He built that business up to $19 billion of enterprise value, sold it to Dow Chemical in March 2009 and joined us the next day. So we now have a specialty chemicals team, of which he is a member. He is suggesting niches within chemicals, a type of insight that I couldn't have afforded to have on my team 12 years ago, when I was starting with much more of a skeleton crew. We also have for example, a Pulitzer Prize-winner who was an investigative reporter at the *Washington Post*. He works for us full-time and had been at Goldman Sachs before he went to the *Washington Post* 30 years ago. He has written books on a range of subjects. He has his life experiences and his ideas, and can provide valuable independent-minded analysis on a range of topics.

We try not to get 55 clones of each other. Rather, we try to get people with a wide range of backgrounds who are all intellectually focused, who are all just trying to come up with the right answer, and we put the thoughts of all those people together in one organised way.

MB: You have 55 people and do three or four deals a year; that is a much higher ratio of people to investments than most GPs run with.

SK: That is true. Some firms have stayed very small, the same five or six people for 30 years, because they don't want dilution from anybody new to cut into the take-home pay of the people who are already there. We have built this place with a different attitude, which is that we want the firm to be around for a long time and want it to just keep getting better and better every year.

I joke that I started with 100 per cent of nothing and so the dilution has come from me. As the firm has gotten bigger, my percentage has gone down. But we say good people are profit centres, not costs centres. We have brought people in who have made the firm stronger, which in the long run, we think, is good for our investors and good for us. And we do try to have a mix of skills so, for example, we intentionally recruit about half of our younger people out of Bain- or McKinsey-type consulting firms and the other half out of more traditional KKR- or Goldman Sachs-type backgrounds. We blend operating and financial skills. And then at the senior levels when we bring people in laterally, from a whole range of different directions, anyone we think can supplement what we do.

The other metaphor I use is that, 12 years ago, when I started the place, before I had called anybody to come and join my team, I felt like I was the guitar player on the sidewalk with a hat, waiting for someone to throw in a quarter and I would play my song by myself on a guitar. Now I feel more like we have an orchestra with a string section and a horn section and we have really built the skill-set out. The basic song has never changed, the basic approach has never changed, but the ability to execute it has got better and better.

MB: Does everyone have carry, including the Senior Advisers?

SK: I am simplifying now, but generally everybody shares in the carry, and from the Vice-Presidents up they are formally partners in the partnership. Below that level, everyone, including the receptionist, also effectively gets carry, but it is done on more of a phantom bonus-type arrangement, where they theoretically have carry, but they are not formally in the partnership.

MB: You talked about making a decision once a year to staff up to explore certain sectors in more detail for the next year. Is there a tension between sticking with sectors for many years and getting depth of knowledge and breadth of networks within them and changing sectors frequently as opportunities change?

SK: It is not so much changing as deepening, and it is like putting more fishing lines in the water. For example, as I mentioned, our very first investment was in education where we bought Strayer Education. Then we put in our own people as the team, I was chairman, so we have deep experience in that sector. Now we continue to look at education over the last 12 years, and we have never done a second investment in the space. But we haven't gotten amnesia about the sector. What we don't want to do, though, is have someone who says, 'Hey I am the telecom guy' and then feel this huge psychological pressure to find a telecom deal, whether it makes sense or not. So everything we know we still know, and we repeat spaces over the funds, but we don't want to get stuck in a rut where we are never freshening the list or focusing for the current conditions. We are trying to find the best blend between very deep specialisation and staying fresh.

MB: In addition to your focus on defensive growth sectors, you are known for not relying heavily on debt. A lot of people would say that if you are acquiring control stakes in businesses that are low in capital expenditure, are profitable and likely to remain so whatever the macro-economics, those are exactly the kinds of deals that lend themselves to being leveraged up, because they can be relied on to throw off cash to service debt.

SK: We don't have some theological opposition to debt. We just don't subscribe to the view in private equity that risk, and debt, create returns. We think making a business better creates returns. So we think the use of debt is just a corporate finance decision, the same way you would do it for any other company. If it makes sense to use some debt, we will. If it makes sense not to use debt, because you are either endangering the company or slowing up its growth, we don't use debt.

For example, with Strayer, the way to grow that business rapidly is to get admission into new states. The state regulators do not like to see campuses with debt on the balance sheet. If we had used debt, we would have slowed the growth up tremendously and had lower returns, even though we would have taken more risk.

To give you another illustration, we owned a business called MailSouth, which was the alternative to local newspapers in the USA in the small town markets where, as circulation of the local newspapers were declining, advertisers wanted a more efficient option. We bought MailSouth debt-free, and later Wal-Mart came along with a giant order and asked us to double our production. This was a good business decision for the long term but meant we had to incur significant losses for the first year or two to get the expansion started. We were in a position to take on this growth, because we didn't have to service a lot of debt or obtain lender approval.

We would rather make the returns through growth than through financial structure risk. We think risk is something to be avoided whenever possible. The typical chart you will see in a traditional finance textbook is one where risk and return go up together on a graph, where they rise up to the top right corner, but these type of charts are based on the assumption that there is no skill involved in the game. In a gambling game like roulette, for example, if you want to make more money, you have to bet more and take a bigger risk, because it is all luck. It is passive. If you are in a game of skill or an event of skill, it doesn't work that way. If I go into the boxing ring against the heavyweight champ of the world, I will have all the risk and he will have all the return, because he has skill, so risk and return don't go always together. We think private equity should be a skill sector based on business building, not a luck sector or a risk sector. And we think private equity is a form of business, not a form of finance. So we capitalise our activities as a form of business to maximise the long-term value with the least possible risk we can incur.

MB: You've spoken about the importance of growth, both at the level of the sector and of the individual firm. How do you and your team work with managements to help accelerate value creation?

SK: There isn't a single formula, because every company has a different situation. But I can give you some examples.

I will start with Strayer, because it was our first transaction. It had been around for about 100 years, was just in the Washington DC area, offered very high academic quality up to Masters level. It was accredited by the same regional accrediting bodies that accredit Princeton and Cornell, and had very high operating margins. So it was a very nice business but growing very, very slowly because it was just in the Washington DC area and it was controlled by a former professor at the school who had gotten sick and had no team to succeed him and no real energy on his team to build the business forward. He had majority control, and was ready to sell. So we went in and bought majority control from him, and put in our own in-house executives as CEO and COO of the business. I went in as Chairman, we built a whole new board. And we greatly expanded the new campus opening programme and the online education programme. I think we doubled or tripled the organic growth rate of the business. And not only does that lead you to higher earnings, but it also leads you to a higher exit multiple because a faster-growing business deserves a higher valuation multiple than a slow-growth business.

A second example is Ikaria. Ikaria makes a medical device and pharmaceutical gas that saves the lives of the 'blue babies' in neo-natal intensive care units. When the babies can't breathe and are turning blue, they inhale the gas and it opens their lungs and saves their lives. The research behind it won the Nobel Prize for medicine in 1998. It was a solid, healthy business but again very sleepy, and was a very small division of a big European conglomerate that was more focused on other businesses. We were able to put in an entirely new management team, a much higher-powered, pharmaceutical-oriented management team. They got the product licensed into Japan, are now building up the Australian and Canadian markets and have built up the acceptance of it in the USA.

The other thing we did was to team up with some of the best life-science venture capital firms in the USA, who invested in the transaction along with us. And we now have four major new products under development that were never on the drawing board when we bought the business. We are still waiting for our FDA [Food and Drug Administration] approvals for these products, but they could be major upsides that never existed before. The earnings before research are up very significantly and way ahead of plan, and the research budget now is very high-powered, where there was essentially no new product development before.

Just one other example. We sold a business in 2011 called Connextions. Connextions works for the healthcare insurance companies in the USA to sell policies to individual consumers. When we bought the business, it was mostly a traditional call centre, where they had operators on the phone to sell insurance. Under our ownership, it developed into a top-quality software company where they have all the software and technology that the healthcare insurers need, whether they use our call centres or not. We sold the company to United Healthcare, which was one of Connextions' clients and therefore knew how good the software is. Again it is a 'good to great' transformational approach, of taking a nice safe business and building it into a 'new mountain' in the industry.

Every business is different, but generally we will put in the management, we will give them a strategy, we will make sales calls for them. We will be their M&A staff, we will build their boards. If you look at our website, the homepage says one thing, 'New Mountain: Building Great Businesses', and that is what we take the most satisfaction in.

MB: It seems to me that changing managements is an important part of your approach. Does this not create tensions with incumbent teams?

SK: Generally, management changes are pre-agreed when we buy businesses. For instance, we acquired a 75 per cent stake in Deltek, an enterprise software provider for project-based firms, from an 80-year-old father who was long retired and a 50-year-old son who wanted to retire. With their blessing, we went out and recruited the executive who was CFO [chief financial officer] and Co-President of PeopleSoft, which had just been acquired for $10 billion by Oracle, to run this much smaller business.

I grew up in a family business, and so did a lot of the other people at New Mountain. Psychologically, we think of every investment like the new family business. When a family owns a business, you give every piece of energy you have to make the business better. One of the people in our team used to help run the operations and transformation practice at McKinsey. He is now a full-time MD with us and he is not supposed to find deals but instead to work with the companies we have to help the managements execute their transformation strategies.

MB: So do you have a formal separation within the firm between people who are looking for the next deal and others who help add value to portfolio companies?

SK: No, because even among the people who are out looking for the next deals there are people who have had 30 years of experience owning and running businesses. So they may find a new business to acquire every two years, but in the meantime they spend the bulk of their time working with the companies that they are responsible for, which they have found and recommended. They are then also leading the oversight team, but they are now supplemented with experts who are not supposed to find deals but are focused on helping the team help the business grow.

MB: Do you always do control deals?

SK: That is our standard model, except that there have been a couple of financial services start-ups which were essentially billion-dollar or bigger deals, where we teamed up with other financial firms to start the companies and share control with the other founders. Validus Insurance, for example, was a $1 billion start-up of a new Bermuda re-insurer after Hurricane Katrina. We were one of the founders of the business, got founders' warrants, but we were not big enough to put up the majority of the equity cheque back then – this is fund two. We are one of the largest holders of EverBank, but we don't control it, there is no single shareholder who does. But on the other ones, on the non-financial services deals, we have been the control shareholder in every case.

MB: You've also diversified into the management of other types of asset – public equities and corporate debt. How come?

SK: New Mountain Vantage Advisors, the public equities arm, came about when one of our biggest LPs, a big state fund, came to us and said, 'You are one of our strongest private equity managers, you don't use debt really in your investments, you are all based on research and business-building, so why don't you apply that strategy to the public equity markets where you are not trying to acquire control of the company but you are just try-ing to make good public equity investments?' And after we had thought about it for some time, they asked us to apply for capital. We eventually did apply, and they have been one of our investors since the beginning. We have built it up so that is essentially a long/short hedge fund, but using private equity-style research and a private equity ability to actually work with the management in some cases, and to improve these businesses in a friendly way.

MB: The idea of becoming a strategic shareholder and working with manage-ment interests me, because I think one of the arguments for why private equity tends to outperform the public markets is that, increasingly, public companies tend not to have actively engaged shareholders.

SK: We engage where it's useful – not in every case, but in a number. The best example that's on the public record is National Fuel Gas, a NYSE-listed [New York Stock Exchange], 100-year-old gas utility out of western New York State, near Buffalo. When we found them, six years ago, they were very sleepy, just trading off the dividend to people who like utility div-idend stocks. We realised they owned about a million acres of land in the Marcellus Shale Basin of Appalachia which they never actively developed, never did reserve reports on, never really gave it any value or attention. We hired Schlumberger, we did months of work, came to the conclusion that it was very valuable land which should be developed. And we have now encouraged them to follow that strategy, and as a result their share price has risen considerably. We worked closely with that management team, and one of our Senior Advisors is now on the board.

Other examples have been more low-key, where we just try to teach the managers how they should present their data to Wall Street or advise them to do a stock buy-back. It is just another sweetener, hopefully adding additional return for all the shareholders by giving good advice when we can.

MB: You also have the New Mountain Finance Corporation, which invests in various types of corporate debt.

SK: It is mainly senior and secondary debt. It started as an investment for New Mountain Private Equity Fund Three. As always we were focused on defensive growth, acyclical companies. After Lehman Brothers collapsed, the financial markets were in free-fall and in a panic. We saw that even the senior debt of the very safe defensive business we had studied but that some other firms had bought was selling at 60 cents on the dollar – even though the companies were on plan. So we got permission from our LPs to take a piece of our fund and buy debt instruments in other people's transactions. We didn't really have debt in our own companies, but we bought debt in what we believed were the safest companies we had studied that other people had bought.

As the debt markets recovered, you could make a very good return on that type of purchase, and we have since taken it public on the New York Stock Exchange. It is a BDC structure, a Business Development Corporation, which means that when interest is collected by the company on the debt that it owns, there is no corporate tax, and the interest just gets passed out as dividends to the shareholders. And they pay their tax as individuals. So it is essentially for people who want to get a good current yield.

MB: It seems to me that what those two developments have in common is that they are leveraging the thinking and research that you do for private equity to offer investors the opportunity to diversify into other asset classes. On the topic of diversification, have you considered expanding New Mountain outside of the USA?

SK: We do that in, we think, a risk-controlled way, which is that we have been doing more work in emerging markets, not as standalone investments, but rather as add-ons to our existing investments. For example, we have a laboratory chemicals business called Avantor, which is headquartered here in the USA. In the past year we made a significant acquisition in India to broaden its distribution and manufacturing capabilities there, which is a big growth opportunity for them. And we bought a smaller business in Poland which gives them a very efficient manufacturing base and a better ability reach the emerging markets of Europe. So rather than do a standalone investment in India and say we are an Indian private equity firm, we made those acquisitions but they are managed by the team who already manages the Avantor transaction with the stability of being part of a bigger team and with much more strategic upside than if we had just bought those businesses stand alone.

MB: Is there a case for opening offices and making direct investments in other continents?

SK: We could, but I think the current strategy will suit us for some time because I think it is the most logical way for us to invest in the markets. In time there could be something standalone in an emerging market, but the point is we are not trying to open overseas operations just to say we have done it.

Our decision-making process is very much about getting all these people with different skills around the table to analyse whatever decision the team is recommending, and we don't want a fractured process where a handful of people in one country send memos in and nobody else understands or has an intuitive feel for what they have been working on. Our decision-making process has been quite cohesive from the day a sector is picked to the day the investment comes in; we are all together here debating it as a group, and that is something we are trying to preserve as long as we can.

MB: I guess with your business model, opening offices outside the USA would be quite a big strategic decision because you couldn't just put two or three people in offices in, say, London or Mumbai; you'd need a fairly sizeable team, because you'd want to do a lot of analysis pre-investment and be hands-on post.

SK: I think we could do it if it was a sector we knew extremely well, like laboratory chemicals, where we have a big enough team globally to understand the situation. What we don't want to do is what I call the Supreme Court model, where three people work in Singapore, get the deal negotiated, send in a formal memorandum to the investment committee and eight people start reading the memo on Monday morning and someone says, 'I don't like it', or 'I do like it'. Either way, they don't really know what has been going on, they haven't been part of the process the whole way through. We want to be, as a firm, intimate with the process; we don't want to just have two people say 'Let's do it' and then do it or don't do it. We want to really try to get good quality control on the decision by vetting it in a more systematic way.

We are lucky in that our investors are pretty flexible. We can pursue as many international add-ons to US companies as quality determines. We can also have over 20 per cent of our assets headquartered internationally if we find good opportunities. We can also analyse pretty much any industry, as long as we don't do anything that is immoral.

MB: Given that the defining characteristics of your firm are high growth and low debt, does it annoy you that the industry is often lumped together and criticisms levelled at it that really only apply to the buyout guys?

SK: I believe there are approximately 2000 private equity firms globally, so there is a whole range of styles. Private equity doesn't require that you must use excessive debt. Obviously, if anybody is doing something wrong, you hate to get grouped in with them if you didn't do the same. Over all, I think we can make our own way and set our own record. Our social dashboards over the last four years show that our portfolio companies are significant net creators of well-paid jobs and that we are major investors in R&D, software development and capex; in addition, we have never had a bankruptcy or missed an interest payment. When you are buying businesses and building them in an intelligent, defensive way, we think that is a very good activity for everybody. And we are on record saying it, and that is what we want to keep doing.

9
Wol Kolade, Managing Partner, ISIS Equity Partners

While their approaches are different, my previous two interviewees have much in common: both are growth investors, headquartered in the USA and playing in large markets where the opportunity to roll out portfolio businesses drives returns. Can growth private equity work in a much smaller geography, such as the UK?

My next interview is with Wol Kolade, the founder of ISIS Equity Partners, a relatively small (around £650 million under management), lower mid-market UK growth investor, the track record of which – returns of two and a half to three times capital – suggests that there is a profitable niche for such a firm. ISIS's success can be credited to an approach to both deal origination and value enhancement that is, if anything, even more focused than TA's or New Mountain's, much of which I think could have relevance for other GPs, combined with a baked-in culture of working empathetically with entrepreneurs which, being intangible, is hard to copy.

Kolade is the Lagos-born, UK-educated son of a Nigerian diplomat. He began his working life in 1990 on the graduate scheme at Barclays Bank, before moving three years later to asset manager Ivory & Sime. Shortly after its takeover by Friends Provident to form Friends Ivory & Sime in 1998, Kolade pitched to the CEO the idea of creating a more sizeable private equity division. He got the green light, and £20 million of risk money to test the concept, on condition that he also turned round the firm's legacy venture arm.

A couple of very successful early deals resulted in the parent wanting to invest a lot more capital, but Kolade took the prudent decision to avoid becoming a 'captive' (a private equity firm that derives all or most of its capital from a single source, normally a financial institution), instead opening up the fund to external investors. After a re-branding to ISIS when Friends Ivory & Sime took over RSA's investment management business in 2005, Kolade and his management team bought the firm from Friends Provident after changes in accounting policies would otherwise have compelled it to consolidate the activities of the private equity funds' portfolio businesses into its accounts.

Kolade is refreshingly honest about the fact that his lack of a traditional private equity background led him to think differently about the industry:

> I thought what we were doing as an industry is rather curious. We were backing, on a generous basis, anything that came through the door. We were responding to deal-flow by going, 'Well OK, it's an interesting business. Is the market any good or the sector any good? Are the macro-economics any good? Yeah! Do the deal!' So you wouldn't quite know what you were going to do until it arrived.

> I didn't want to invent everything from scratch so I spent a lot of time travelling in the USA and on the Continent, talking to anyone who'd talk to me about what they did. It just seemed to me that we weren't really addressing the opportunity in the right way. I thought we should turn things on their head and do a lot of work ahead of time to decide what sectors we wanted to be in and why, and which businesses looked good within that, so we could benchmark what we saw against what we thought was good.

Kolade's observation that proactively identifying attractive sectors and businesses is preferable to reactively assessing on-market transactions is familiar growth-investor fare. But his approach to doing so contrasts with both TA's long-time specialisation in a handful of verticals and New Mountain's annual poll to select new industries and sub-industries to study. And his philosophy for staffing the firm and enhancing value is equally original.

ISIS selects broad investment themes based on the macro-economic, technological and social trends it expects to see developing over the next five or more years, which means its sector focuses are always evolving, as opposed to being static or constantly added to. Kolade says a colleague describes their approach as 'arriving in a sector before the hot money gets there, and selling it when it does'.

As with TA, a separate team is responsible for getting appointments with entrepreneurs, and the firm has a database of around 8000 firms it has approached. And, as with New Mountain, ISIS has team members who focus on value creation in portfolio companies, but it intentionally sets up an intriguing dynamic between them and their colleagues responsible for deal origination, and it also has a particular focus on preparing firms for exit.

*   *   *

MB: How did you develop your theme-based investing approach?
WK: I did it by looking at private equity in the USA, the UK and Europe. The USA is a lovely market, more than 300 million people, so you can do well by finding, say, a small business in Florida, and provided you've got the right

capabilities and what it's doing is new, awesome and different, the whole country is there for the taking. Here in the UK we have less opportunity to do that. But I liked the fact that they segmented things and thought things through in a rather more scientific way than we did over here.

The mainstay of private equity in the UK back then was buying into, say, a metal-bashing business in Birmingham that made parts that went into Rover or Ford cars. The trouble is, those sorts of businesses are commoditised and often under pressure to invest in more capital equipment. So all their cash is going to fund capex, and you end up having to break it up for the property.

I met a German private equity guy back in 1998 or '99 who asked me if I could put a pin in a map of the UK, draw a 50-mile radius and find ten world-class, privately owned manufacturers within it. I couldn't, but of course he could do so for Germany. So that got me thinking that the UK was focusing increasingly on services, and the lovely thing about those sectors is that you can obscure pricing, or if you're selling people certain things, such as food in a restaurant, they don't care what it costs to make. They aspire to something different and judge you on the value you bring.

I thought we were in for an interesting ride, given that there was a lot of high-technology stuff going on and I believed that the internet was going to act as a massive deflationary force for the long term. For commoditised products, the internet was bringing greater transparency, which would empower customers to better understand your costs and your competitors' prices. So unless you picked sectors where the customer didn't really care or know what it cost me to make or provide the product or service, their automatic response was going to be to attack me on margin. So that's one axis – pricing capacity.

That still left a big universe to go after. Then we thought about stage. We only want to put our money in once. I didn't want to invest in businesses that aim to create new markets, because the hardest decision for an investor is whether the follow-on money you provide is really good money after bad. That steered us away from early-stage. And I wanted businesses that generate a very high return on capital so they could sub-generate their own expansion capital. Those two axes lead you to services.

The job is then to break services down into its component bits and start doing the work to build sector focus and become sector experts. Initially this is quite an easy, top-down exercise, because there are lots of brokers' and industry reports. The trouble is, if I've got access to them, so has everybody else, and actually insight into a company comes from the bottom up and also a lot of the brokers' reports and industry stuff go 12 or 18 months forward, max. What we try to do is go five years forward, ideally more. What we're really trying to identify are sectors that are cold today but will be hot in five years' time. That's really about doing the hard yards, getting out and talking to people.

MB: How did you do that?

WK: This really brings me on to the second part of our strategy. We were the new kid on the block, because we were building up from a very low base. As a consequence we had no portfolio to offer to advisers. We had limited experience: I was 31. I had barely built relationships with people, and they weren't doing us any favours, so we were being offered the dross.

I recognised that we needed to get closer to entrepreneurs, so we opened an office in Birmingham. Later on we opened in Manchester, with a satellite office in Leeds. That helped because we wanted to be part of the community rather than being in London, because deals people didn't want to do in Birmingham just drifted to London and that's what we were being shown, deals that ten people had looked at it in Birmingham and said no. I said, 'Let's go and be part of the Birmingham community.' It was great fun to open in Birmingham, going in 1999, 'We're ISIS, we're completely new, just opened an office. And by the way, we're not doing manufacturing.' The huge derision that greeted our arrival in Birmingham was hilarious, particularly from people who now bang the drums for sector focus. Back then they just thought we were nuts.

Way back in '93, when I first got involved in private equity, I used to regularly get calls from entrepreneurs saying, 'My friend who's a lawyer or a bank manager says I need some private equity. What is it?' Then we became lazy as an industry, and the accountants became very enterprising and decided they needed to act as the guys in the middle. The minute that happened, we gave the game away because we became a commodity. Suddenly it was just about how much money you could put on the table, with the classic auction process having been developed to the point where there was no difference between one private equity firm and another. How high a price are you going to pay? Or what are the best terms of the deal? And how much are you prepared to lose?

I decided I was not enjoying that world. So why not go direct? Why not build a capability to create our own deal pipeline then re-establish the connections we used to have with entrepreneurs? This was about 2001. It was laughable, a naïve approach. We charged investment professionals with making cold calls based on having read a trade magazine or been to a trade exhibition and got a name in a sector they thought was interesting. We got told no the whole time, and instinctively when that happens, most people stop making calls. It just didn't work.

Then one of my colleagues had a blinding insight, namely, 'We're not very good at making calls, are we? So why don't we get people who are good who are?' 'But they don't know anything about private equity!' was the response. 'So? That's a good idea!' We hired a team, and now there are three of them, and what they do is they get us meetings. The buzz for them comes from getting past the PA to the meeting with the entrepreneur and then building a relationship over time. And they do it on the strength of our research and industry credibility. It's not a 'Hi I want to do a deal with you' type of cold call, it's 'Hi, we are involved in the sector. We've done some deals. We understand what's going on. Let's have a chat. We can share some ideas and swap stories about what's going on.'

This is a very skilled, very different job from the ones that we have as investment professionals. If we get it right, we can build something really interesting in terms of how we go to market and it's been really successful. Mostly because we've actually built our own CRM [customer relationship management] system. Most of this isn't visible to the rest of the industry, but since 2003 I think we've researched around 8000 companies. We've probably contacted 6000. The numbers are big, and there's not much that happens in the sectors we like that we don't see. It's because we've created a system and a process that makes it work. It's an important part of our business. We think that if our pitch is to be part of the entrepreneurial community, then we have to have a hot line to it.

Today, we work with advisers all the time. Two-thirds of deals come from our direct approaches, the other third come from advisers, but sometimes we'll get to a company and the adviser will get there at the same time as us and actually say let's work together on it rather than fight each other. There's not much that moves in our size and our sector that our people don't understand.

MB: It seems to me that your combination of top-down, thematic sector analysis combined with bottom-up identification and assessment of individual firms has more in common with small-cap fund management – perhaps reflecting your background with Ivory & Sime – than with conventional private equity.

WK: The difference, though, is that a small-cap fund manager tends to have a fixed view of a finite universe, whereas ours is sort of unlimited in the sense that I don't think you can put a limit on entrepreneurship. We still see businesses where we go, 'Ahh, I didn't know you could do that!' Or, 'I didn't even know that kind of business existed. Wow! There are people who actually make money doing that!'

All the time it happens, and it means I don't have to do the work to figure out where the UK is going, because I'm backing people who know. That's for me much more fun, investing in tomorrow, whereas the higher up you go in quoted equities, the more you're buying yesterday. You have to, because they're big players in their marketplaces and your first job is to establish whether a company has a consolidated, solid management and a strong market position. To find that out you have to look backwards, and then question whether it's sustainable by just looking a bit further forward. But they're historic businesses, they're not innovating. Innovating within a market to change the way people buy or the way they use a service, that's what we find exciting.

MB: You mentioned changing the way people buy. A lot of people would say that ISIS has been closely associated with innovative retailers, fashion brands, travel companies and food and drink businesses, where intangibles such as brands and relationships with consumers are critical. But from what you are saying, that's only because you've identified these as areas where margin erosion can be avoided and there's a high return on capital, and your chosen sectors could change over time?

WK: That's true, but we already do a lot more that just isn't as visible. We do a lot in healthcare; we are the front end of – what's a nice way of putting it? – the increasing efficiency of the UK social sector. We can't afford the public services we've got, delivered as they have been to date, most people know that. Quietly, governments of all political colours have been wrestling for the last 20 years with ways of improving the efficiency of the public sector.

There are lots of entrepreneur-led service businesses trying to find more efficient ways of delivering public services. We've invested in businesses involved in fostering, in domiciliary care for people with learning disabilities, very high-end schools for people with special educational needs – stuff that the state does really badly and really expensively that we know how to do better. A lot of it is just managing processes and a bit of technology which they don't have or they don't know how to get hold of and bringing these skills into the sector.

MB: Did this come about as a result of you doing an analysis and identifying a mega-trend and therefore going out and looking for businesses to buy into? Or was it the other way round, with people knocking on your door saying they owned businesses that were growing really fast and wanted to take on a supportive shareholder and they happened to be in this sector?

WK: Very much the former. About ten years ago we looked at the healthcare sector and concluded that the NHS was a proxy for it. But we didn't want to deal direct with the NHS. People that make money dealing with the NHS are big; they have to be to resist the monopoly pricing power. We could see that there were lots of people coming into the NHS from outside who were good at purchasing. If you had any excess profit, it was going to get squeezed out at some point.

So we said, 'If we can stop people coming in, that helps them because then it doesn't increase their cost base, so they'll allow us to exist. Or if they're already in, we'll pull them out faster. Again, that helps them.'

So we concluded that's where they'd have to be: small businesses that outsource functions, and do them better, quicker and cheaper than the state can manage it.

It's the classic entrepreneurial model, backing people who've been employed in a big organisation and spin-out because they see a way to do it better. For example, we backed two social workers who were frustrated working in fostering in local government and needed to be freed from the constraints they were operating under. They hadn't been trained that way or exposed to the wider commercial world so needed our help to take it beyond a certain level.

The issue was that there aren't enough foster carers in the UK, which leads to kids being placed in utterly inappropriate settings in high-cost children's homes. If someone expresses an interest in fostering, it can take the local authority literally 24 months to approve them. By that time they might have lost interest. We asked how we could make the process more efficient, where the bottlenecks were in the process.

We identified that the business was very similar to recruitment, that it was important to understand what forms of marketing generated what results and how much to spend on advertising. So we got in some people from the recruitment industry, and it really paid off. Another aspect was how to put together the panels that assess people's suitability. We cut that process down from 18 months to three or four months. Suddenly, for the same amount of money being provided, we had a much more productive business.

We then took it further, by looking at what social workers actually did. The way they work in local authorities is mainly nine-to-five. Where are the problems likely to be for foster carers? It's not going to be nine-to-five, because the kids are mostly at school then. It's going to be weekends and evenings. So we changed the contracts so we could provide the foster carers with a 24-hour support service, because they told us that what really worried them was what happened at weekends. The local authorities would say, 'It's all about the police, and we'll support them', whereas we said, 'Don't worry. Which social worker would you like to work with?'

We also asked what a social worker actually needs to do. Is it the admin? Absolutely not! And yet if you go to the local authorities, that's what they're doing. So strip the admin out. Use IT to make it more efficient. Make it easier for them to do the job they love doing. What you find is that their attention increases, their ability to deliver increases, their productivity increases. This can be replicated for a whole swathe of sectors across local authority provision.

MB: You must spend a lot of time doing analyses to work out which niches to target.

WK: We tend to think about sectors and themes, meaning concepts such as healthy living, patient choice, an ageing population, technology-driven services, waste and recycling. We overlay those on the sectors and ask, 'What does this do to sector?' Then we go into to the sector and talk to people, asking, 'How is this affecting you?', because most people think about things this way only when you really ask them to. That's why they like meeting with us, because we add something to their conversations. We build a picture about what's going on and then decide which company we are going to get involved with.

MB: It sounds to me like you and your team are pretty actively engaged in your portfolio companies. How do you balance that with sourcing new deals and getting exits?

WK: We never forget there are three aspects to earning our money: you have to buy a business, grow it and then exit it. The typical private equity model still seems to be for the guy who handled the initial acquisition to say, 'I did the deal, I built all the relationships with the people. As a result, I sit on the board and manage it for my company. And because I've been the rock star who did the deal, I will also be the exit specialist, a great one.'

I thought, OK, but what happens if you're busy doing another deal? I've done the job, and I know that there were times when I was running around like a lunatic trying to convert deals, spinning plates all over the place, trying to catch them before they dropped. How much time, especially back then, did we give looking after entrepreneur companies? Back then, I was doing four deals a year, and managing that was insane. I just thought I don't want to deal like that. Why don't I get a group of people whose sole job is to look after the portfolio and work in parallel with the new investments team, so that we cover all the waterfront?

The job of investing is two-fold: on the one hand, we try to create value through looking at the upside, but on the other hand, I want my money back so I'm looking at the downside too. I think different people have different attitudes to investing: some see the glass as half full, others as half empty. I don't know a single individual who is both at the same time. It's almost impossible. Solution? Get two people who are slightly different to look at the same thing. Bingo! We've covered both upside and downside.

The people we employ to look after the portfolio tend to be a bit more downside protection. Why? Because they haven't been involved in creating the transactions. To create a transaction, you have to have some optimism, you have to have some upside thinking otherwise you'd never do anything. Yet together, they build the complete picture. Together they help manage the interface with the management in the company so that deal-doers can be off doing deals. That's fine because ISIS is still fully engaged with the company, and it's a seamless contact because the transaction guy is always around. There's also the fact that, a lot of the times, we're actually adding to our companies in terms of new management coming in, developing and old and new. It's almost impossible for one person to manage those relationships and have the same level of intense relationship and sort of trust. So our view is that you should have two people who build different relationships with different views for ISIS as a whole to cover the whole waterfront. That way we are set up to add more value to our underlying portfolio companies.

When it comes to working with portfolio companies, we've codified our philosophy into what we call the three Ps: people, platform and position-ing. I'll take them in turn, using the example of Fat Face, the own-brand active fashion retailer. It was a critical deal for us.

The company was set up in 1989 by two ski bums, Jules Leaver and Tim Slade. They were phenomenal entrepreneurs, selling T-shirts out of a van. Got a bit older, came back to the UK, set up a shop. Using the mailing lists they'd created from their customers over the years, they tapped into this aspirational, outdoorsy thing, which was a marked contrast to either the US Timberland brand or M&S and Gap, which were about the only other options for leisurewear back then. After ten years they had a business that was growing at 50 per cent a year compound, way out of control. They wanted to sell it, and we gave them the option to sell us about half, let us bring in more management and grow it with them and all exit together five years later. Together between 2000 and 2005 we took it from 20 shops to 110, maybe £10 million sales to £80–90 million, £1 million profit to £10–12 million, 200 people to 2000.

Some of my colleagues in the industry were saying, 'How can you write a cheque for a few million pounds to someone? What gets him up in the morning? Why does he continue working?' They missed two things. One is how conservative most entrepreneurs actually are. If pretty much all of your personal wealth is tied up in your business, you're inclined to manage it very cautiously; if we buy half the business from you, you're liberated to take some more business risk. The other is that they don't only care about money. They go to work because they really believe in what they're doing and how they're going to build it, and they care what happens to their businesses next.

When we bought in, Tim and Jules didn't even have formal jobs. Every-thing about how the business ran was in their heads. With the business so reliant on them, any buyer would have wanted to shave the price, and most of the price would have been deferred into never-never land. When we looked recently we found that we've added an average of five senior management people to each of our portfolio companies.

After about three years we brought in a CEO called Louise Barnes, who used to run Monsoon in the UK. If she'd come in on day one, it would have been a disaster because there were no levers to pull. It was all in Tim's and Jules's head. So they had to spend three years getting it out of their head into the people systems, processes that we built around them. Which brings me on to platforms. If you're growing a retailer to ten times the number of shops, you're going to break at least two EPoS (electronic point of sale) systems. You can't graft on top, you literally have to start again. And you have to think a bit ahead and put in some of the people in place ahead of any big step-changes. Again, entrepreneurs are nervous about putting in cost without any return on it until tomorrow. We tell them to relax, it'll pay off.

We also think you should look to introduce some debt. Why? Because it keeps people on their toes. Fat Face used to run with cash in the bank, because suppliers to a small business worry about getting paid, and the thought that the world might all end tomorrow is actually in the minds of most entrepreneurs, which doesn't give the best impetus in the universe for the finance director to manage the cash. We think by putting a bit of a strain on it you have to think about where the bottlenecks are and how you collect cash, and to make it more efficient. The platform theme runs through the whole operational infrastructure, how the business runs, the pricing, the buying, the salespeople's incentives.

The third and final area is about positioning the firm correctly for the buyer. It keeps you honest, because all the decisions you're making, whether they're about investing in people or infrastructure, you're designing it with one purpose in mind. Otherwise you end up making excuses for why things should carry on for longer. In the case of Fat Face, we created a business that had a platform fit not just for the UK but for international expansion, and we started opening sites in overseas airports and doing a few flagship wholesale operations to give the next buyer the feeling that there was a lot still to go for: all they had to do was sign the cheque.

MB: I'm interested that your approach to debt is more relaxed than some other growth investors. Did this cause any difficulties when the financial crisis hit?

WK: No, because we saw it coming and because we're diversified – in addition to consumer markets we have healthcare, education and IT, which are much less cyclical. I remember in 2007 sitting here and watching a run on a UK bank for the first time in my lifetime. A few months later people were saying 'It's fine, it's all sorted.' No way! At that point we shifted our whole focus towards the assumption that we were going to hit a really bad period. We couldn't have dreamt how bad it was going to be, but by the time Lehmans hit we had already got our portfolio companies to bed down, take their costs down and pay back their debt. We also sold quite a lot of stuff, shed about a third of our portfolio and got our bank debt down to levels where some of the companies had net cash positions. And we had taken overhead out, so that we could then use the strengths we'd created in 2009 to take over any competitors and re-invest in growth.

MB: Given the intense focus you have on working with entrepreneurs to create value and the separation in roles between cold-calling, deal origination and portfolio management, I'm interested to know how you employ people, what backgrounds they have and where you get them from.

WK: It's diverse. They're a mixture of accountants, bankers and consultants. We're a small business, and it tends to be people we know, have worked with and can build a level of trust with. The partners with me in ISIS have been working together since 1999, and we've all stayed and we know each other extremely well. One of them I worked with when I was at Barclays, and that's how he came across. One a guy worked at Deloitte, and he had another friend of his who used to work there and he brought him in, and beneath that you then hire based on people who know people. It's very rare for someone to write in; it doesn't work. If you put an advert in the paper, you get 200 responses. We find it easier to just go and look for what we want from the various different talent pools. It's worked very well for us, and we've got some good long-standing people.

MB: And what qualities make a good ISIS person?

WK: I take the basics for granted: financial modelling, business acumen, entrepreneurial mindset. Beyond that, an interest in business, a love of what we do and the way we do it, engaging with entrepreneurs, that sort of thing. I think what marks us out is that we're quite curious and questioning of people. We don't really sit there and go with the majority view. We ask, 'What about those who aren't saying that, over there somewhere? What are they saying?' That's ISIS.

It's also a very open environment where no one has offices, it's completely open-plan. We debate, we talk, we engage at all levels, whether you're CEO or a junior. We grow our own, we have very rarely gone outside to get senior people in. We've got a very strong culture. I guess that's the slightly different way we approach life.

MB: You used to chair the BVCA. How did you feel about defending the industry against allegations of asset-stripping and shedding jobs, which aren't characteristics of the part of the industry that you come from?

WK: I would say that I chaired the association at the worst possible time [2007]. But in a way it was easy for me, dealing with MPs and unions, because I could honestly say, 'I don't recognise what you are saying, it's not like that in my day job. And I'm a private equity guy. You're tarring us all with the same brush.' The trouble is, you can't just say to them that they should just be talking about a small group of people such as Blackstone, that they shouldn't be using the words 'private equity' to describe the actions of the big buyout firms, because it means they'll just go and have an argument with them separately. But 'asset-stripping'? How do you do it and still sell a business for more?

MB: Especially if you're mainly buying service businesses that are asset-light anyway.

WK: Because their assets are their people! You've got to deal with the people, which means you couldn't do the deal unless people trust you. So half the stuff they're talking about is nonsense. A few years back someone spotted that 14 per cent of the private sector workforce was in private equity-controlled businesses, and some union leader picked up on it. We had to justify ourselves and start talking about the returns and how they benefited pensioners, that sort of thing.

The truth is, for a while the industry as a whole did very well and it seemed as if private equity was magic, but actually it was a combination of a lot of hard graft and the fact that a lot of people, particularly at the top end, were using a lot of debt. But when debt doesn't work, it really takes you to the cleaners.

We operate in an area where we haven't had the opportunity to take lots of debt. It's not what banks give us, but if I'm offered the chance to take something really cheap with limited covenants attached to it, then why wouldn't I? Providing I never kid myself that I may not have to take my hand out of my pocket again if things take a turn for the worse, and I'll reserve some capital just in case. What I wouldn't do, and which is what happened a few years back, is basically to build your operating structure as if it was going to last for ever. That's the mistake the industry made, because it didn't take a genius to see the leveraging system was getting out of control, in the same way as it's gone too far the other way, currently. The banks are so risk-averse, it's ridiculous.

MB: Some studies have said that the buyout guys have under-performed public markets recently, and that the GPs' returns have been higher than the LPs', with most of that coming in the form of management fees.

WK: The great irony of our industry is that we get 2 per cent on our funds, and we manage about £700 million. I think Blackstone gets 1.5 per cent, and they manage, what, £30 billion? We've got 28 investment professionals here, and they've got probably between 30 and 50 in Europe. The economics are completely different. We make money through the carried interest, which happens only if we make better companies. It's about being aligned with the investors: we make money when they make money.

MB: ILPA says that management fees should be set at a level that covers the running cost of the general partnership.

WK: Yes, but they're the self-same investors who gave billions to the big guys! In their defence, the trouble is you get into this bidding war for talent, and the industry has to compete with the investment banks and consulting firms. Over the past few years, the best and the brightest went into investment banking. The only way you could nick them for private equity or stop them from going there was to pay them a lot of money, because carried interest was just too far away for people to think about. Then the thinking was that if the industry could do bigger deals, raise larger funds, it could afford those huge salaries.

We're in a vicious circle now where even at our level, we absolutely have to be on market. Our competition is the bigger guys who'll drop down and can afford to pay our individuals two or three times what we can. I now cannot hire people and keep them unless I pay them, not the same, but not far off; otherwise they just get taken because the underlying jobs of course, are similar.

MB: I'd argue the jobs are actually more challenging here than in a big buyout firm. More interesting, but more challenging. Anyone who has worked in investment banking can buy an on-market company, put together the financing and sell it. Not everyone can work with entrepreneurs to create enterprise value.

WK: You could say that, but I couldn't possibly comment. The bigger you go in this industry, the truer it is that if you have a problem with people, you just write a big cheque and tell someone to sort it out. If you need a new Chief Executive, you get a head-hunter to go and find you the best manager in Europe for that kind of business. We don't have that. Very often we're creating management teams for sectors which are emerging and actually we have to mentor them. We have to make it work, and that's about us having to do the work. Thankfully we've been quite successful at that.

10
Matthew Collins, Founding Partner, Hutton Collins

In Chapter 7, TA's European boss, Ajit Nedungadi, observed that 'When there's less of one form of capital in any market, there's more opportunity for the other forms of capital.' With debt very much less available than it used to be, particularly in developed markets, there's no doubt that some growing businesses that might previously have funded expansion by borrowing are instead teaming up with growth private equity firms, such as those featured in the previous three chapters.

There is another option open to certain types of high-growth business, and it is also one that is forming an increasingly large proportion of the funding structure of many buyout transactions. I'm talking here about the various ways of funding a company that sit on the spectrum between conventional senior debt and ordinary equity.

In particular, since 2008, there has been a growth in instruments that blur the distinction between equity and debt: mezzanine debt with options attached and preferred stock that does not carry a current yield (i.e., where the yield is rolled up and paid on exit, albeit that it is technically a form of income rather than a capital gain). Some call this intermediate capital, a term that brings to mind the UK-based, publicly quoted finance provider, Intermediate Capital Group (ICG). In fact, ICG provides a much wider range of instruments, including senior debt and high-yield bonds, and its structure does not really lend itself to being regarded as a private equity firm, so I have instead focused on one of its competitors, Hutton Collins, which specialises in this middle ground between debt and equity, has no debt in its own structure and is set up in the conventional, GP/LP private equity mould.

Hutton Collins was established in 2002 by Graham Hutton and Matthew Collins, who had previously worked together in Morgan Grenfell's London-based structured finance team. Their firm is also based in London. It currently manages around €600 million of committed capital, typically investing between €35 million and €100 million in firms valued between €100 million and €500 million. As you would expect from the preceding series of Euro signs, it is focused on the European market, driven by an identification of an opportunity to offer the more sophisticated range of funding instruments long available in the USA to firms on the other side of the Atlantic.

Hutton Collins is fascinating because it is both a supplier or partner and a competitor to conventional private equity houses. On the one hand, it participates in the funding structures of other PE firms' transactions, enabling them to close deals when the metrics would not permit the use of more senior debt or ordinary equity; on the other, it raises capital from the same pool of limited partners as any other GP and it does primary deals with managements that might otherwise have sold equity to growth private equity firms.

This last point merits a little clarification. If you've read the past three chapters, you will know that the ideal transaction for most growth PE firms is to acquire existing equity in an asset-light business that requires minimal capital expenditure. The reasons are obvious: such a firm can be scaled with less investment and can start to repay the acquisition capital sooner through dividend flow, resulting in a higher internal rate of return – the primary measure on which LPs judge GPs, and the crucial figure on which GPs' carried interest is calculated.

Preferred capital – Hutton Collins's favoured term for its specialism – is, in effect, a mix of debt and equity, often provided in situations in which lenders consider the risk profile too high for senior debt but management does not want to be diluted as much as would be the case in an all-equity deal; therefore the mitigation of risk is critical. Preferred capital is thus more likely to be an attractive option for growth companies that want to put cash onto their balance sheets in order that they can spend it on the acquisition of tangible assets or bolt-on businesses that will contribute to their future expansion, and which represent security for the finance provider. But the instruments can also be used as an alternative to conventional private equity for secondary transactions, buyouts and refinancings, so while its relevance to corporates is undoubtedly growing as an alternative to debt in today's de-leveraging environment, it is also an increasingly useful tool for private equity for certain kinds of transaction.

I met Matthew Collins, co-founder of Hutton Collins, in the firm's office on Pall Mall, close to St James's Palace. A modest man, he was anxious that the interview should not come across as a 'hard sell' for his firm; rather, he wanted to make the case for the type of funding that his firm provides.

* * *

MB: Why did you and Graham set up Hutton Collins?

MC: We felt that there was a gap in the market in the grey area between conventional mezzanine debt and private equity. We took what we thought was the most interesting and scarce bit of the capital structure and raised money to make those kinds of investments in order to be in a unique position in the market.

MB: How would you describe what you do to someone who is not in the industry?

MC: I'm going to take the irritating approach of first defining what we don't do, before talking about what we do. When we set the business up in 2002, if you looked at the conventional funding spectrum, you'd see the senior debt business, then the mezzanine business, which was a very identifiable product, a loan that ranked junior to the senior debt and generally carried some payment of cash interest and some roll-up, and in those days you could get it to carry some additional return in the form of an option to acquire shares in the business for a nominal cost, and there was a pretty set formula in terms of the security package and the relationship with the other creditors, and then there was equity, which was provided by people who were willing to take a greater degree of risk than senior and mezzanine, but in return wanted control of the enterprise.

Our feeling was that there was a gap in the market in that as soon as you went to a mezzanine provider and said that you couldn't afford to pay interest because you had a company that had a big capital expenditure requirement, you pretty soon got to the point where the mezzanine market said, 'Well, that's not a mezzanine loan.' And yet the risk wasn't a pure equity risk.

We believed there was an opportunity to provide something that felt like it was in the mezzanine risk area, but in a more flexible way. We also believed that there was a very jerky drawing of boundaries between the various items in the capital structure. Looking at the equity account in many transactions, there was the opportunity to shade it in a slightly more subtle way so if, for instance, 40p in the pound was equity, and someone was required to put up the first 10p or 15p on a first-risk basis, then that's probably a tangibly different risk for which you ought to be prepared to charge accordingly.

Product number 1 is really about junior, junior debt, so some more exotic form of mezzanine. And product number 2 is about senior equity, a slightly less exotic form of equity. There are two main applications for these products. One is private equity firms that don't have all of the 40p equity component. Another is finding entrepreneurs that want to go out and acquire other businesses and have a lot of the equity they need, but not all of it, and don't want to give control to a private equity firm to raise that money.

Other people have subsequently set out to do things in broadly our part of the market, but they have a lot of leverage in their structures. We've never had any leverage in ours, not a CLO [collateralized loan obligation], not a CDO [collateralized debt obligation]. We're not a hedge fund or a leverage mezzanine.

MB: In lay terms, you've sought to bridge the gap between debt and equity, with a mix of equity-light and mezzanine-heavy products, and you've done this without debt because you have a private equity-type structure in which the capital you provide is coming directly from limited partners?

MC: Exactly.

MB: And you do this not only for private equity firms, as part of the capital structure of buyout transactions, but also for owner–managers wishing to raise development capital?

MC: Yes. We differentiate ourselves from debt providers by saying this is more patient money than the debt world. And we differentiate ourselves from the equity providers in the sense that we say, 'We believe that by being offered the opportunity to sit at the point that we do in the capital structure, we're not taking the same risks you are. So in return for having a position of one seat nearer the door than you, we're willing to live with a slightly lower return and critically, we're willing to live with not being a controlling shareholder in the investment.'

MB: Looking at your returns, are they essentially a form of rolled-up coupon? Payment-in-kind-type returns?

MC: It's a combination: most of it is rolled up, but we also have equity interests. If you look at every investment we've ever made to see where our return is coming from, roughly 60 per cent would be from rolled up interest and 40 per cent from participation in the equity upside of the business. We've never really been on a fixed income, and we're definitely trying to find businesses that offer the opportunity for upside returns.

MB: If you typically hold a small minority position, which can be a mix of a class of equity that carries a lower risk than the principal equity provider's position and options you've received in return for providing mezzanine debt with deferred payments, are you a relatively passive investor, more like a debt provider?

MC: I wouldn't use the term 'passive'. It's a very active form of investment, although we try to restrict the activity to areas that we know and feel that we can contribute to. We have quite significant minority protections, but there are an awful lot of things that we don't control in this business. Certainly private equity firms would say, 'I like that business. I like the sector it's in, but I'm not sure I like the manager. I'm going to buy the company and we'll take it from there', whereas at the due diligence phase, we're more likely to say, 'We like the plan, we like the manager, we like the business, we want protection to make sure the management carries on doing what we want it to do.' The difference is that the people that we're backing have always got significantly more money at risk than in a conventional management buyout, and because they're making that statement, we're more willing to see it through with them. We bring a bit of a lending approach to private equity investing, which is that if things go as you tell us they're going to be going, then you can get on with your life. Talk to us about big decisions, refinancing, acquisitions, disposals, major new lines of business. Absent that, you're running the show.

MB: I'm conscious that you have two categories of transactions. In some you are completing the capital structure for a private equity firm, in which case they'll do a lot of commercial and human due diligence and will oversee the business and the management team post-transaction. But in others you are working directly with a management team, so presumably you have to be more actively engaged there, both at the due diligence stage and once the deal has completed.

MC: Yes, a critical part of what we do is making an assessment of our partners in these transactions. There are some cases where our partners are a management team and they are doing a secondary buyout. They made a lot of money out of round one and if they're willing to put that money into a second round, in a big way, it helps a lot. But it's still crucial to assess them. What are their motivations? What are their capabilities? How good is our alignment?

In other cases you're backing a management team and a private equity firm. The assessment of the management team is always the critical thing, but you also need to understand the ability of whichever private equity firm it is to steward the investment.

MB: Are there preferred private equity firms that you like to deal with, or are you happy to work with anyone on a case-by-case basis?

MC: Definitely the latter. Graham and I have been in the buyout world since the late '80s, so we've reasonably good knowledge of the individuals out there, but we will always consider working with newcomers on their merits.

MB: Presumably your LPs are the same kinds of investors that go into conventional private equity funds?

MC: Yes, they are a mix of insurance companies, pension funds, funds of funds. Our list of investors looks much like the list of a typical UK midmarket private equity firm.

MB: Do you ever get situations where you are funding a private equity transaction in which the same LPs are participating both in the equity component and in the preferred – that's to say, they're invested in both your partnership and the private equity firm's? If so, does that concern them?

MC: It does happen, but not that often. And they're already well diversified, so it doesn't worry them.

MB: How do your returns compare with other private equity?

MC: There's a spectrum to what we do. We're anywhere between mid-teens and mid-20s IRRs, because some of what we do is much lower-risk than private equity, but there are also private equity-type transactions where the returns are similar.

MB: Presumably your volatility is lower – that's to say, you don't have so many transactions where the return is negative?

MC: That's the aim.

MB: On one level, you're private equity's friend, you help them finance transactions, and on another you're their competitor, in that there are entrepreneurs who can choose between going with growth or development-type private equity or working with you, and generally what you offer is more appealing because it's less dilutive.

MC: In a sense that has always been true, ever since we started, but only in a limited number of cases. Some management teams are willing to invest much more heavily in the business than a commercial private equity team would, and they're willing to do that to have more of a feeling of building a substantial privately-owned company, rather than being just an MBO [management buyout] with a series of different backers.

If you compare the financing markets in the USA and the UK, in the USA there are a great many businesses that you wouldn't call management buyouts; they're just privately owned businesses of some size that finance themselves in the bond or mezzanine markets. They would never dream of selling control to somebody else to raise money, and I've always thought that over time this is something that will develop more over here than it has hitherto.

MB: I think the same could be said of the German *Mittelstand* [family-owned medium-sized businesses], many of which seem to be in capital-intensive sectors such as engineering and the success of which is widely attributed to their long-term stability of ownership. Here in the UK it seems that our options for companies wanting to grow are debt, the public markets and private equity, and at times when debt is hard to secure, as they are now, and the public markets are challenging for small caps, that pretty much pushes firms toward private equity, which then wants an exit, resulting in at least two changes in ownership, into and out of the hands of the PE firm. In contrast, if they could access a less dilutive form of funding, which they later paid back from future cash-flows, they could have greater stability.

MC: Exactly. We're very comfortable working with a private company that has a capital expenditure project that in this climate the banks won't finance. And even if they could, a lot of private owners are very nervous about raising money that could kill the business. We might find that the money we were putting in is relatively small compared to the overall enterprise value of the business, we might own 5 or 10 per cent of the equity.

MB: Can you structure a deal like that in a way that enables the firm to fund your exit through future cash-flows, rather than having to force them into an exit?

MC: Often, yes. Everything tends to be debt-like when we invest, so there's a repayment date of our underlying capital. It tends not to be cheap capital, so once the company is in a position to repay it, it generally likes to do so. That tends to deal with how we get back our initial capital and accrued return. As for our equity interest, we do have drag-and-tag rights, and obviously we don't want to cap our returns, but we have on occasions given people the option of buying back our equity interest.

MB: It seems to me that what you're offering is an attractive proposition for roll-out businesses, where you've got a core formula that is successful and profitable, but rolling it out requires capital expenditure and working capital, and the provision of preferred capital would enable it to accelerate its growth, until one day the decision is taken to slow the rate of growth, turn it into a cash cow, then everyone exits.

MC: Yes, and if you look at some of the sectors we've invested in, they fit that description. In particular, we've made a number of investments in the restaurant sector [Loch Fyne, Caffè Nero, Wagamama]. We've also backed roll-outs in healthcare, financial services, cinemas, TMT [technology, media and telecommunications], not all of them ourselves but alongside private equity GPs.

MB: And what about geography? Do you do deals throughout Europe, or focus on certain countries?

MC: We concentrate on what we call old buyout Europe: France, Benelux, Germany, Italy, Spain and of course the UK, which is about half of what we do. Central and Eastern Europe we think is a different skill-set from ours. We can invest, and have invested, in companies that are essentially global, but we have to feel that the epicentre of the business is somewhere in old buyout Europe.

MB: Presumably with the structure you use, where you have minority provisions with covenants and warranties but you don't actually own very much of the businesses you back, being confident that the legal system is one that enables you to enforce your rights is pretty crucial.

MC: Yes, exactly.

MB: What about the USA? Is that a market you've looked at, or is there too much competition?

MC: A fair amount of our money comes from the USA or from LPs that are already picking specialist managers to invest in the USA. We've invested in businesses that have a US element to what they do, but I don't think we would ever set out to go and invest in a US business. I don't think it's what our clients would want us to be doing.

MB: Would you say that your market has become more or less competitive in the past few years?

MC: I would say it's less competitive than it was four or five years ago. Back then, the hedge fund industry would make some of these kinds of investments, and there's a lot less of that now than there was. And the banks were in this business back then, and probably now they're not. There's always competition, but it's a pretty orderly market now.

MB: I guess the famous – or notorious – example was Peter Cummings's integrated finance team at the Bank of Scotland. A lot of money was thrown around, on pretty lax terms, and there are all kinds of rumours about some of the things that went on.

MC: I couldn't possibly comment!

MB: Deal-flow must have been pretty easy for him, just a matter of identifying high-growth businesses that banked with them. I imagine you get a lot of deal-flow from private equity firms, either asking for help funding buyouts or considering you as an option for a secondary transaction. But how do you get deal-flow from managements?

MC: Word of mouth is important. Some really interesting deals come our way because we've backed a management team that has done well and they've told their friends that we were different backers and could maybe help them do something similar.

MB: Doing the Loch Fyne deal in 2005 must have helped you build up a profile in restaurants, hospitality and leisure.

MC: Yes, and it means you can connect far better when you're talking to owners of those kinds of businesses. I can have a discussion with the owner of, say, a casual dining restaurant business in the way that someone who hasn't done deals in the sector would find difficult.

MB: You've also done several deals in healthcare. Do you also see that as a specialism, and if so, why?

MC: Yes. We're looking for businesses that have fairly stable revenues and are cash-generative, we don't want businesses that might fall off a cliff or might be worth 100 times the price. Stability and cash generation go a long way to ensuring that you get your money back and get some return on it, but they should also have some growth prospects and potentially the liquidity that we provide can help achieve that growth. So I think the industry theme is really about funding businesses in sectors where we've found those characteristics.

MB: What other sectors or themes appeal to you?

MC: The banks are being de-levered, and there's a whole raft of good companies out there with sensible prospects, and if you're in consolidating sectors you'll get the opportunity to pick up smaller businesses at historically very attractive prices, but it's quite hard to get the capital to do that. I think this theme is going to be with us for quite a while.

MB: So that points you toward a roll-up, as opposed to roll-out, model? And presumably if the quality of earnings and multiples paid for the acquisitions are attractive, it's the kind of low-risk model you like?

MC: Exactly.

MB: It seems to me that the challenges around bank de-leveraging not only present opportunities for the deals you do direct with managements but also provide more intermediate types of capital for other GPs' buyouts. And you also face less competition than you used to. So will you be raising a much bigger fund next time round?

MC: This is a very difficult environment to be raising capital in, and that's part of the reason why the opportunity is attracting so much interest, but it also means it's a challenging time to raise new funds. Generally, when it's difficult for private equity to raise money, it's comparatively easy to invest it attractively. And when it's easy to raise it, it's difficult to invest it well.

That said, I think there's a tendency to assume that after a big bust like the one that we've had, there'll be a boom and the world will be full of fantastic opportunities to invest in things very cheaply and make fabulous return. I personally don't see that. You've got to work hard in this environment to find good opportunities, but if you work hard, you can find them, as opposed to four or five years ago, when there were so many people chasing these opportunities. So I don't think there's going to be a great bonanza for private equity returns, but I think we're be back to an environment where it's a pretty orderly market.

MB: It seems to me that, for right or wrong, things have been managed in a pretty orderly way so far, and Darwinism has not been allowed to run riot. With the possible exception of public equities in late 2008, early 2009, there hasn't been a spectacular revaluation of assets that represented a once-in-a-generation buying opportunity.

MC: That's true, the air is being let out of the tyre very gently. I grew up in leveraged buyouts, and when I started, you had a couple of years' grace before you started servicing your debt and you started making significant repayments from about the end of year three. If you look at the big buyout structures set up in 2007/8, look at how much of the debt is non-amortising, then of the amortising debt, when does it really start. You really only had to think about starting to make some serious repayments at about year six or seven, or even eight. Nobody back then was forecasting LIBOR [London Inter-Bank Offered Rate] rates of half a per cent. So you're not going to be failing to pay your interest unless things change pretty dramatically. And the covenants were all incredibly weak, so the biggest problem you've got, which you can't escape from, is just the level of debt. That only bites you when you've actually got to repay it, and you don't have to start doing that until 2013/14 at the earliest.

So there are a lot of private equity-backed businesses where the banks don't have the right to take away the keys because nothing has happened yet, but on any sensible view about the valuation of the business and where it might go, you have to ask how it could ever create enough value to be able to repay the debt.

MB: I suppose it depends on your view about what the real intentions of the UK and US central banks, and the ECB [European Central Bank], are. Certainly in the UK and USA it seems to me there could be a hidden agenda to quietly inflate our way out of our debts. And if we go down that route, it could be the salvation of those big buyouts done at inflated valuations with a lot of debt. As long as the companies have reasonable pricing power, which is likely because their scale means they are probably number one or two in their markets, they should be able to raise prices, and hence revenues and earnings at or ahead of inflation, whereas the debt remains at its pre-inflated level. So in cash terms you can exit at a price that lets you repay the debt and maybe even give a decent return to investors, even if in real terms it might not be worth as much as they'd hoped.

MC: That's right, that's where the bank balancing act is. I'm not a macro-economist, but it seems to me that you let the brakes off inflation but try to avoid an inflationary spiral or pushing retirees into poverty and hope you can maintain that balance long enough to deflate away much of the country's debt. Inflation is good for leveraged businesses. If you look to the early buyouts in the USA in the late '70s and early '80s, it really helped to inflate away the leverage.

Right now the picture in private equity is one of extending the hold periods. I don't think it's because they're hoping to inflate away the debt component, although that may happen, it's more that it is taking longer to create the increases in value needed before exiting. There's also not a great deal of new buyout activity. But there are a lot of private-equity-owned companies out there that are going to need money to achieve all their plans and achieve growth, and that's potentially an opportunity for us.

MB: Providing development capital to existing portfolio companies of other GPs, as opposed to secondary transactions?

MC: Yes. The GPs will be saying something like, 'I've owned this business for five years. I'm probably going to need to own it for another couple and I'd like to make an acquisition. Five years ago I would have gone for bank debt for the money, but I can't, and I don't want to put in more equity money or I don't have it, so where else can I go?' It's a different proposition from the initial funding of a buyout, where a GP might get five or ten firms all pitching for pieces of business; it's a much less perfect market.

Another trend we're seeing quite a bit is private equity firms undertaking transactions with low or no debt, effectively using their own capital, then refinancing it at a later stage, when they can demonstrate stability and the impact of management actions on cash-flows. We like that model because we like predictability and seeing whether managements can do what they say they can, and we prefer high operational leverage to high financial leverage.

MB: Are there any other developments that could change how your business will look in perhaps five or ten years?

MC: Not especially. The private equity firms that I admire are the ones that really stick to their guns, that didn't go from being a £300 million fund to a £7 billion one. They've plugged away at doing what they set out to do, very, very well. I would like to think it's the same for us: keep the discipline, stick with the model.

11

Garry Wilson, Managing Partner, Endless LLP

So far in this section of the book, we've seen three different approaches to growth private equity and a fourth firm that combines growth investment with a funding model for buyouts that avoids over-reliance on debt. But it would give an incomplete picture of the flourishing niches within developed-market private equity to leave it at that, because there's another sector that is both gaining scale and achieving good returns: turnarounds.

I touched on this area when I interviewed Jon Moulton (Chapter 2), since his quoted fund, Better Capital, inhabits that space. As the straight-talking elder statesman put it: 'People made good money at Dunkirk clearing the beaches, so there's always some angle.' Before moving on to look at how private equity is evolving in emerging markets, I want to revisit the turnaround model by looking at a firm that is also notable for the non-standard backgrounds of its team, the innovative way it raised its first fund and the profiles of some of its backers.

The manager in question, Endless LLP, is probably now the UK's leading turnaround investor and also the generator of what are almost certainly the highest repeatable IRRs in the industry. While my interviewee, founder Garry Wilson, is coy about the numbers, an analysis of the returns on the first two funds and industry speculation about the third suggest that he and his team have consistently achieved an internal rate of return on limited partners' money of close to 100 per cent per annum. And yet, prior to 2005, no one in the senior team had ever been employed in private equity, investment banking or management consultancy – albeit that many had provided services to private equity firms.

An accountant by training, Wilson and fellow Endless co-founder Darren Forshaw specialised in restructure work at Arthur Andersen. Wilson became a junior partner around 18 months before the firm hit the buffers in the wake of the Enron scandal, running the Leeds office. After Andersen's implosion he received an offer to move the entire team to Ernst & Young, which he describes as a proud moment because it enabled him to preserve the employment of everyone in the office, many of whom he had recruited. But the incident led him to re-evaluate his future career path.

Among Wilson's most lucrative clients were private equity firms seeking turnaround advice on under-performing portfolio businesses. Looking back, he describes the situation thus:

> We weren't just trying to recover banks' money in restructures, we were trying to recover shareholders' positions, rescuing and creating equity value. Crucially, that trained us to think like shareholders. We realised that in the world of private equity, everybody wants to be associated with the successes, but failure is a very difficult thing for people to deal with. We were the guys who were willing to embrace the failing investments, I think because we were emotionally detached from them. But recovering money when a private equity firm has written it down to zero is a fantastic win for them.

Around the same time, Wilson and Forshaw had another, very different client: a high-net-worth individual who had made money in property and had secured their help in buying and turning round several businesses. Wilson is coy about the identity of that individual, on the grounds that he does not seek the limelight, but a few seconds' work on Google will tell you he is called David Newett.

Wilson says that the co-founders of Endless 'went with a couple of pages of A4 and pitched the idea of doing this more seriously', raising a first fund consisting solely of Newett's money, on a pledge basis. Given the structure, it is difficult to compare the fund size with a traditional raise; the most capital employed at any one time was £37 million, but the total deployed was around £100 million. Subsequent funds have been larger (£164 million and £220 million).

The second fund, the firm's first conventional partnership, continued the theme of including unconventional backers: among the investors was HRJ Capital, an investment vehicle established by three high-profile former professional American football players: Harris Barton, Ronnie Lott and Joe Montana. Another unusual characteristic of the fund was that the GP, the general partnership consisting of the investment professionals who manage the capital, was the largest investor in the limited partnership, having rolled into it the profits they made in the first fund.

The third fund, raised in the difficult market of summer 2011, is also notable, for two reasons: it was closed unusually quickly (just ten weeks; according to industry data provider Prequin, the average time firms spent 'on the road' raising capital for funds closed in 2011 was 16.5 months); and the firm received serious commitments for approximately double its target but chose to cap the fund size because of concerns about its ability to deploy additional capital without reducing returns.

Endless does not publish an equivalent of New Mountain's social dashboard, but in my view it should: all too often, the alternative to rescue by a turnaround private equity firm is liquidation, so there's a strong argument in favour of the proposition that much of the employment in the investee businesses and of the tax receipts they generate are societal gains. Nevertheless, Wilson provided me with a breakdown of the current portfolio businesses, indicating that they employ more than 7000 people, while an analysis of its exits points to around 10,500 jobs having been saved.

Endless shares with UK growth investor Isis Equity Partners a belief that getting into the regions is crucial to deal-flow. To that end, its first office was in Leeds; subsequent bases opened in Birmingham and Manchester, and it is only in the past couple of years that the firm added a London office, in a Georgian townhouse in Mayfair. Unlike most firms with premises in such a prestigious location, it does not refer to that site as its head office, preferring to retain that designation for its original base in Leeds.

It was in the basement boardroom of the London premises that I interviewed Wilson. The floor has a surprisingly contemporary feel, more like a fashionable boutique hotel than a corporate office. I asked Wilson who chose the décor: it turns out, in typical Endless style, that one of the team, associate director Simon Mason, has a friend who specialises in fitting out clubs and bars and was able to do the firm a good deal. Large photographs on the walls depict scenes from past and present portfolio businesses: a carpenter working on some timber at office furniture specialist Neville Johnson and a futuristic, robotised warehouse operation at stationery distributor Vasanta Group. It is difficult to escape the conclusion that Endless is about a relentless focus on operational and financial efficiency in real businesses in the manufacturing and distribution heartlands of Britain.

* * *

MB: What was it like managing a pledge fund initially, rather than a conventional limited partnership?

GW: We made the money go as far as we possibly could, because we didn't have a lot of it. When we bought a business, we gave intense focus to how we could get some or all of our money back. If we didn't do that, we wouldn't be able to do another deal. We'd concentrate on efficient working capital management, we'd look at the receivables, the inventory and the payables and think, right, how can we squeeze some cash out of this? That enabled the company to repay the money that we had loaned it to get out of difficulty, and that returned capital to us to enable us to go and do another deal.

MB: Presumably at this point you were paying next to nothing for the equity in the businesses, so the capital you were committing was largely working capital to enable the businesses to trade out of difficulty?

GW: That's right, the companies we were buying didn't have equity value because they were generally loss-making or not making much money, and there was a fresh cash need which existing shareholders did not have the appetite to fund or they had lost the confidence of their banks.

Because we didn't have a formal fund structure, we didn't have lots of capital at our disposal so for us, cash was a scarce resource. We treated it accordingly and wanted our companies to do the same. We quickly learned, however, that you couldn't do turnarounds on a shoestring. We had to properly capitalise our businesses because that would give the companies, their customers and suppliers and employees, confidence that they had a stable base to go forward. We had to strike a balance between recovering some of our capital and making sure that the outside world could see that there was a stable business there.

MB: What was the first deal you did?

GW: It was a business called Speedframe, which was a uPVC window man-ufacturer. Ultimately it went wrong. We bought it in December 2005. We fixed the business. We moved it from a £4 million operating loss to a £2.5 million operating profit, but then the collapse of 2008 happened, housing starts plummeted and its market completely dried up. So we turned it around, only for it to go back in the wrong direction before we exited, which was a shame. I think it showed that once we turn something around, we ought to consider exiting at once. Our core skill is turnaround, not turnaround and growth.

If we hadn't gone through the credit crunch with that business in the portfolio, I think we would have made a good capital gain but we didn't. We came out of it with a small loss – I think we lost just over £1 million. When you don't have much capital, it's painful to lose that.

MB: When you are doing turnaround work, there must be a higher level of volatility than when you're buying businesses that are very well established and on a visible trajectory. I guess as long as there are others that have done correspondingly well, the occasional loss is acceptable within the overall business plan.

GW: Yes. In the turnaround game you've got to limit the losses to small num-bers, and you've got to aim for high multiples on the ones that do very well. Thankfully, we've been able to do that so far. [Wilson subsequently shares with me a confidential breakdown of present and past portfolio companies segmented by expected or actual returns. Almost a quarter of the deals resulted in, or are expected to lead to, Endless losing most or all of its capital. In another 15 per cent, the firm came out, or expects to come out, with its capital back. A further quarter of its investments generated, or were on track to deliver, the kinds of returns normally associated with private equity. The performance of the remaining investments – a little over a third of the total – are best described as super returns, in the sense that they ranged between 50 and 300 per cent IRR.]

MB: What were your initial investment criteria?

GW: We weren't sector-specific but we wanted to focus on businesses that had some asset backing for the money that we were going to inject, in the knowledge that if we weren't successful in achieving a turnaround, at least we could get some or all of our money back. That led us towards more traditional businesses, so instead of software and business services, we found ourselves dealing in manufacturing, engineering, retail.

MB: I'd noticed, looking at a list of your investments to date, that quite a few of your deals were in manufacturing and warehousing, in the Midlands and the north of England. It seems to me one of the quirks of corporate accounting is that businesses that own buildings and land tend to be undervalued because few of them, especially those trading in difficulties, tend to revalue upward these assets because it increases the tax charge, so instead they sit on the balance sheet at a written-down value that bears no relationship to their market price. Which presumably makes them fairly low-risk turnaround propositions, because unless they need a lot of working capital, if things don't work, chances are the break-up value will be less than you've put in.

GW: That's exactly what we looked for, and it's still important to us today.

We also looked for businesses that had to do something. What I mean by that is that we had so many approaches for funding we had to ask ourselves, 'Do they really need to do a deal?' If they didn't, we decided to focus our efforts elsewhere. We were running towards things when everyone else was running away. If it had cash-flow pressure and the bank didn't want the business in its portfolio, then that was our type of deal, whereas everyone else was saying this business isn't in a good place. That to us was good, because it meant that company had to deal with us or someone else, and it meant we weren't wasting our effort. We learned early on that sometimes we spent a lot of time on things but they could muddle their way through themselves or they didn't need to do a deal and it was just wasted effort.

MB: So an insolvency event is what triggers your interest?

GW: Or a pending insolvency. Sometimes if the business is in administration or threatened with it, that's a tick in the box for us. If the parent company had withdrawn support, again, another tick in the box. All those danger signs are motivators for us.

MB: How do you get deal-flow?

GW: It's not difficult spotting companies that are in trouble. A lot of it is in the public domain. A lot of it is market gossip and rumour. The difficulty is spotting the troubled companies where there's a viable turnaround plan that can be executed, and to do that you need to get into the next level of detail.

MB: Your job must entail kissing a lot of frogs. Plenty of companies are in terminal difficulties because there's no market there for them or there's upward pressure on the costs or something else that can't be solved that means there's not a viable business there.

GW: Yes. Sometimes we get approached just two weeks before an administrator is due to be appointed, so we've got to decide very quickly whether to run at it. If we do run at it, we've got to get a team in place to do it very, very quickly. This isn't something that happens over six or nine months. The alternative sometimes if we don't do it is the company closes or goes bust. So it's very binary.

MB: One of the criticisms levelled at private equity is that they're asset-strippers and get rid of a load of staff, but actually in your case there's quite a compelling argument for saying that you save people's jobs because you may be the alternative to the company closing down.

GW: Yes. The biggest winner from Endless since 2005 has been the taxman. The taxman has made much bigger returns than our investors have made, because almost every company we buy has millions of pounds of tax arrears, and of course we only get to continue to trade these businesses if we pay off those arrears. That can take several months to do.

Assuming the company survives, we're paying PAYE and national insurance month in, month out and VAT every quarter, and there are various other duties and taxes on top. On one of our businesses, Vasanta, a company that was at risk of closure, paid more than £20 million in taxes in the 12 months between July 2009 and July 2010, and the taxman also got his £7 million arrears of tax. If I look back since we founded Endless at the taxes our portfolio business have paid and how the companies we've saved have boosted the local economies we've operated in, it saddens me that we never get any credit for that.

MB: I'm surprised that you've continued to trade distressed companies where there have been tax arrears, rather than doing pre-packs [pre-packaged sales of assets and goodwill to new companies, usually taking place almost simultaneously with the appointment of administrators].

GW: Our preferred choice is not to do pre-packs. If we avoid them, we can generally continue with the support of our suppliers. They will continue to give us credit, which reduces the amount of capital that we have to put into place. We don't have to deal with a crisis. If we have taken a business in and out of administration very quickly, we have a crisis on our hands and sometimes companies don't survive that. If we can avoid that pre-pack, we've got a stable business that can be stabilised and properly capitalised and continue with the support of suppliers and customers.

Sometimes, of course, there's no option other than to do a pre-pack. To give you an example, let's say we were buying a £20 million revenue business that has a £20 million pension deficit and £5 million of tax arrears, it's just not viable; the capital structure needs to be reset for the business to be able to continue.

MB: Presumably many distressed companies that owe money to creditors have meaty tax losses that can be carried forward and can benefit the ultimate buyers.

GW: Yes, you can then trade for perhaps a few years without paying corporation tax, whereas you would lose the tax losses if you went into administration.

MB: You've talked about buying cheaply, identifying businesses where there's little or no equity value, and managing cash so you don't have to have too much capital committed for two long. What about the value creation side of the equation?

GW: We look very closely at cost control and operational efficiencies. We go through the cost structure line by line – it can be how much are the pens and pencils costing, to who are the best-paid employees and are we getting very good value from people who are costing us six figures per year.

When we bought Crown Paints, we started a project on day one called Project 15. The aim was to take £15 million of annualised cost out of the business, which lost £11 million in 2008, when we bought it. Our attitude was that we thought it was loosely controlled and that it could be much better managed. Project 15 ultimately ended up producing £17 million of annual cost savings, so in that one act of cost control we moved the business from losing £11 million to creating £6 million of profits. Cost control is not a popular thing to do, people hate change, but it's a fantastic way of getting a business to a more stable place and securing employment.

MB: Taking that firm as an example, what were the biggest areas of cost control, or of previous over-spend?

GW: It was in every aspect of the business. Surprisingly we didn't have to institute a huge redundancy programme. Of 1500 people we made 110 redundancies, less than 8 per cent of the workforce. Looking at every cost line from raw material expenditure through to amounts paid for office supplies, we made savings in every single area.

A big thing I'm strong on is customer and product profitability. Some of our products we just didn't make any money on. We were selling them at a gross loss. Some of the customers we supplied, we didn't make any money from. These are people we would spend huge money on, entertaining and building relationships. We were selling products to them for less than it was costing to produce them. I am keen to do that analysis in every company we go into. Are we making money from every one of our customers and every one of our products? A theme that I would put forward would be simplicity. Simplify the business, because over time with different practices, different management, they can become incredibly complex organisations.

MB: It seems to me the age-old tension between marketing and operations. Marketing people dream up new products and find new sectors, and sales people find new customers without actually thinking whether these things are going to be profitable to serve, because they don't always understand the operational challenges and costs involved.

GW: That was a huge cultural challenge in Crown Paints, getting sales and marketing to speak to the operational people and bringing the organisation together as a team, rather than relying on matrix management. For instance, if one of the large sheds [warehouse-based DIY retailers] wanted to run some promotional activity, it made a big difference to profitability if we could get them to do that with some paint we already had in stock or a core product line, rather than giving them a huge variety of product to promote.

MB: It seems to me that your team need not only financial skills, because they have to do due diligence and forecasting on distressed businesses against tight time-scales, but also operational capabilities in helping to turn them around. What is your recruitment strategy?

GW: I'd had the benefit at Andersens and Ernst & Young of working with top-quality restructuring people, and I wanted to cherry-pick the very best restructuring people in the market. It was crucial that they had turnaround experience, because those guys look at the world in a different light to traditional M&A people. I need people who can understand what an asset is worth, what the downsides might be, and if a business goes bust, how we can get our money back. I need to know what we really think of the management team. That's not a case of conducting some due diligence; that's working alongside them day in and day out. It's getting their hands dirty. It's working from 7 a.m. to midnight in the first six weeks of the project to get it under control. That's what I wanted, and I was lucky enough with my background to know some of the best people in the industry for that.

There are a lot of spreadsheet jockeys in the market, and frankly their financial modelling skills in Microsoft Excel are stunning. Getting them to go out and see a business and assess a management team is a completely different matter. I'd rather see guys that have been to the business, spent some time there, interacted with the management team and brought me some figures on the back of a fag packet, rather than a really fancy, all-singing model. If the model's too fancy, they haven't spent enough time at the business. That's my personal view.

MB: And what's your view on remunerating the team?

GW: I have a belief that everyone in the team must share in the carry. That's my personal style, and our team ethos. When a deal goes well, it's a fantastic place to be. When everyone in the team, and I mean everyone, shares in the upside. When a deal goes wrong, it hits everyone. It produces a fantastic team atmosphere. Everyone gains, and everyone loses.

I'm also a great believer that GPs must take risk, they must invest their own money in the deals. At Endless we insist on being one of the biggest investors in our funds, and one of the reasons we are being able to grow so quickly is that we've reinvested the profits we have made into our new deals and into our new funds. That gives our LPs confidence. We're putting our money where our mouth is. They can see that we are totally aligned with them. In fund two we were the biggest investor, in fund three we're the second biggest.

MB: I'm surprised more LPs don't insist on this practice. Otherwise, the carry is only an incentive when things go wrong, there's no alignment of interests when things go badly, because only the LPs suffer wealth destruction at that time unless the GP has real money in the fund too.

GW: When I'm sat in an investment committee meeting and we're making a decision, it involves a huge personal commitment from the team around the table. That makes you think a lot more carefully about which deals you accept and which you reject.

MB: I'm interested that the firm began in Leeds, then went to Manchester and Birmingham, and London came last, in 2010. What is behind that approach?

GW: We started in the north of England and then the Midlands because we were interested in sectors such as manufacturing and engineering that aren't in London. It makes it easier to have relationships with advisers, banks and company directors in the regions that can bring us proprietary deal-flow.

But having an office in London is bringing us larger deals, typically two or three times the size of the things that we see in the regions. And the businesses are often more international in nature; they might be UK-headquartered but of a size that means they have operations abroad. The size of the market is hard to contemplate, so we have to take different approaches to marketing. In the regional markets you can know everyone; in London there are so many people you can't, so we work a lot harder to make people know that we're here and available. I think showing hunger and motivation and appetite down here brings rewards.

MB: I suppose one big difference with London is that it's where most UK and European private equity firms are based, which perhaps makes it easier to network with them and get secondary deal-flow from over-leveraged buyouts that go wrong.

GW: That's right. We offer an honourable exit for private equity firms. Instead of businesses going bust, they can sell to us, OK for not much money, but it's a better headline to say they've sold to Endless than it is to report that an administrator has been appointed. In some cases we have not been able to turn it around, and therefore the winner was the private equity house and not Endless. In some cases we have managed to turn it around, and we have won from it, but I never publicise who we bought the business from or crow about what price we paid for it because, in terms of repeat deal-flow, if I can provide the private equity houses with an honourable way out of a difficult situation, that's a good place to be.

But of course it means that the reputational risk lies with us. If a mid-market buyout house makes an investment that fails, it might mean that the bank takes control, or they sell to us or a trade competitor buys it – there are options other than closure in many cases. Failure for us means administration and adverse PR. I would liken it to a surgeon who specialises in the most complex forms of surgery on the most fragile patients. Sometimes we have to walk out of the theatre and say, 'I'm sorry we couldn't save the patient.' Most of the time, thankfully, we come out and say the operation was successful. But when you come out of theatre and say it hasn't been successful, unfortunately there are a lot of upset people.

In 2011 we acquired a discount retailer called TJ Hughes, just before it went into administration. We spent a few months and a lot of money trying to save the business, but fundamentally it was too far gone. That business was previously private-equity-owned, but we were the owners when it finally fell into administration, so any press coverage was about our ownership. That's difficult to deal with, but as I said to a lot of journalists at the time, don't criticise us for giving a business a last chance when no one else would. The coverage we had was fair, and we recovered the vast majority of our capital. We gave a dying business one last change, but unfortunately in that instance we couldn't save it.

MB: Who do you see as your competitors, and how do you differentiate yourselves from them?

GW: There is one competitor that dominates, and it's the banks. Forget any other private equity house, our primary competition is banks and debt-for-equity swaps. All the major clearing banks have hundreds of equity stakes in troubled businesses; it will be interesting to see where that goes in the next few years.

MB: Currently they are under a lot of pressure to appear to have strong balance sheets, so they are reluctant to write down some of those assets or sell them for less than book value.

GW: Yes, but I would give them more credit than that. I think there is a genuine desire among the banks to take a creative approach toward troubled businesses. RBS, Lloyds, HSBC and Barclays are fundamentally the economic owners of a lot of over-leveraged buyouts. In the recessions in the '90s and early 2000, such businesses would have gone to the wall or been sold off cheaply, but this time they have decided they are not going to make those mistakes again. They are going to support businesses through the tough times and hopefully realise some value as the economy recovers. The difference this time, of course, is that it isn't a short-term recession, it's a long-term depression, so I think a lot of them are looking at their strategies again to see how they are going to exit instead of just keeping on building equity stakes.

MB: Do you blame the banks, buyout firms or both for what happened up to 2008?

GW: I think the private equity industry rode the wave of a growing worldwide economy and growing debt markets for too long. The smart guys got out in time, but some people joined the crest of the wave as it was crashing, and I think they are stuck with investments that aren't worth any money and never will be worth any money no matter how long they keep them. I think the industry is now facing up to perhaps generating lower returns overall and having to roll up its sleeves and get its hands dirty again. I think it will need a new generation of private equity people to do that because a lot of the guys who helped grow the industry are, frankly, worth a lot of money now, and I'm not sure will have the appetite to do that.

MB: I guess that points to growth in the secondary market.

GW: Yes, but a lot of those will be driven by banks and not private equity houses. Low interest rates mean even troubled companies can service debts at the minute. If the economy gets tougher and it wipes out any spare cash, or when interest rates finally do go up, there will be a spurt of deals.

MB: Presumably a lot of those will be distressed companies that could come your way?

GW: Yes, I see it as a big area of activity.

MB: From time to time since mid-2008 the debt markets have opened up again and there have been some fairly highly leveraged buyouts done. Do you think the banks or the private equity industry have learned any lessons?

GW: If a bank is prepared to loan a private equity company the vast bulk of the money to do a deal, the positive is that the firm doesn't lose very much if the deal goes wrong. It's the banks that are the losers.

MB: It makes me wonder why they do it: they get lower returns than equity providers when things go well, and take the lion's share of the losses when they go badly. People were being paid a lot of money to arrange those kinds of loans, but they weren't really good deals for the banks, were they?

GW: I think you've touched a nerve there, in that there's potentially a conflict of interest between teams and individuals on the one hand and corporates and their shareholders on the other. So you've got teams and individuals driving for bonuses which are evaluated on short-term metrics, and they may not necessarily be around when the deal goes wrong.

A lot of people criticise private equity for being short-termist, but to make a lot of money in private equity you've got to see a fund through for ten or 12 years. You don't get big bonuses for doing deals. You make good money for generating good returns for your investors. That's not necessarily the case in banking. Can you imagine bankers sticking around for 12 years to see whether their portfolio of deals have made money or not?

MB: In an era of lower growth, and in the main less leverage, with firms having to be more hands-on with portfolio companies and with funds being harder to raise, will private equity be less profitable in the future?

GW: I think LPs' return expectations may have to come down. The typical hurdle rate in private equity is an IRR of 8 per cent. Interest rates have been at almost zero for a few years now and could stay that way a while. There needs to be a recalibration of return expectations down several per cent and the carry adjusted from a straight 20 per cent to a structured layer focused on different levels of return.

One of the challenges I see is that a lot of GPs have got rich off management fees over the last ten to 20 years. LPs are now expecting greater transparency. I don't necessarily think the fees will come down, but with GPs having to staff up more, they will no longer be a profit centre. All our LPs see our operating budget, we are a break-even business that is entirely focused on capital gain rather than management fees. I think GPs are going to have to compete a lot harder to attract investors, and a key element of that is building trust with LPs and having a reputation for transparency.

MB: So what level of information do you give your LPs?

GW: We report quarterly; our reports are an inch thick, and there's far too much information in them, but our investors know that whatever they want to know about our businesses, they can access straight away.

MB: Another dynamic is how much money is going into emerging markets funds, especially Asia and South America. Will that continue?

GW: Maybe, but they still have the challenges of whether investors can feel safe investing there and whether there are enough regulations and protections for investors. At the same time, developed market private equity is a mature scene, where growth will happen only if people fundamentally come up with new ideas and strategies. There's also the risk that too much regulation, particularly from government and the EU, could mean that the UK is no longer the natural place to be based in Europe.

I think that would be a great pity. Taking just Endless, in just three and a half years of taking on external investment for funds two and three, we raised over £300 million from US and European investors and brought that money to the UK to be invested in troubled industries. Can you imagine trying to get that money from the EU or the government? That £300 million is creating huge value for the UK economy. If politicians make it harder for people to invest in the UK, or for GPs to be based here, that money will find a new home.

MB: You mentioned the growth of niches in developed markets. Turnaround may be one of those. Do you see competition for deals increasing, and if so, how will you handle that?

GW: It's already happening; I don't see mainstream private equity groups moving to special situations, but I see new groups being set up. That's inevitable as people see firms like Endless doing well. Our response is to demonstrate to the stakeholders that we are excellent at turning businesses around operationally and at creating value on exit. No one else has a track record like ours in these areas. Doing turnarounds can be emotionally draining and hugely absorbing. We've developed a framework for being able to do it several times at once. Let's see whether other firms are able to do that.

MB: Do you plan to change or diversify your strategy?

GW: We will continue to be focused on special situations but may add new products. For instance, we might create a credit opportunity fund or an asset-backed lending fund, other ways of helping troubled companies that perhaps do not generate the large returns we seek under the core fund.

MB: I assume you see those kinds of opportunities among firms that don't actually reach a liquidity point where they have to do a deal or go into administration, and see an opportunity to offer your investors a lower-risk alternative to the main fund.

GW: Yes, and we would see it as being an opportunity to bring some of our operational skills to the companies, rather than just money.

MB: Do you think economic recovery could make it harder for Endless to source good deals?

GW: No, because we have operated through both good and bad times. In 2005/6 the economy was booming, and we weren't short of opportunities. As the economy improves, I see the banks offloading more equity stakes and I also see companies struggling to cope with the increased demand and the increased working capital needs. I am looking forward to the day when that happens as it'll bring more opportunities, but I also think it'll be easier to turn businesses around in that climate.

Section III
Emerging Markets

12
Introduction

A helicopter view of the geographical spread of private equity since KKR invented the buyout model in the late 1970s would show the industry gradually extending its sphere of influence east and south. It had become established in the UK by the early 1980s, and from that bridgehead expanded into Europe over the following decade. Meanwhile private equity in Asia and Africa came into being around 20 years ago, initially dominated by Development Finance Institutions (DFIs), but with humanitarian capital gradually taking a back seat in those territories and for those investment strategies that have been proven to generate commercially attractive returns. US GPs made tentative forays into Latin America in the late '90s, again often alongside DFIs, got their fingers burned in the meltdowns at the turn of the millennium, but returned with more sustainable approaches around five years ago.

Since the financial crisis of 2008, the macro-economics of private equity have changed, perhaps for ever. The risk weightings traditionally attached to mature and emerging economies have had to be re-assessed: no longer are the USA, UK and Eurozone necessarily seen as safer than, say, China, India or Brazil, whether in terms of their vulnerability to economic shocks or currency risks for overseas investors. And a major distinction between developed and developing countries – the availability of debt – has been blurred, and even where high leverage is selectively available in mature economies, the wisdom of using it has been undermined by the decoupling of the positive relationship between gearing and returns.

Small wonder, then, that the third quarter of 2008 marked a defining moment in private equity: for the first time in history, according to data provider Prequin, more capital was raised by funds focusing on Asia and the rest of the world than those targeting Europe ($15.4 billion versus $14.0 billion).

Fast-forwarding to the most recent period for which data was available while I was writing this book, the final quarter of 2011, reveals an even more intriguing picture. At first sight, emerging markets appeared to have tanked, attracting less than a third of the capital that went to Europe. But the geographical split is overshadowed by a hugely significant trend: the growth of the global fund.

As we've seen with TA Associates, there are attractions to funds that provide managers with the flexibility to invest anywhere, provided the underlying businesses meet a set of broad criteria – principally scale, stage and sometimes sector – that have been pre-agreed with LPs. First, they offer at least the potential for higher returns than single-territory funds, as managers can allocate capital dynamically across a number of geographies as the macro-economics change. Second, provided the invested capital is in actuality distributed fairly widely by territory, such funds offer investors diversification without having to be in a number of different limited partnerships. And third, as a result of these two factors, global funds potentially represent a tempting proposition to potential investors – especially in uncertain times.

In 2011 Q4, global buyout firms attracted $18.4 billion – almost twice as much capital as those focused on Europe and two and a half times as much as those concentrating on the USA. The rest-of-the-world figure was tiny – less than 10 per cent of the figure for global funds. Seeing a higher figure for Europe than the USA rings an alarm bell: many of the global buyout funds are in fact the big US firms, repositioning themselves as global investors. Time will tell how much of the capital raised actually gets deployed outside the USA, or in emerging markets. Being charitable, for reasons I will expand on in this third section of the book, which explores the investing models that are getting traction in developing markets, developing economies are not necessarily places to which the buyout model is well suited. But similar trends are observable in other sectors, particularly growth funds, where the $2.5 billion raised for global pools was more than four times that attracted by funds targeting territories or regions in the rest of the world.

I'm optimistic that much of this growth capital will genuinely be put to work in emerging markets. For a start, there's now an ecosystem of investment professionals and lobbyists behind the trend. Sarah Alexander, founding President and CEO of the Emerging Markets Private Equity Association (EMPEA), is overt about her organisation's objective:

> Our aim is to have emerging markets private equity be considered an asset class. Once it's considered an asset class, it has to be allocated to. It is only going to be an asset class when people think that they have to be in it, or it has some characteristics that provide a diversification element within their portfolios. It doesn't have to be an asset class just within the private equity sphere, because one of the things that's unique about emerging markets is that you cannot get the same level of exposure through the public markets as you can in developed markets. I would argue today that it is pretty close

to being an asset class. Not all institutions are doing it, but most would like to if they had the human capital and the fund size to do it.

The focus on asset-class promotion extends to the trade associations set up in recent years to make the case for investment in specific emerging regions. For instance, when I met Cate Ambrose, President and Executive Director of the Latin America Venture Capital Association (LAVCA), it was at an industry event in London, where she told me that she had also recently visited Abu Dhabi, Hong Kong and Israel to present to investors on the merits of her region as a place to invest. Her organisation publishes an annual scorecard for each country on the continent, produced in association with the Economist Intelligence Unit. It rates nations on a wide range of factors spanning the regulatory and judicial, fiscal and cultural factors that determine whether each represents a good environment for private equity investment.

LAVCA's scorecard raises several points, illustrative of the broader private equity environment, that merit discussion. First, Ambrose is candid about the fact that some countries, including 2011's front-runner, Chile, and middle-ranker Colombia, actively work with the association to improve the environment for private equity in the hope that their scores will increase and that this will lead to capital inflows. Second, her scorecard includes some developed-market comparators, and it is chastening to note that only one point separates Chile and a large western European economy, namely Spain, in the 2011 rankings. Third, putting these two factors together, it seems to me that with Spain already suffering faltering domestic demand and an unemployment rate nudging 25 per cent, the comments made by a couple of my interviewees about the risk that over-regulation by the EU could drive investment elsewhere should not lightly be dismissed.

The professionalisation of emerging markets private equity encompasses not only the way in which it is being presented but also the actuality of the proposition. Not only are some governments working to improve the legal, judicial and fiscal environment for private equity, but general partners have been reinventing their *modus operandi* to improve returns in these markets. No longer are investments made by fly-in, fly-out teams of North Americans or Brits; increasingly, general partnerships are either set up and owned by nationals of the countries in which they are investing or, if the GP is a familiar, developed-market name, the investment professionals are predominantly native, and live full-time in the regions.

Unsurprisingly, people who have grown up in the business communities in which they are making and managing investments, and who have not been schooled in a standard US or UK private equity model, have been creating their own adaptations of that basic formula, and have developed entirely new formulae of their own. As a minimum, these overcome any challenges that are specific to the territories in which they are working; at best, they may represent entirely new thinking that the industry in both other emerging economies and developed ones might wish to consider adapting for and deploying in their own markets.

One of the many criticisms levelled at private equity in the USA and the UK is that the industry fishes for talent in a very shallow gene pool: very few people working in general partnerships at a senior level are not Caucasian men, from relatively advantaged family backgrounds, who boast career histories in investment banking, accountancy or top-tier consulting firms. Indeed, on a personal level, I find it chastening that, while I am deemed qualified to write a book about private equity and co-founded a professional services firm linked to the industry, few GPs would see me as an obvious match with their hiring profiles: my career history is too entrepreneurial and insufficiently blue-chip, and I'm not enough of a 'quant'.

While I have reservations about the concept of affirmative action – and believe that the industry would, almost universally, push-back against pressure to make its recruitment policies more inclusive – I do think there is merit in the observation that teams of people with very similar backgrounds may be more prone to 'group-think' than are more diverse ones.

So I see it as positive that private equity in developing countries is evolving an identity and a distinct set of approaches that, for the most part, has latterly resulted in returns that equal or exceed those generated in mature economies. For the beneficiaries are not just the people who manage and provide the capital and live in the communities in which it is invested, but also private equity firms in developed countries, because they now enjoy, for the first time, the opportunity to benchmark themselves against and learn from a parallel set of professionals in emerging markets.

I accept that some of the approaches that are proving successful in Asia, South America and Africa and the Middle East might not be applicable without heavy modification in the USA, UK or western Europe and acknowledge that the higher growth rates in many of the countries in which the GPs operate constitute a very different macro-economic environment (although not, necessarily, an advantageous one). But I think that each of the firms whose investment and value enhancement strategies I've tried to capture in the interviews that follow exhibits, at the very least, a series of nuggets of thinking that could be adopted in developed markets and, in some cases, that present entirely new and potentially very attractive management paradigms.

13
Derek Sulger, Partner, Lunar Capital Management

If I had to pick one country that embodies the extremes of the opportunities and challenges of emerging market private equity, it would have to be China. Home to 1.35 billion people – close to one in five of the world's population – it boasts an economy that has grown at approximately 8 per cent per annum for more than a decade. And yet concerns about corruption, intellectual property theft, government interventionism and a possible bursting of a property and banking bubble together present a risk profile almost as formidable as the market size and growth trend are exciting.

There are people I've interviewed in the course of researching this book that view the country as too much of a frontier market – John Hess called it 'dangerous as hell'. Others, including my next interviewee, founder of Chinese private equity firm Lunar Capital, Derek Sulger, believe that the negatives are overstated and that they can do a lot to mitigate them by pursuing particular investment strategies and operational models. The same can be argued for most, if not all, emerging economies.

In Chapter 6 I observed that fund managers are in pursuit of 'alpha' – genuine out-performance in returns, even after adjusting for risk. Private equity as we know it has existed in China for barely a decade, so it is too early to say whether or not those risk-mitigation approaches will succeed in the long term. However, to date, the best China funds have performed at least as well as their Western counterparts. And many of the GPs I've interviewed who work in emerging markets are pretty strongly embedded in the business communities of the countries in which they operate, have often made money for themselves and investors as entrepreneurs in those territories before moving into private equity and in many cases have significant personal money tied up in the funds they manage – factors that lead me to believe they are alert to, and on top of, the downsides.

Although I observed in Chapter 12 that one of the trends separating the current boom in developing market private equity from the first wave in the

1990s is the preponderance of funds raised, or at least managed, by natives, Derek Sulger is, by some measures, an exception. At first glance he appears to be the epitome of old-world private equity: half-American, half-British, educated in the USA and then Harvard. In the early 1990s he joined the definitive US investment bank, Goldman Sachs, moving to its London office in 1993.

What sets him apart, and eventually resulted in him setting up one of the best-regarded private equity firms in China, was a chance observation he made in the late 1990s. He saw that the uptake of mobile phones was much higher in Europe than in the USA due to the latter having chosen a legacy technical standard. He researched the idea of starting a business relating to mobile phone usage, initially in the USA. In order to explore the idea he hired a few interns from Imperial College, London. By chance, they were Chinese. At the time, China had only 5 or 10 million mobile phone users, and analysts expected that figure to grow to about 50 million in three to five years.

Sulger's research led him to believe the forecasts massively understated the likely growth – he predicted 300 to 500 million within five years. So in late 1999 he resigned from Goldman and relocated to Shanghai, where he launched three companies in the sector. One, Intrinsic Technology, provided the back-end billing systems and software systems for mobile operators. The second, Linktone, provided consumer-oriented mobile services such as email, messaging and text messaging services. The third business, Smartpay, helped mobile phone companies collect the money that was owed to them in what was, in those days, a largely cash economy. Linktone became one of the first Chinese companies to list on Nasdaq, in 2004; Intrinsic was sold in 2005, and Smartpay remains privately owned.

Today Sulger explains his decision thus:

> The businesses I was involved in from 1999 to 2006 were predicated on one simple thesis, which was that I thought China would have more mobile phone users than Goldman Sachs and Morgan Stanley and Credit Suisse did, and I thought that if I was right and they were wrong, we were going to make a lot of money.

The first Lunar Capital fund was, in effect, the holding company through which Sulger and others invested in the three mobile telecoms businesses. The second fund, LCP2, was raised in 2007 and was the first conventional fund in that, although a significant part of the capital came from Sulger's and his team's successful exits to date, external investors also came on board. LCP3 followed in late 2010/early 2011. They are small funds – $60 million and $150 million respectively – but Sulger actively encourages co-investment, and believes that making smaller investments is the optimum strategy in China.

Sulger sees his strategy today as an extension of the one that worked in mobile telecoms: 'The only reason we got into the sector was because it was a good proxy for growth and consumption … Since I moved to China, it has gone from maybe 100 million to 400 million consumers, and that number will probably be 800 million in ten years' time. That will change the landscape of China in a way that's very hard for economists to model or investors to think about. So we look for very simple domestic consumption stories, and we focus on the next 400 million rather than the current 400 million.'

This focus on the next 400 million means that Sulger's investment strategy is concentrated on the provinces inland of those in the eastern coastal belt of the country that have experienced the greatest urbanisation and economic growth to date.

Crucially, Lunar Capital leverages everything that Sulger and his team have learned first-hand about entrepreneurship in China and their knowledge of best practice in business in developed markets. The firm takes an exceptionally hands-on approach to portfolio businesses, typically implanting at least two of its own people into each company to accelerate growth, and control the purse strings.

* * *

MB: It seems to me what sets you apart from most Western private equity operators in emerging markets is that you've started, run and exited businesses in the country where you now invest.

DS: Yes, and it doesn't just apply to me but to my team – a lot of us have run businesses in China, whereas most private equity firms are more dominated by bankers and financiers. I look the part of a private equity guy in China because I went to Goldmans, but I think what our firm has that's unusual is having actually had to go in and get our hands dirty. It's a business where we can see some money to be made by actually just being willing to go and help run the companies.

MB: What were the dynamics of private equity in China before you started Lunar Capital?

DS: In the late '90s there was a fair amount of early-stage venture capital, mostly people flying in from Silicon Valley. Most of the investments turned out to be very successful, sustainable companies, but the capital was a product of the dotcom bubble.

Next there was a four-year drought. Then our company [Linktone] went public, and I think that re-opened the fascination with companies going public in China. That led to a big part of the private equity community being growth capital looking to do pre-IPO investments based on multiple arbitrages: investing in companies that were about to go public and hoping to float at a higher multiple after a few months.

The number of people willing to be traditional private equity investors, focusing on the value-add, was more limited, and that's the hole I felt we should fill. I still think that hole exists dramatically in China. I think the next decade will be one of more specialisation and value creation.

MB: You've said your strategy isn't early-stage or pre-IPO, so how would you describe it?

DS: It's profitable companies that are a little bit too early to be public, but are profitable, have very steady growth rates, so it's realistic to assume that if a company just keeps doing what it's doing today, it will be a scale of a listed company two or three or four years down the road.

Our thesis usually is not to rush it out to go public. It is more to get actively involved and capture more of that growth. We tend to take larger stakes and be more actively involved in the company in areas where we can actively drive value creation. That includes being involved in the management of our businesses. So if we're going to be a minority investor, we want it to be pretty substantial and we are majority investors in more businesses than most PE firms in China. We operate in a market where the number of private equity deals that actually are majority in nature is minuscule. It's probably 1 per cent of the total. More and more of our deals are those majority deals, because that's how we feel we can really get the control and involvement.

It's not like we're going in and kicking management out. Mostly it's that we're going into companies where management just happens to be a minority. So it's almost like they were married to someone. In many of the companies they started the business, they married a bunch of investors, maybe they went public, maybe things happened, maybe the company grew and all of a sudden they find themselves minorities in their own companies. So it's almost like they're looking to get married once again. For example, we invested in a company recently where the founder of the business only owns 20 per cent, so when we came in and owned 60 per cent, we became the majority controlling shareholder, but it's not incompatible with still working with the woman who started the business.

MB: So is your capital used mainly to buy out non-management shareholders, or to finance growth?

DS: We've mostly put to work new money to grow the businesses, but we're getting more confident about buying out older shareholders. Up to three years ago, that strategy was a little tricky in China because everyone had irrational expectations of what an IPO meant. In a year like last year when the Chinese equity markets dropped 27 per cent and there wasn't an IPO for months, a lot of these secondary shareholders' expectations are far more rational and so the ability to selectively buy them out, if it facilitates a transaction, becomes less risky and more logical.

For instance, looking at one recent deal, the founder owned 20 per cent, the management team owned 10, and the other 70 per cent was owned by three individuals who didn't like each other very much, so we bought out the two that were not adding any value, left in the one that was, left in management and *voilà*! We end up with 53 per cent, and it's almost like we we're coming in as like the referee! That's the kind of majority strategy that I think really makes a lot of sense. So what you're putting a little money in people's pockets, but in that case we were actually solving a problem.

MB: But excepting the buyout of non-management shareholders, it's principally development capital – providing cash that can be used for growth or acquisition, in return for new shares?

DS: Yes. Private enterprises in China have a very difficult time raising money from banks to fund expansion. Larger firms are forced to go to the equity markets, but that's a lot harder for smaller companies, which presents the opportunity for us.

For example, we bought 30 per cent of two parallel fruit juice processing companies that were owned by a family. We spent two years working to merge them together to create one of the biggest firms in the sector, then we wanted to buy a third processing plant that was a dormant state-owned asset. It was well built but was never run properly. So our money was used first for the working capital to bring two companies together, then to acquire this other plant. The company was profitable, but the profits needed to be kept in reserve to run the operating cash-flow, because in China it can be difficult to get even simple vendor-financing. As firms grow, it's often hard for them to use their profits for new expansion because the cash might be tied up sourcing more raw materials or buying more electricity or whatever is needed to run the business. When it comes to undertaking expansion, they have to turn to equity providers like us, and I hope in the case of the fruit juice business we got in very cheaply because we were able to add a lot of value, put a lot of people on the ground and help them solve a lot of problems.

MB: You've mentioned being very hands-on and working proactively with management. How do you structure and resource your team to achieve this?

DS: We divide our team into investments and operations. On the investments side, there's one of the early investors in one of our telecoms business, who has more of a banking background, but had also started a company in China, but probably didn't run it to the same degree I did mine. We have three investment GPs and a slew of analysts. The idea is just three teams; each team has a focus and that's why we're only really going to focus on three things maximum because I want each of those teams to be more specialised over time.

The other half of our company is people with operations backgrounds. One is a consultant, one was the COO [chief operating officer] of a large company in China, and their team is comprised mostly of in-house, consulting-type analysts and associates, but they also oversee all of the people that we hire and then second into businesses. Our model is generally hire the person first, then put them in as our person into the companies later. So right now in their team we have a former controller of a Coca-Cola bottling corporation in China, and he's seconded into one of our beverage businesses. Last year we hired the former MD of Vitasoy China, a popular Chinese drink, with the intention of seconding him into one of our beverage businesses if we closed the deal. We hired him first. Had we not closed the deal, our payroll would have swollen for no apparent reason.

MB: Are you saying that you second one of your people to each investee business?

DS: Usually more than one. We try to second someone with operating experience and someone with financial controls experience. If I had to write it as a paper formula, we would second a financial controller and a CFO, but those titles are meaningless. The financial controller is usually someone who basically makes sure that we basically have daily financials from the business. We report to our LPs monthly, whereas most private equity firms only report quarterly. That job also extends to things like information systems roll-outs. For example, we had one mining business where we put in an ERP [enterprise resource planning] system or in a retail business we'll have to roll out a big point of sale system because they might not have very good internal information control systems.

The person we put in that we call the CFO usually is more someone who can run the business. More someone who is actually the co-CEO, but we don't want to call him that. In the West we think companies are all supposed to have CEOs, COOs and CFOs. In Chinese companies they don't really have that. They have general managers and finance directors. Those are usually the two most important. There is a lot of expectation of hands-on involvement. In Chinese companies the CFO is really considered to be the right-hand man, so we hire CFOs who have more operating experience so that they could actually step up and run the business, whereas the group financial controllers we hire are more the guys who actually do what we in the West think of as the CFO job.

Those are the two secondments we make if we have a real minority stake. In a case like a retail business we recently bought, we actually hired those two plus five other, much more specific, functional people. We want them to be our people, we want the perception to be that we pay them, so there's a loyalty to our firm.

MB: Are these permanent hires?

DS: Yes, the rule internally is they have to spend 110 per cent of their time on the portfolio company and then 30 per cent of their time on the other stuff, but in practice they call into our Monday morning meetings or will attend our Monday morning meetings if they happen to be near by, but other than that, they're in the portfolio company full-time.

MB: And how many of them are native Chinese speakers?

DS: All of them. I'm the only foreigner, and the only one who speaks non-native, bad Chinese.

MB: I understand you welcome co-investment.

DS: We push ourselves to have co-investors in our deals. Some of them are the LPs in our funds, because we've taken the strategy of trying to keep smaller and more focused funds, but they're all where we both want to give the company new money and buy out old shareholders that our funds can't do alone. They tend to be people who are either industry experts or other LPs who we would like to get to know better. So, for example, a co-investor in a recent deal was a big global fund of funds because we wanted them to get to know us better with a view to investing in the next fund, and sometimes the best due diligence is coming in and seeing how we work.

Philosophically, I find this to be a good thing to do because, while it does add a layer of complexity, it challenges our team. It forces them to have to go through pretty extensive due diligence and to answer the same questions ten times, which probably means I don't have to do as much. For instance, we recently had a really smart Middle Eastern fund wanting to co-invest in a deal, and they were peppering our team with excellent questions. This added to an already heavy workload, but deep down I think it's really great that someone is in there asking them 100 tough questions, because it keeps them on their toes.

MB: How do you incentivise your teams?

DS: My philosophy tends to be to give them economics in everything – in the firm as a whole, then in the funds and in some extraordinary cases on specific deals. I'm a little nervous on the deal-specific because on the one hand it's a very powerful incentive, but it also can create a lot of fiefdoms within the firm. Generally speaking, I think the best formula is exactly what the banks are moving away from: low base salaries, high potential upside, solely and only if it's performance-based.

MB: How is the competition for deals? There have been some sizeable Asia funds raised in the past couple of years.

DS: That money is trying to head towards China, and I think it will end up there. But it's still challenging for those firms, because most of them have a proven recipe of how to do things in Western markets, or other Asian markets outside of China, and it has been a real struggle to translate it. One or two have given up and pretty much announced that they weren't going to do any buyouts or majority deals in China, that they would do all minority growth capital deals.

I also think that private equity in China is low, relative to the size of the economy. There are funds coming online, but until you see $10 billion funds it's hard to argue there's a lot of money. In the USA and Germany and elsewhere, everyone can name $10 billion funds. So I think there's a long way to go before there's too much money. I think there's a perception that it's a huge economy with a lot of opportunity, but what is private equity really allowed to do? Therefore it's hard to determine what is the right amount of private equity, but I think time will prove that there's actually too little money, rather than too much, right now.

MB: The question of what private equity is allowed to do is quite important in China, isn't it? What's your view on where we are now and where things could go?

DS: I think what private equity should be doing is adding value, and I think that if you think of the regulators as keeping score of the industry, the government bureaucrats don't like to see private equity funds acting as get rich quick firms. They know there's this arbitrage because it's difficult for Chinese companies to go public, but they don't like seeing headlines that a firm goes in and makes three times its money in a year, just because it happens to take a small stake pre-IPO.

They like deals that facilitate consolidation, knowledge transfer and value-add, so I think it's good to stick to those old-fashioned principles and also given how big the economy's getting you're going to have a very easy time to keep your head well under the radar and not get caught up in the crazy political times. The challenge for most of these larger private equity funds has been that they all want to do what Goldman did with ICBC, they all want to invest a billion dollars in something, and they all want to go into things like financial institutions, where it's easy to put a lot of money to work, but that are completely closed off, so that's a very different challenge. That's where their strategies haven't worked.

The opportunity in China, what China needs and wants, is for private equity to finance private enterprise, because that's the area that they don't really feel comfortable allowing the banks to finance. I think, deep down, they think the banks don't know how to do it. You're filling that gap and no one's going to criticise you for doing that.

MB: You mentioned that there may be unease in Beijing at Western private equity firms making a lot of money quickly from pre-IPO deals. Is that model not under threat from the reduced appetite for IPOs and the more realistic valuations we're now seeing?

DS: I think historically one of the problems with the pre-IPO investing is that everyone paid too much, because the only way you made money was if the company went public. People didn't want to do M&A because they'd bought in at valuations that were predicated on going public. Doing an M&A deal was like coming last.

I think that perception should and will change. I think people underestimate how fast consolidation and M&A activities can accelerate domestically in China. It's always been there, but it's just been a bit haphazard and it's usually been foreigners trying to acquire Chinese companies. Now Chinese-on-Chinese M&A is going to accelerate, so I think increasingly it's easier to know that there is a price for every company.

In our firm, with most of our businesses, we first think of what we could make in a roll-up or a consolidation. The market in general puts 99 per cent weighting on an IPO and 1 per cent on a trade sale, where I think you should think trade sale first, IPO second.

MB: How far and fast could private equity grow in China?

DS: I think the ultimate size is mainly a function of how the capital markets liberalise. It's not that easy to go in and buy domestically listed shares, for example, the bond markets are almost non-existent and the banks don't lend to private enterprises. All this creates opportunities for private equity, but it also limits it – it's why you don't see large leveraged buyouts.

I don't think in ten years' time it'll be like London or New York, but I do think that it will just get better over time. It'll mean that, three or four years from now, you'll hear more about people routinely doing $200–300 million deals, which then justify having $3–4 billion funds.

I also think this decade will be one where players in the Chinese market will have to define more narrowly their strategies and specialise. Historically in China it was mainly about pre-IPO and growth private equity, so almost every fund is looked at as being the same, whereas I think by the end of the decade you'll have LPs asking whether you are a small or a mid-market buyout fund, a growth capital fund or a late-stage venture fund.

Right now I think the LPs maybe aren't pushing the Chinese GPs to specialise enough. I think even with us, we are trying to specialise, but sometimes we feel a bit like iconoclasts doing it and I would like to think that what we're doing is going to be more typically done in five or ten years' time.

MB: You made the point that there's not much leveraged buyout activity in China, because there's not much of a debt or bond market. Could you get it from non-domestic sources in the region, Standard Chartered or HSBC?

DS: It's hard; you can for some dollar-based deals, mostly privatisations of listed companies, but it's tough. We get approached by the banks to do it, but I think it's because not that many people are doing it so they're looking for people to try. What the terms would be, how aggressive they would be, I have no idea.

MB: What about the denomination of private equity funds? There seems to be this feeling that the RMB funds [raised in Renminbi, traditionally from wealthy Chinese citizens, but which have recently received limited approval for issue to external investors], are able to do deals in sectors that external funds can't touch.

DS: There's definitely that component. It's that black and white, because I think it falls into two categories. The first category is deals that they can do purely because the regulatory catalogue prevents foreign investment. But a lot of those industries that are banned to foreigners are sort of banned to private enterprise in general; they're more state businesses. The second category is the idea that it's easier regulatorily to do a deal with RMB. I think the jury's out on that. I think it's easier to do it quickly, but I don't think that's necessarily a good thing. I think in years like 2006/7 people were really infatuated with the idea of RMB funds because they thought you could move quicker, but moving quicker is not a great idea if it just forces you to make sloppy decisions, and I think that's what has happened.

MB: What are the implications of certain industries being off-limits?

DS: It can sometimes present opportunities. For example, forestry is the only agricultural line you can currently own. So we're in that sector. We have a really great business that's doing really well [Yunnan International Forestry]. If we could acquire farms, we'd consolidate them together and invest in automation and all the things we can do to drive efficiencies in forestry. But we can't. So we tapped into it in a different way with our juice business. The company actually made money because agriculture in China is so fragmented. We could produce, for example, pineapple juice for half what it would cost us in the Philippines because we could buy from 50,000 farms that have no pricing power, whereas in the Philippines we had to buy it from one landlord, who would be a lot more aware of our prices.

Ironically, if the government relaxed its policies, it could accelerate the urbanisation trend because making farms worth more money and more efficient would help people move to the cities.

MB: I get the feeling that you see the change in affluence and spending patterns as people move from the country to the cities as the key driver of your investment strategy.

DS: Since I moved to China in November '99, it has gone from 43 per cent urbanised to about 50 per cent. So all that growth happened on a shift of just 7 per cent, and it's got a long way to go. One of the reasons it hasn't happened much quicker is because there's still a lot of people tied to the farm, and agriculture's very fragmented in China, so you can't yet have consolidated agriculture. You still have a hundred families on a plot. There should probably be one family farm. That's another one of the obvious things that people overlook, if you read economists' articles about this whole issue about urbanisation, it'll always point to urbanisation as being people coming from the countryside to work in factories in Shenzhen to make iPods. That was true. That was urbanisation from 1998 to 2006, but now urbanisation is people going from rural and suburban parts of Chengdu and Chongqing to Chengdu and Chongqing. It's no longer migrating half-way across the country.

It's a completely different type and flavour of urbanisation, and it's far more powerful because unlike the old one, which was the man leaving the family and moving a 12-hour train ride away, the new one is just getting enough money to move the family into the outskirts of a big city. That's going to accelerate. That's why I think people underestimate the transformational aspects.

I think what people in the West are usually wrong about is they just can't grasp the size of China. Even if they go there, they see Shanghai and they say, 'Oh, it's fully developed, there's nowhere left to go', but there are 292 cities in China of more than a million people. They still think of China in terms of Beijing, Shanghai and Shenzhen or Changchun, and they just can't grasp that all these cities of 2 and 3 million people that they've never heard of can actually become hubs of consumption.

We recently invested in a retailer that has 700 stores, and it's only in 138 of those 292 markets. In most of those markets it has only one or two stores, whereas in a city like Shanghai they have 60 stores. The number of cities where they have more than ten stores is just five.

When we talk to people about maintaining 50 per cent revenue growth rates in that company, they say it's mathematically impossible. I say they should think of it another way and ask how many stores they should have. They're doing to have one in all 292 cities at some point, right? And the number they have more than ten stores in is going to grow substantially. So how many stores are they going to go from 700 to? 1000? 2000? 3000? There could be 8000 stores. That's the thing I think people don't grasp.

Of those 292 cities, almost all of them are bigger than, say, Birmingham or Manchester are in the UK. And they're geographically close together, like in the UK or western Europe, rather than spread out, like in the USA. Populated China is pretty crunchy. The longest flights between these places are two hours. The furthest west large Chinese city is arguably Chengdu. It's a two-hour flight from Shanghai. Economic China is a pretty small area, and it's shrinking because they're building high-speed rail networks. All these cities around Shanghai – like Nanjing, Suzhou and Ningbo, which I used to dread going to because I hate sitting in a car for four hours – now you can get there on a train in 40 minutes.

When I started those three telecoms firms in 1999, it was as a proxy for the growth of the Chinese consumer. Today, even people investing in our company don't believe me when I say that nobody back then thought that 50 million Chinese people would be able to afford a mobile phone, or to use internet services on their phone, by 2005. [Sulger subsequently emails me a link to a *Washington Post* report on the launch of the first of the three businesses; it ends with an analyst's comment that 'Anyone who believes that significant numbers of Chinese consumers are going to be spending lots of money for mobile Internet services anytime soon is going to be very disappointed.']

MB: It seems to me that the scale of opportunity you are describing will require a fair amount of capital. Will you be increasing your fund size next time you go on the road?

DS: It could be as small as $250 million or as big as $500 million. We will want to do a similar scale of deals, but inflation means they will be that bit bigger in cash terms. And we'll want to take down more resources to do more of the deals single-handedly. But I don't want the fund to be so big that we ever feel pressured to invest. I think one of the keys to our success is never having too much extra money lying around.

Part of my thesis is that smaller is often better, because it forces people like me, running the business, to have more of our own money on the line, and I think there's a high correlation between that and success.

MB: There also seems to be a negative correlation between fund size and returns, especially lately.

DS: I think the law of big numbers would just suggest that the larger the fund, the more you're really looking at it as trying to outperform an index. For a very large European buyout fund, what you're probably hoping is that you beat the FTSE by a few per cent. It's really hard for those large mega-buyout funds to do substantially more than that. It's easier to do if you're more focused. I want to be intellectually honest about what we do, and I think that if you want to add value, there's no way we could actually be helping actively run more than a 20 companies at the same time. We're 29 people, for God's sake, and right now we are focused on only about ten companies.

I think as those businesses get successful and our team grows, we'll have more bandwidth and then we'll be able to do more, but more being going from doing two or three $25–50 million investments a years to maybe three or four at $50–100 million.

We try to look at a lot of projects, but not to do too many. With our strategy, the dating process is long, but I think that length is necessary, because if you're going to get comfortable about buying out a secondary shareholder, for example, you don't want to do that with a company that you've known for less than a year in China.

The way you gradually increase the number of deals you can do, in my mind, is to do what no one else in China is willing to do right now, which is to focus and specialise a bit. For example, I've spoken about the juice producer we invested in; we then bought a large beverage bottling business and more recently a branded beverage business. Because they are in related sectors, it's much easier to do due diligence and to have confidence in our people's ability to go in and run them, much like how in 1999 my one mobile telecoms company turned into three. The idea is to have three beverage businesses that are so tightly related that it's almost like having one investment.

MB: The approach you describe reminds me of Citadel Capital [an innovative Egyptian private equity firm profiled in Chapter 20]. They try to build vertically integrated chains of related businesses and exploit the synergies between them.

DS: I think one of my roles in the company is being the one that always reminds people that the best pipeline deal is actually the deal that isn't really like a separate pipeline but is more like funding another part of the business.

MB: How do you find the culture of entrepreneurship in China? I'm intrigued that it is perceived to be a highly entrepreneurial place, and yet not so many years ago private enterprise was almost non-existent.

DS: The first generation of Chinese entrepreneurs have gone from being perhaps 35 years old to 55 or 60. They've seen the growth of professional management classes. They've seen what it takes for certain companies to get public or get acquired, and they're not stupid. There's a stereotype that says they are megalomaniacs that want to create dynastic businesses and are hard to deal with, but that's because people are projecting what the economy looked like in 1995 or 2000 onto today, and they don't factor in things like getting old and the fact that some of the most famous entrepreneurs in China who are still talked about today don't own majorities of their businesses any more because they've gone public or they've been sold to strategic partners.

They want to succeed, and there's no doubt that for some people success means controlling the business, but for some people it means going public and for others it just means making a lot of money; the good news is, it's fragmented. Some people it's all because they really are control freaks and they really do want to be the chairman, CEO and major shareholder. Others like the idea of being the chairman but don't really want to run the business. I think it's good news for private equity, because it means there are plenty of opportunities for us to work with good entrepreneurs.

14
Niten Malhan, Managing Director, Warburg Pincus LLP

Having begun the emerging markets section of this book by interviewing an entrepreneurial fund manager investing in the world's most populous country, China, it is fitting that this next chapter should be devoted to a conversation with a GP active in the second biggest, India.

This time I'm talking with someone whose fund more closely fits the profile I described in Chapter 12 – a single pool of capital, raised by an established US manager for deployment anywhere in the world. Likewise, the individual I've interviewed is more typical of the current generation of developing market investment professionals, being a national of the country in which he puts capital to work. But he shares with Chapter 13's Derek Sulger a career that spans developed-market professional services experience and exposure to new-economy entrepreneurship.

The firm in question is New York-headquartered Warburg Pincus, the roots of which go back to venture investing in the late 1960s, but which evolved into the growth sector long before other large US private equity became largely synonymous with leveraged buyouts in the late 1970s and early 1980s. The individual, Niten Malhan, was born and educated in India, then joined McKinsey, working initially in his home country, followed by stints in Indonesia and the USA. His time in the USA coincided with the tech boom of the late 1990s, where friends from the Indian Institute of Technology, where he had gained a computer science first degree some years earlier, invited him to join them in a start-up that provided server security services. It was VC-funded, which gave Malhan an initial exposure to a field related to private equity.

Progress from concept to 'beta' was slow, and Malhan concluded that he was not contributing hugely to the product development side of the business, so decided to move on. In 2001 an ex-McKinsey colleague, Pulak Prasad, who had by then joined Warburg Pincus, sounded him out about a role in the firm's Singapore office, investing primarily in India. At the time Malhan retained a desire to do something entrepreneurial, but he accepted Prasad's invitation when it became clear that the role would involve working closely with owner–managers in high-growth businesses.

Warburg Pincus was one of the first Western GPs to become heavily involved in Asian private equity. Chip Kaye, who is now co-CEO but was then a young partner in the firm, moved out to Hong Kong to build an Asian presence in 1994. A Singapore office was added several years later, targeting South and South-East Asia, but with the growth of the firm's investing activities in India the decision was made, three years after Malhan joined, to relocate to Mumbai. So although the firm's physical presence in India dates back around eight years, it has been one of the country's largest private equity investors since the mid-1990s, having deployed a cumulative $2.6 billion.

Having raised a $15 billion global fund – the tenth in its history – in 2007, Warburg Pincus has the firepower to operate as a buyout firm in the USA and Europe, although even in those territories it remains principally a growth investor, specialising in sectors such as financial services, healthcare, TMT, energy and consumer, industrial and services.

Intriguingly, India is one market in which private equity will remain principally about models other than leveraged buyouts: the law prohibits the use of debt for acquisitions. But there are significant differences between the approach employed by Warburg Pincus in India and that which I described Lunar Capital applying in China in Chapter 13. Malhan's firm acquires mainly minority stakes in larger businesses, and its capital is used principally to enhance the capital bases of the firms in order to accelerate organic or – crucially, given the ban on debt-financed M&A, acquisition-led growth.

Another key difference is that the Mumbai office co-headed by Malhan is able to call on expertise within any of the firm's 12 other centres – in places as diverse as San Francisco, Frankfurt, Beijing and Mauritius – and to leverage relationships with portfolio companies and the firm's networks in the other territories in which it operates; the firm believes this enables it to make smarter investment decisions and to help investee businesses grow faster.

*   *   *

MB: How do your colleagues describe the early days of private equity in India, in the mid-1990s?

NM: What I'm told comes from Chip [Kaye] and Dalip Pathak, who was the first person Chip hired to build the India business. I understand that a lot of time that they spent in the early days was educating entrepreneurs and potential investee companies as to what this asset class is, because India had not seen this form of capital.

This is not a leveraged buyout-type market. It is about providing entrepreneurs with growth capital. Historically in India, people only really understood public market funds, mutual funds and banks, but people didn't quite understand what was this asset class was that provided equity capital that was not public-market-driven, but was longer-term in its outlook.

The other big question that entrepreneurs had then, and still have today, is how a private equity firm would behave if it became a partner in a business that had previously been 100 per cent owned by an entrepreneur. Much of that initial time was spent in explaining how we think about life because over a five- to seven-year period, businesses can obviously go through ups and downs and you want to make sure, as partners, you have a common view of how you're thinking about the business.

If I go back to when I joined in 2001, 11 years ago, and recall the kinds of conversations we used to have then versus today, I'd say there's been a huge evolution in terms of the acceptance and the understanding of the asset class over that time, and I'm sure in the five or six years prior to that it was even more nascent.

MB: I'm interested that Warburg Pincus is now a sizeable player in private equity in Asia but that it has built that position from a global fund, rather than by raising a regional fund, or country funds.

NM: I think two of the really distinctive features of the firm are first that growth investing is a large part of what we do, including in the USA and Europe, and that we have historically always raised only one pool of capital. It invests across industries, geographies, stages of companies, and we think this gives us the flexibility to dynamically deploy capital where we think the opportunities are most interesting, as opposed to slotting ourselves *a priori* into categories that we think might be interesting over the next three to five years and then being somewhat forced by virtue of that allocation to live to that mandate.

MB: So do all of the 13 offices, including yours, pitch to a central investment committee for funds?

NM: That's broadly correct, the only nuance being that while we have a 15-partner central executive management group that provides the leadership function to the firm, the reality of how we run the business in terms of investments is more decentralised compared with how some other large global firms tend to run things. A lot of the investment decision-making is pushed down to the partners of the firm that are closer to the deal. Obviously there is oversight and central controls and systems that are established, but it tends to be less centralised.

For us, an investment committee is not a formal monolithic structure. It's almost an investment committee that gets decided specific to an investment. The firm is organised around certain domains in the USA: we have very strong investing practices in healthcare, energy, technology, media and telecoms, industrial, financial services and so on. Depending on where the investment resides, part of the role that someone like Chip will play is to ensure that we are connected to the relevant group. Part of his role, other than approving the investment and being counsel to local partners, is to make sure that the dots are connected, so while we are being local in our approach of thinking about investments, we are also leveraging the firm's global capability in terms of institutional knowledge. And then for that investment, the investment committee essentially becomes the couple of partners that are most relevant to the idea or opportunity that you are pursuing.

To give you an example, in 2010 we made an investment in a pathology lab chain in India called Metropolis. This was a business that we had identified here [Mumbai]. I was the partner on the ground. We realised that Warburg Pincus had made an investment several years ago in Europe called Euromedic, which was a chain of diagnostic labs that we rolled up into a larger enterprise and did very well at. One of my partners in Europe who had worked on Euromedic was an integral part of the team, and he came over for some time to help us think through the issues and make sure we were learning from our experience at Euromedic. Chip and Dalip [Pathak, from the London office] were involved since they have been involved with India for the last 16–17 years and one or two people from healthcare in the USA got involved because they had some perspective, so that became the decision-making approach.

The balance that the firm is trying to create is to ensure that, in order to be successful investors in different markets, we do not try to replicate the same models of success that may have worked elsewhere blindly, but rather that we learn from them, and apply them in a manner that is most relevant for the local markets in which we are operating, without losing sight of the fact that different markets in different economies are very different and what works one place may or may not work elsewhere.

If I look at our India investment record over time, there are businesses that the firm has invested in here that we would find hard to invest in other parts of the world. For instance, some time ago we invested in a very efficient cement manufacturer called Gujarat Ambuja. Typically in the Western world, cement is a mature commodity business where it would be hard to figure out how it could make an interesting private equity investment. But India is a very different story in terms of the nature of real estate and infrastructure growth and the unique characteristics of how this company was doing business meant that we were able do the deal.

Each of our offices is run and staffed by people that are local and have been in that market for a period of time, and each works like a local business, but with very strong global connections, being part of one fund and one global economic pool for the individuals; and while we have separate legal entities for different countries, we are governed as one firm over all, but with relative independence for each office within that framework.

MB: As I understand it, whenever you look at a potential investment you put together a virtual team comprised of a mix of geographical specialists who are from an individual market and know the territory well and domain specialists who have had previous involvements in that industry, even though they may be from a different geography.

NM: Correct, but it's a needs-based requirement, rather than a tick-the-box exercise that says 'The geography has to say yes, and the industry group has to say yes.' It's much more, 'Here are the facts on the table, let's understand what we've learned in other markets.' There are situations where we would say, 'You know what? Even though this was not a successful business model in the USA, we think it's actually very different in India and might work well', and that's how we collectively build a consensus, as opposed to having a more bureaucratic process which I sometimes see in other places, where two groups must formally say yes for an investment to be cleared. We take decisions in the way that is most relevant to the situation, and more often than not, it is led by the people who are closest to the situation, which is the local office.

MB: I imagine that having a single pool of capital and also giving people economics in that pool rather than the deals done by their office helps a lot when it comes to calling on each other's time and expertise.

NM: Yes, absolutely. These things go hand-in-hand and all work together. One is obviously the one common fund with one common economic pool which, like you rightly said, means that while it is important for me to be focused on what is happening in India, if a colleague asks me a question about some investment elsewhere, I'd be as focused on saying, 'Let's make sure that that is a success', because my economic incentives are aligned with his. I think the second element of working together in a seamless manner but with local offices taking the lead in terms of investment judgement is possible only if you have one common partnership pool that has mutual respect and has known each other for a long period of time, because in a sense you are entrusting partners of yours with capital decisions that impact you as well.

The way we make that happen over a period of time is by being connected as a group. We meet up as partners every six months in New York, sometimes more often. In fact the entire firm connects up twice a year. That's about 160 or 170 professionals now, and part of that exercise is simply to ensure that there is enough connection between people.

We also have a dynamic where a lot of the people have grown up in the firm over long periods of time and we tend to therefore observe and watch each other over long periods of time, and what builds up is therefore a mutual respect between partners in the firm, which enables us to say, 'Look, here is my view on a situation, but obviously you are closer to it. If what I said was sensible, I'm sure you will take that into account, but I don't need to do anything more than offer my perspective on it.'

MB: You mentioned two healthcare transactions: Metropolis in India and Euromedic in Europe. I wonder whether the two businesses typify the different approaches the firm takes by territory, because Metropolis was backing an entrepreneurial founder in a roll-out, whereas Euromedic was more of a roll-up of mature businesses.

NM: Absolutely correct – very different approaches, but at some level a somewhat similar hypothesis around saying why we think the space is interesting.

If you think about India, and why this is predominantly a growth investing market, it is that we are a rapidly growing economy. We are a highly entrepreneurial country over all, even though we had many decades of somewhat socialist leaning. Post the early 1990s, there has been more of a free market-based economy in India and that has unleashed entrepreneurship, and I think the smartest entrepreneurs in India are people who see that growth opportunity and want to grow their businesses. They are not looking to sell their businesses typically if they are in interesting categories and see the potential for further growth.

The opportunity therefore for people like us is to identify those distinctive entrepreneurs, be partners of choice to them, provide them with capital, be helpful to them in any other way that we can and be participants in that growth that the economy offers and that the entrepreneurs create. We occasionally come across businesses that we can buy and control, but they're rare because of where the economy is and the mindset of the entrepreneurs. They'd rather be participants in the growth story than sell their businesses, except where it's a generational change or they just feel that the business has gone to a certain scale and that a larger owner can take it further, or valuation that they may be offered is just so compelling that it makes them want to exit.

Part of being successful in markets like India – maybe worldwide, but I can speak more for India – is being flexible in how you think about your role as investors and not getting too dogmatic about what style you follow, but thinking of your role as being providers of capital, providers of help along the way and partnering with distinctive managements and entrepreneurs. That's how we at Warburg Pincus define what our business is.

I'll give you an example: a company called Alliance Tyres. It is an off-highway tyre manufacturer. These are tyres that go into agricultural equipment, into earth-moving and construction equipment ... not passenger and truck tyres. We got to know this entrepreneur when he was running a similar business in India, an export-oriented business in off-highway tyres. We didn't invest at the time, but a couple of years subsequent to having met him he came out of that company with some capital and he said, 'I want to get back into the off-highway tyre business. I have some capital, but my aspirations are significantly more than that. Would you like to partner and create a business?' At that point, other than some capital, he had nothing, so we said, 'We've seen you operate your other business and we have been quite impressed by what you've done. Let's think together what we can do.'

The off-highway tyre business is, simplistically, a low-volume-run, high number of SKUs business. There are a large number of variants of tyres and therefore a more niche business than passenger and truck, which tend to be more volume-driven. So there's a lot of value in having a product library, because each new product variant that you create has to be tested for a certain period. We went through all of that analysis and said, 'It probably makes sense to acquire an existing platform rather than to start greenfield and try and build something because it will probably take a long period of time. You've been in this industry, why don't you identify some potentially interesting targets that we could go and acquire?'

He found something in Israel. That company was called Alliance. It was listed on the Tel Aviv exchange. We don't have a local presence in Israel, but several years earlier we had an investment in an IT company there, and one of the founders was helpful in navigating some of the local issues that we faced when we wanted to take over Alliance, and is now on the board of its Israeli arm.

That's how Warburg Pincus came to back this Indian entrepreneur, bought that company from its principal shareholder in Tel Aviv and took it private. Subsequently, we invested to set up manufacturing capacity in India so they could use lower-cost manufacturing capability here and take a larger share of the global market. So it was an export-oriented business. About four years ago, when the world went through the financial crisis, a US-based tyre distributor called GPX went into bankruptcy. We acquired that company – 'we' meaning Alliance Tyres – so today, about five years from when we started with nothing, it is close to a $500 million revenue company and we think a very successful global manufacturer of off-highway tyres, which in a few years should be an even more sizeable company.

This is a company that Warburg Pincus controls, but, from an entrepreneurial perspective, the guy who runs it is in charge. He owns a piece of it, and in our mind, although it is a control investment, it's heavily predicated on growth. It's not driven by leverage as being the driver of value, but it's essentially a combination of using capital for greenfield capacity build-out, being opportunistic in acquisition, using our global footprint to be able to help an Indian entrepreneur navigate first the Tel Aviv-listed company complexities, then buying a company out of bankruptcy court in the USA. It's a question of how can we be helpful to Indian entrepreneurs in realising their aims, and capital is only one element of it.

Admittedly a large number of businesses that we invest in India are more local, because, frankly, that's the bigger opportunity in our mind, and they don't necessarily therefore have these linkages to the rest of the firm, but when they do, being a global firm helps us play that card very well.

MB: I'm intrigued that debt cannot be used for acquisitions in India. Presumably that means that private equity is well placed to acquire equity in businesses that, for whatever reason, don't want to or can't access the public markets, but nevertheless want to acquire?

NM: The way it works in India is that the central bank over the years has not allowed the use of local leverage to further acquisitions. I'm not entirely clear what the genesis of this regulation is, but whether you are a trade or financial buyer, the banking system is not allowed to lend to you if the purpose of that lending is to acquire another company. In the case of trade buyers, sometimes there are ways round it, because if you have a corporate balance sheet, capital can be fungible and it sometimes is not entirely clear what purpose a certain amount of debt is for, and you can in an overall corporate balance sheet therefore reallocate capital and provide a little bit more flexibility to use leverage if you are pursuing an acquisition. But for a financial buyer where you are essentially going to set up an acquisition vehicle to buy an asset, it is very clear that the purpose of any leverage would be to acquire the company in question. So the leveraged buyout model that is practised overseas has not typically been available in India to date. If you have an already levered company that you are buying, inherently you can create the economics of an LBO [leveraged buyout] though, by virtue of the company being already leveraged and you buying into it, or buying control of it.

MB: Can you, as a financial buyer, purchase an unlevered company that has a lot of assets, then borrow against them?

NM: Yes, you could take leverage in the company itself. There are restrictions on how much of that money can be upstreamed and in what period of time. There are ways you can work around them over time. It is not as efficient as it would be if you could simply borrow in an acquisition vehicle.

MB: So private equity may sit at a disadvantage compared with trade buyers when doing a late-stage buyout, trying to buy a mature business?

NM: Compared with a strategic buyer, there are two issues. The primary one is the cost of capital, which for the strategic may be lower than for private equity. The second, as you suggest, is that the corporate buyer typically has more flexibility around capital structure because they have an existing balance sheet, which provides more fungibility.

But if I step back and think about our presence here, the reality is that it is not a very vibrant part of the market. Yes, there are M&A transactions happening between trade buyers, but often those are strategic acquisitions on terms that may not make sense for private equity, and there's an active minority market that is where a lot of private equity capital is placed. So while people talk a lot about these issues as being things that should and likely will get sorted out over time, my own view is that it will not fundamentally change the nature of the investing market in the medium term.

In India it's harder to do traditional roll-up strategies, because sellers are also looking to grow their businesses and there are not that many that are for sale. It's a conundrum that in a lot of sectors in India you have fragmented businesses which you would argue over time would lead to consolidation, but the pace is usually much slower than you might expect. So the bulk of the investments that we make are essentially around companies investing in capacity or build-out, or in acquisitions overseas.

MB: And how do you typically exit? Is it by IPO, or trade sales to Indian or international strategic buyers?

NM: I'd prefer to categorise exits as public markets versus trade sale. Sometimes when a private company that we invested in lists, the IPO itself may only be another financing event – we may exit at a later date via the markets. And in some instances, given the nature of India and the fact that there are over 6000 listed companies, many of our investments have been primary capital infusions into companies that happened already to be listed, in which case we again exit over time through capital market transactions.

Not many of our exits have been by way of trade sale. The reason is that, because these are essentially minority investments, in most cases even at the time of our exit, the entrepreneur is not selling the company, he is continuing to build it. Most of the companies that we've partnered with have continued to be interesting companies; they may at some point decide to sell, but not necessarily when we exit, so in most cases our exit has been to financial investors on the capital markets through block trades.

This may change going forward. For example, for Alliance, the range of exit options may be a combination of taking that company public and exiting through capital markets. But it could equally be a trade sale to someone in the business or to financial buyers who think of it as an interesting cash-flow business that can be bought as a more traditional mid-market LBO. So I think with positions that you control, the options may be more varied. For the more typical minority investments, I think the more likely outcomes that we budget for at the time of investing involve the capital markets.

MB: Coming from the UK, I think the decoupling between your and the entrepreneur's exit points is unfamiliar. Generally when minority deals are done in the UK, the private equity firm has drag-and-tag rights so it can offer up the entire equity in the company to a trade buyer. It sounds to me like you may not have or need that, because there are plenty of buyers for minority shareholdings in Indian firms – not least, investors in the public markets.

NM: I think that's fair. First of all, it is fair to say that in many situations, minority investors in India will typically not have drag clauses. More importantly, even if you have them, the enforceability of that and what success you are going to have at the time that you actually want to enforce them, is not entirely clear.

When we initially think of investing, we have to feel comfortable that the entrepreneur that we are backing is looking to create a business with the same ultimate objective as us, which is value creation, to the extent that these are growing businesses and will continue to need capital to grow. There is a natural alignment for him to want to get listed at some point, to seek public market capital to continue his growth. You will typically have the ability, at least in contract, to force an IPO, although again, if the entrepreneur and key shareholder doesn't want to do it, you get into the issue of whether it is truly an enforceable clause, but it's a moral commitment to saying ultimately we'd like to take the company public.

I think more important is that, as minority investors, we spend a lot of time with the entrepreneur to understand what is the ultimate objective of the guy, not just in relation to the exit but also, ultimately, to governance. That doesn't mean we will not have disagreements along the way, but we must have enough conviction to say that the thought process of the individual is rational, is based on facts and taking account of the reality on the ground, and that history has been consistent in getting us some comfort that he has behaved in a certain way.

I think that's the element of art, in addition to the business analysis, of a potential investment in India. How do you align yourself with the economic interests of that individual so that you are taking decisions that are naturally in your favour and aligned with him, as opposed to trying something which comes out of yours and goes into his, or vice versa?

MB: Do you think that, compared with private equity in mature markets, there's much more of a people side to the industry in India?

NM: I think that's true. In fact, a large part of our analysis around whether an investment opportunity is interesting or not, is an assessment of whether this is a partner that we would like to do business with. And it has many elements. One is whether the individual is looking for the kind of engagement that we'd like to have. Because there are certain types of entrepreneurs who may be very successful, but who are not necessarily looking for a partnership approach to running a business.

There are others though who seek involvement, who say, 'How can we do better? And can you help us in certain ways?' And who have a more engaging mindset. I think a lot of what our screening for companies is about being disciplined around saying that, as minority investors, we have to recognise that ultimately this is much more of a partnership. It's much more of a marriage than it is simply buying a business, and you need to be very comfortable that, as individuals or as firms and individuals, you really are seeing eye to eye.

But equally, this applies on the other side as well because from the perspective of an entrepreneur who is selling a portion of his business, if he is smart and if he is thinking about it the right way, his criteria for evaluating investors ought therefore to be not simply the price that he can get for his asset or for a portion of his asset, but also who it is that he's inviting into his company. And I think that over time, as more investors play for longer in India, the conduct of different investors will be clearer. There will be differentiation and entrepreneurs will be asking, 'OK, so who are the investors that have truly been good partners to companies? And who are investors that have essentially not been good partners, because their conduct has not been fair or because they've panicked when things have not gone well or even though they talk about being long-term investors, they haven't behaved in that manner?'

I'd say our strong distinguishing factor today is the fact in India that we are probably the most referenceable firm, in terms of having been here for a number of years and in having had a large number of investments in which, irrespective of what the financial outcomes have been, we are proud of the relationships we have struck with these entrepreneurs and how we have conducted ourselves through the period that we've been partners.

It doesn't mean that – like I said –you agree on everything or that you are easy in terms of just taking everything that comes your way, but it does mean that you operate with a certain fair sense of value. You operate with a sense of doing what is best for the business. We've had many instances where, even when we've been exiting, we've been conscious of the fact that although we've wanted to maximise the value of the 20 or 30 per cent we've been selling, there has been the potential to be disruptive in terms of who we sold that ownership to. I think all of those elements are equally important on both sides because ultimately, for the entrepreneur, this is usually his crown jewel: he is partnering with us in something that has been his, and now we are a shareholder with a seat at the table and, to put it bluntly, if we were not going to behave ourselves, we could be a nuisance.

MB: There seems to be quite a bit of LP money heading towards Asia in general, and India in particular. Is this intensifying competition for deals?

NM: India is definitely a competitive market, more so than it was five or seven years ago. How do we deal with that? Are there situations where we would want to do business and we're finding that we are not able to because there were five other people chasing the deal and we were outsmarted?

The answer is that, while we have to keep working hard, we haven't yet felt that impact. There will be situations where the terms of the deal will be such that you will not be prepared to do them, but I think not dissimilar to what my colleagues in Europe or the USA will say, that there are certain times in markets where there are great businesses, great assets, but prices don't make sense and you say, 'Fine. We'll walk away.' There may be periods in time that feel frothy, but frankly, you have to look through that and say, 'Longer term, is the market interesting and creating enough opportunity?' And I think the answer to that is yes.

Also, I think all of us focus a lot on the supply of capital, rather than the demand. We now have a $1.5 trillion economy, growing in real terms at 7 or 8 per cent and in nominal terms, depending on what inflation is, that could be 12–14 per cent. We are adding meaningful chunks of the economy every year just in absolute numbers, and therefore in terms of the number of young companies that are bubbling up that need capital to scale up to the next level, we have ourselves seen a dramatic shift in the last six to eight years in the range of opportunities that can absorb, say, $40–50 million of equity.

While there's a lot of capital that is finding its way to India and I think will continue to, frankly there aren't that many places in the world that have a broadly stable macro-economic outlook, very compelling demographics and strong growth, a broadly functioning regulatory and institutional system, language benefits. We tick most of the boxes. So you ask, 'Do you think capital will flow here?' Absolutely. But on the other hand, the demand for that capital is pretty real too, so my own view is that if we stick to what we do best, which is be good, value-adding, fair partners to good entrepreneurs, that strategy should continue to reap rewards.

MB: Do you see your approach changing at all?

NM: Historically India has been a generalist investment market where we've tended to cover the full range of sectors and leveraged our global pool wherever relevant. We are consciously making an effort, as we grow in this market and as the market gets more sophisticated, to specialise and become more domain-focused. It may not mean that we will have professionals that spend all their time in one vertical, but at least there are one or two areas that they proactively spend time, build their networks, get to know people, have insights about how the industry's likely to evolve. This helps us in two ways. It helps us identify the interesting players in that sector and be able to screen them and react and move quickly when required. And it helps us to be better partners to them, because we can have a more intelligent conversation with them around their businesses and what the likely evolution is. That's an investment that we are making in terms of ensuring that we have adequate capacity to be able over time to create a little bit of that specialisation.

I don't think, at least in the next five years, that this sector focus will be as rigid as it is in, for example, the USA, where we tend to be organised very strictly around domains, but I think it will be much more than it was in the last five years and that I think will hopefully continue to create interesting competitive advantage for us.

The other thing that I think will happen is that we will increase our coverage in terms of going deeper into the country, beyond the top five or six cities, building stronger relationships with intermediaries and, through them, companies in the next level of cities and towns, because as the overall economy is growing, we are finding today that many of the companies that we meet that are potentially interesting targets come in the next tier of towns.

15
Martin Escobari, Managing Director, Advent International

I mentioned in Chapter 12 that South America has a boom-and-bust, famine-and-feast reputation as a destination for private equity investment. At the time of writing, the market was exhibiting both characteristics simultaneously: boom in that investors' capital continued to flow into the region and, in Brazil especially, owners' valuation expectations for private businesses remained frothy; bust in that the region's key stock market, Brazil's Bovespa, remained subdued, trading at a PE ratio of less than six on the back of sober projections of Asian demand for the commodities and energy that comprise much of the index, due to concerns about anaemic recovery in Western consumer markets.

This paradox highlights two of the central questions about investing in South America, and in varying degrees, all developing markets: where does each country's economy sit on a continuum from being dominated by exports to being driven by domestic consumption and, irrespective of the relative sizes of those parts of the economy, which is the better investment thesis for private equity.

We've seen in Chapter 13 that Derek Sulger's strategy for China is the latter; indeed, he is more interested in targeting the basic consumer staples requirements of the next tranche of urbanised, salaried workers, than the increasingly sophisticated discretionary spending of the established urban elites. Niten Malhan's approach to India (Chapter 14) is more diversified: he has invested in sectors dependent on consumer affluence, such as medical technology, but also in staples such as non-highway tyres and in infrastructure and export themes, such as ports.

China and India are the largest beneficiaries of emerging markets private equity, as you would expect of the two most populous nations on Earth. South America is probably the third biggest but defies easy categorisation because it consists of a collection of nations, each at a different point in terms of its economic development and transparency of doing business. And because a number of those countries – not least the largest, Brazil – have historically been hyper-cyclical, investment strategies tend to vary widely by territory and by time.

For instance, at the time of writing, GPs were acquiring stakes in quoted companies in Brazil, benefiting from the valuation arbitrage that saw them being valued at typically half the multiples of private businesses, while also pursuing growth strategies with private companies in smaller countries that lack significant public markets.

Another characteristic of South American private equity is that local GPs and LPs represent a larger proportion of the market than in many emerging regions. This is in part because the large-scale flight of US managers and capital after they got their fingers burned a decade or so ago left a relatively clear field for the locals, during which time they built up relationships and track records. A second reason is that, when local LPs invest, they like to be hands-on, typically demanding seats on investment committees and the right to veto specific deals. This is culturally unacceptable to most international GPs, which bars them from attracting much of the local capital. And finally, the providers of that capital are able to invest with greater confidence than the big North American LPs because, unlike the latter, they are not exposed to what have historically been significant currency risks.

So private equity in South America is unlike its counterparts in China and India: there is a much greater diversity by country and by theme, with a lot more local GPs and capital. But where Western GPs have got in early, stayed, developed country-specific approaches based on hiring locally and not imposing a top-down approach, they have done well. Among these, Advent International stands out. Probably the single biggest private equity investor in the region and the firm to have raised the largest regional fund ($1.65 billion, in 2010), it has been active on the continent since 1995 and has offices in four countries in the region: Argentina, Brazil, Colombia and Mexico.

Created in 1984 as a spin-out from TA Associates by TA's founder, Peter Brooke, Advent's approach is in some respects similar to Brooke's original firm's, but it is very different in others. It has an almost identical set of sector focuses: business and financial services, healthcare, industrial, retail, consumer and leisure and technology, media and telecommunications. It shares TA's commitment to high-growth businesses and tends to use debt sparingly, even though it is better placed to lever up, since it tends to do control deals. Another differentiator is that, like New Mountain, it identifies macro-economic themes and applies them to its chosen verticals to identify high-potential sectors and businesses. It also has a particular focus, perhaps unsurprisingly given its geographical spread (at the time of writing, the firm had offices in 16 countries, with affiliates in a further six), on internationalising its portfolio businesses. And yet, unlike TA or Warburg Pincus, it raises funds by region (USA and Western Europe, Central and Eastern Europe, Latin America).

I interviewed Advent's São Paulo-based Managing Director, Martin Escobari. His background, like Malhan's in India, mixes local heritage with

US experience, blue-chip consulting with entrepreneurship: Escobari is a Harvard alumnus who subsequently worked for Boston Consulting Group in both North and South America, before spending a brief spell in private equity in its first big wave in South America (GP Investimentos, in the late 1990s), quitting to co-found what subsequently became one of South America's largest online retailers, Submarino, exiting that business in 2005 and joining Advent.

Shortly after our interview, Escobari moved to a similar role heading up the South American activities of another GP, General Atlantic, which adopts a wider range of investment styles – including PIPEs (private investments in public equities), which, as previously mentioned, appeared to offer potential at the time of writing. Escobari's comments remain highly relevant both to Advent's activities on the continent and to the overall investing environment, and indeed the fact of his departure is testament to the competitive, fast-changing nature of the South American private equity industry.

* * *

MB: How did it feel, being in private equity in South America in the late '90s? It must have been pretty nascent.

ME: Yes, there was the Exxel Group in Argentina and GP Investimentos in Brazil, and at the time GP was the largest private equity fund for emerging markets. GP1 and GP2 were $500 million and $700 million, which for the time were humungous.

It was a volatile time. We had no debt, but there was a lot of currency volatility and some expectation of inflation. There were no capital markets to speak of, and it was the middle of the privatisations, so a lot of money was going to the telcos [telecoms companies] and the railroads. The guys that invested in the privatisations tended to do OK despite the devaluation of the Real. The people that at the same time were investing in start-ups, media companies and internet companies for the most part didn't make much money, and most of them left the region.

MB: You're talking about the first wave of US money?

ME: Yes, I think the problem was that they were flying in as opposed to having permanent offices, so there's adverse selection – the deals they got to hear about were the ones that had been punted round and others had rejected. There were a lot of minority deals done without a lot of understanding of the enforceability of governance provisions and a lot of speculative deals in unproven business models, particularly in telecoms and internet. And on top of all that the currency devalued in the '99 to 2003 phase, and it's hard to make money if you're a dollar investor when that happens.

MB: Advent International is unusual in having established a physical presence early on.

ME: Yes, it has been in South America since 1995/6. It opened offices simultaneously in Mexico, Argentina and Brazil, and it was only in 2010 that we opened our fourth office, in Colombia, so it wanted to cover the region from very early on. From the outset it sent very senior people to the region, hired relatively large deal teams, focused on the same sectors as it had globally, and of all the international firms is the only one that has had a non-stop presence, and probably because it has stuck to its sector focus, done primarily all-equity deals and been selective, over the course of the years it has grown very rapidly; we're now on our fifth fund. The first, in '96, was $230 million; the latest, in 2010, was $1.65 billion.

MB: And is it primarily US money?

ME: I think originally it was mainly US, although it's now more balanced with Europe having increased, and we've also had Asian and Middle Eastern groups becoming more relevant. We have not had a big presence of local investors.

MB: Why is that?

ME: In the region, but particularly in Brazil, asset management is less sophisticated, and the real interest rate is so high that there traditionally wasn't much of a culture of investing in private equity or hedge funds. The pension funds have begun to allocate to private equity in the last four or five years, but they want to be on the investment boards and not to delegate; and when you have so many investors that becomes very hard to manage.

MB: Presumably Advent, being an international firm, would not accept such terms?

ME: Exactly, so we mainly draw investment from pension and sovereign funds abroad.

MB: How would you describe your investment strategy?

ME: We invest in five core sectors; we do control transactions, with relatively low leverage. We try to find highly cash-generative businesses and companies that have strong barriers to entry so they enjoy highly defensible positions, and we staff them with great management.

If you have no debt, it means that most of your value has to come through growth. If you look at the sources of our gains over the last 16 years, 85 to 90 per cent has come from growth in EBITDA. So all our skill and focus is on selecting high-growth companies and making sure that they grow faster, and the way you do that is around strategy and processes and also around the people. If you look at the profile of Advent partners and employees, it tends to be much more oriented to those who have had an operational, entrepreneurial or consulting rather than finance backgrounds. The value's not about negotiating the debt package and winning an auction but about making the companies grow.

We've analysed how we've made money and identified the common characteristics of the 30-odd successful investments we've had. We've found that if we identify markets that are growing, that provides a rising tide that lifts all ships. The longer we spent tracking the company before we invested, the more effective we've been when we bought the company. And the more people that were involved in the deal team, the less likely we've been to make due diligence mistakes.

MB: There are other high-growth emerging markets where there are a lot of minority deals, with the founding entrepreneurs remaining in place. Why have you not adopted that model?

ME: The main reason we have not done minority deals in Latin America is that the capital markets are not well developed, and it's very difficult to exit a minority position to a strategic buyer, because a strategic buyer wants strategic control. Most of the time when you have a minority position, your preferable exit is to an IPO, but in Brazil we can go for several years without a single IPO, so if that is your only exit, it's a pretty limited exit. The same problem applies in Mexico and Argentina. It's changing slowly, but it's still pretty bad. If you think about Brazil compared to India, for example, on a GDP basis we're roughly within 10 per cent of each other. India has 6000 publicly listed companies. We've got 300.

MB: Why is that?

ME: One is the limited culture of investing in equities because real interest rates were so high people would just invest in safer deposit accounts. Another is the high level of informality in the economy, so for many companies, it doesn't pay to have audited statements. That's changing as the tax authorities have clamped down. I think it also has to do with the fact that there are a lot of family-run businesses that are very tightly controlled and don't want the exposure and risks associated with letting the world know how wealthy you are.

MB: If you are buying control positions from founders and their families, does that generally mean you are changing the managements?

ME: Most of the time when you get family members working with us they tend to me more on the board rather than as executives. We've had exceptions to that which have worked out well. But senior managers generally remain, and we are strong believers in incentivising them through equity ownership and variable compensation. We've had some companies where we've changed very few people over the course of our tenure and others where we've changed 80 per cent of the senior leadership. Where we add the most value we tend to have a larger team of executives from which to draw on in roles such as CFO, head of M&A or IT. Those sorts of skills are the same across industries, and because we've been doing this for a while, we've got people that we invite over and over again to be part of our deals.

MB: What's the rationale for the four offices? What about markets such as Chile and Peru?

ME: We have a physical presence in the four largest markets. Chile is relatively small, and we cover it remotely out of Buenos Aires. Peru is probably the next country on our radar screen, and today we cover it remotely from Colombia. Already with four offices we're by a factor of at least two the largest team on the ground. We've got roughly 55 employees in Latin America, all in private equity.

MB: I notice you actually invest in a large number of countries, including the first leveraged buyout in the Dominican Republic.

ME: Yes, that's Aerodrom Group, the leading airport group in the country, which we merged into Latin American Airport Holdings. There are certain industries where we make sure we cover the entire region, because we have an expertise and there are few large assets available. One such industry is airport construction and management and airport retail. We also own many restaurants throughout the Caribbean – part of our IPC company.

MB: So it's a platform strategy – owning one asset and then using it to go out and acquire more related businesses?

ME: Yes, in this case around an expertise in travel retail, so either airports or highways. In IMC there are synergies, for example, in joint procurement, and with Dufry [a duty-free retailer, now in 60 countries], the suppliers tend to be the same and there's a lot of knowledge interchange because stores are very similar across geographies. In pharmaceuticals, we own two businesses in the sector and are creating a national company because it turns out they were already selling into each other's markets but didn't have a dedicated sales force, so whenever we can we combine companies across the geographies rather than simply rolling them out. We probably do it in 20–30 per cent of our investments. The value is high, but you have to prove that there are the synergies both ways because there are a lot of integration costs.

MB: You mentioned that getting IPOs has been tough in recent years. So are you looking for trade sales?

ME: Yes, 80 or 90 per cent of our exits have been to trade sales, and it's a very important part of our approach that we pre-identify who the likely buyers are, and more often than not we actually go out to them and ask them if this is something they'd be interested in buying five years down the road if we accomplish X, Y and Z.

MB: Isn't there a risk they would simply buy the businesses themselves, now?

ME: We wouldn't be showing it to them if we felt they were going to be a competitor. Also, most often there are complexities, such as the companies having been under-managed or having some restructuring that needs to be done before it can be sold to a trade buyer, and that's what we're really good at.

MB: Are the strategic buyers mainly from within the region, or outside?

ME: It tends to be multinationals – European and American.

MB: I'm guessing that a local acquirer would have more management on the ground so be more willing to effect a restructure themselves, whereas a multinational wants to acquire a nice, cash-flow-positive growth business?

ME: Yes, we're turning what were entrepreneur-led businesses into nicely presented firms that multinationals can buy and consider they've ticked a strategic box for Latin America.

MB: Does the same apply to LPs, that they now feel they have to allocate funds to the continent?

ME: Yes, it wasn't long ago that even Brazil was massively underdeveloped in terms of private equity as a percentage of GDP. Interest has picked up over the past three years, but still compared to China or India it's probably a fifth of its potential size, so it does feel more competitive than it did four years ago, but when we talk to our peers who are working in those other two geographies it is several step-functions lower in terms of competitive activity, particularly in terms of the number of players. When we get invited to auctions, it may be that we're among three or four, perhaps five, private equity players. When there's an auction in India, it starts with 80.

MB: I'm conscious that there's a big difference in maturity of private equity market between Brazil and many other countries in South America and that the governments of countries such as Colombia are working hard to increase their nations' attractiveness to the industry.

ME: I think Colombia is where Brazil was six or eight years ago in that they've invested in reforms, conquered the sources of instability, but have yet to receive global recognition from strong investors, so we are the first global private equity firm to have a permanent presence there. We signed our first deal there last year. It's a $100 million pharma deal, so not small. And we continue to see a very exciting pipeline.

MB: I understand that you're focused on certain sectors; do you apply that thinking differently by territory?

ME: Yes, in that we'll apply different themes, which take us to different sub-sectors. For instance, the Colombia pharma deal was in generics, which we might not have done in the USA or Europe. Another example would be financial services. We've stopped looking at asset managers in the more developed countries, but we're now looking at ones in Latin America.

Our themes are around fundamental transformations. So, for instance, our interest in travel and retail is around the rise of the middle class, of people wishing to travel more. And airports require considerable investment, and there's pricing power where services are offered. We've spent a lot of time with the payments revolution, the development of the market infrastructure to support the growth of credit and in the rising needs for more sophisticated, technology-intensive educational services.

MB: You've mentioned that you don't use a lot of leverage. What's the typical figure?

ME: About 40 per cent.

MB: And how about providing follow-on capital or refinancing for acquisitions?

ME: Typically we leave space on the balance sheet for acquiring with leverage or internally generated cash-flow, but at least 20 per cent of the time we find compelling cases to make further equity investments.

MB: Other than changing or adding to management and acquisitions, how else do you achieve value creation?

ME: All sorts of things – the right compensation structures, upgrading IT, prioritising R&D spend and product development, looking at channel distribution, pricing strategies, a lot of value-add on M&A, expanding into new niches, balance sheet restructuring, renegotiation of supplier contracts – the full list of tools.

MB: How do you transfer the knowledge that exists within Advent International to the investee businesses?

ME: We are active on the boards. Often we staff up the companies with executives that have worked with us, either permanently or on a temporary basis, and we will send some of our investment professionals in support roles during the first 100 days or six months. In some cases they become part-time, or full-time, temporary CFOs. Sometimes they assume head of M&A roles, for example. We can act as external consultants, and sometimes we hire consultancy from third parties as well.

We see ourselves as providing as much support as possible to management and making sure they get the resources and speed of decision-making they need to operate the business. We're very close to management. On my portfolio companies, I talk to the CEOs every day, just to make sure we're up to date as to what is going on.

MB: It sounds to me like quite a high-cost management model.

ME: It's a high ratio. Here [Brazil], for instance, we have 15 very strong professionals and ten portfolio companies. Our model requires a high level of resource intensity. We don't have people that are 100 per cent allocated to doing one thing, but we try to staff people closer to their strengths. So if someone has previous experience of supply chain, we give them projects that use that, or if someone has been a temporary CFO with knowledge on how you restructure debt, if we go into a debt restructuring, we try to use that knowledge.

MB: Does that also go across geographical boundaries? For instance, if you do a healthcare deal in Mexico and you have someone in Argentina who knows the same sub-sector of that industry, would you ask them to get involved in that deal?

ME: Absolutely.

MB: It seems to me that you have to pay fairly strong multiples to buy control stakes in private businesses in a high-growth region, and you also have significant operating costs as a general partnership relative to the typical deal size [around $100 million], and you are also using little debt, so the value creation has to be pretty significant to give worthwhile returns [the firm is reported to generate a typical IRR of 20–25 per cent].

ME: Yes, but the model works. I'll give you an example. We bought a company called Cetip, a fixed-income exchange in Brazil. It was a not-for-profit owned by 600 financial institutions and we converted it to a for-profit and drove growth. We brought in a lot of operating partners and changed 80 per cent of the senior management. We did partnerships with Deutsche Börse and a US firm called Algorithmics. We took the company public. We invested more in R&D in the first year than the company had in the previous ten years combined. We were able to do a transformative acquisition that doubled the EBITDA of the company.

When we invested in the company, it had a valuation of 700 million Reals. When we finished selling our stake, within three years, it had a valuation of 7.5 billion. This was a tremendous amount of value creation for us and for the shareholders that were alongside us. After taking the company public, we sold our stake to a strategic player, the Intercontinental Exchange, who took our board representation in the company and continues to support the growth. This is a classic Advent deal, in that we put a lot of resources and really transformed the company, which hopefully then translates into a higher valuation, as it did in this case.

MB: What examples can you give of bad deals, and why did they go wrong?

ME: In the early days – 1995 to 2000 – there were a couple of deals as we were fine-tuning our model that didn't perform as we'd hoped. We invested in a Pepsi bottler in Mexico where it proved very hard to enforce contracts and eventually had to go into restructuring. We invested into a soccer franchise in Brazil, believing that soccer was professionalising at the time and that ownership of soccer teams would be a good business. Neither of those worked out that well.

More recently, where we've run into trouble, it has been in consumer markets in Mexico. As you know, the US downturn has had a massive impact on the Mexican economy, and those businesses have lost years of growth, so it is taking us longer than we expected to get to the size we want to be.

MB: It seems to me Mexico is pretty dependent on oil exports to the USA and transfer payments from Mexicans living in the USA.

ME: Absolutely.

MB: How about Brazil? A lot of people talk about inflationary pressures and a property bubble.

ME: We're optimistic about the growth prospects of Brazil. In the past ten years we've had 32 million people join the middle class. That's equal to the population of Canada. So we've got a new Canada appeared and it's in our market. That's pretty exciting.

Every bubble has a debt component, that's the real engine of a bubble, and we don't have a lot of debt in Brazil, even now. Private debt to GDP is less than 60 per cent. Mortgage debt to GDP is less than 3 per cent, so I don't believe we have a property or credit bubble.

There are certain segments of the economy where pricing is high: for example, suppliers to the oil and gas industry, where everyone expects it's going to grow 20-fold over the next five years. In retrospect, the valuations may be proved right unless the growth is slower than people thought. So, with the exception of oil and gas, I don't see a lot of bubble-like behaviours. Some may argue the exchange rate at sometimes has appeared a little overvalued, but these are arguments about 10 to 20 per cent, not 200 to 300 per cent.

MB: How long will it be before you can leverage up buyouts to a significant extent?

ME: Not any time soon. It would need the interest rate to decline. We're at least a decade behind where the USA got to at the peak of the LBO boom.

MB: How about other forms of capital, between equity and debt – preferred equity or mezzanine? Is there much of a market for those in South America?

ME: In theory, there ought to be. In practice, I haven't seen much of it. There were funds offering mezzanine in the '90s, and I haven't seen them kick back in.

MB: When you look at other firms operating in South America, what errors do you sometimes see?

ME: Underestimating the importance of being close to management, buying in commodity-driven businesses and forgetting how brutal volatility can be, trying to supervise companies from abroad. I think sometimes people have suffered from poor governance structures because they've gone for complicated shareholders' agreements that aren't enforceable. And sometimes there are due diligence mistakes.

MB: And how about when you look at private equity in other markets?

ME: I'm not an expert, but I know a little about the Chinese market. I think it's extremely hard to make money because you're very dependent on the quality of the entrepreneur as you're only doing minority deals. And there's a lot of interaction with the government.

MB: And how about developed markets?

ME: I think there's a realisation that large-scale LBOs where all the value is in the debt structure are not going to cut it for the next generation of managers and people are having to think again about value creation. So I suspect there's going to be a move back to basics across both Europe and the USA and a focus on more mid-size deals and growth investing. I think they'll be doing stuff that worked in the beginning of the industry, before the availability of debt distorted some of the basic principles.

MB: What trends do you expect to develop in Latin America?

ME: I think we will see more private equity to private equity secondary deals. There isn't much of that going on now.

MB: Do you see Advent International as a buyer or a seller in that scenario?

ME: I think it has to be both. There are good companies that still have juice in them, and we've got an angle that we think we can take them to another level. I just want to make sure there aren't any major skeletons in the closet, but if a firm has been within reputable private equity for five years, it's less likely to have any major surprises from a due diligence viewpoint. And there are these large major firms that want to enter the market, they could drive larger consolidation-type deals.

MB: Any other trends?

ME: We'll see more club deals as people get together to do larger transactions. And I think over time, however slowly, we're going to see a little more sophistication and increase in the levels of debt. At the other end of the scale, a lot of private equity in South America is done by entrepreneurs and families that snatch up small opportunities. They're fulfilling a need but they're unable to scale, which creates opportunities as economies get larger. I think the greatest transformation that will help our industry is the decline of informality, because so many more companies become buyable when they start producing audited accounts and paying their taxes.

MB: So the opportunity for M&A and roll-ups will increase as a result of companies reporting their true profits as opposed to running two sets of books?

ME: Exactly.

MB: And how do you see your firm's Latin American operations evolving in the next few years?

ME: We need to constantly re-invent ourselves to make sure that we have cutting-edge thinking. More and more we will need to specialise, so we will have partners beginning to focus more on an industry and not just a country. And because I think the markets will become more competitive, we will have to keep improving our game, and to do that well we'll have to integrate even better within the broader Advent network, which is already pretty specialised.

16

Mark Goldsmith, Director and Head of Environmental and Social Governance, Actis

One of the most enduring areas of debate concerning the involvement of private equity in developing economies relates to the balance between achieving financial returns and delivering societal benefits.

I mentioned in Chapter 12 that the industry's first moves into emerging markets were generally anchored by funds from development finance institutions (DFIs) such as the International Finance Corporation (IFC, part of the World Bank), CDC (formerly Commonwealth Development Corporation, backed by the UK government) and Proparco, its French counterpart. These organisations traditionally lent to developing countries' governments and the big-ticket capital projects they endorsed, but increasingly saw an opportunity to deploy some risk equity money as an enabler for greater commercial investment into the private sectors of those economies.

They achieved this through a mix of making direct equity investments as GPs and either providing debt finance alongside or investing as a LP in other GPs' funds, often with the capital table structured in such a way that the DFI money was at first risk or likely to generate less aggressive returns, in order to make it financially attractive for commercially driven LPs to invest in geographies that had hitherto struggled to attract private equity investment.

Over time, this approach led to the emergence of a cadre of GPs able to demonstrate that investing in the most commercially promising projects in many of the countries in Asia, Africa and South America was able to generate returns that were in some cases comparable to those achieved in developed markets. As a result, the DFIs have in recent years been re-evaluating their approaches, leaving investment in the less volatile, more developed and better-governed countries within emerging markets and in the industries deemed to contribute the least to development goals to conventional LPs. Indeed, the subjects of the three preceding chapters, who are among the most respected investors in their chosen markets, do so with either no or minimal DFI money.

Instead, DFIs are increasingly channelling their capital towards specialist GPs that put it to work in the poorest countries in emerging markets or the poorest regions within individual developing nations, or that are focused on industries and investment strategies that are expected to generate the greatest benefits for the communities with the most pressing needs.

A fascinating example of this strategy shift is CDC. Created as the Colonial Development Corporation by Clement Attlee's post-war Labour government to provide loans for infrastructure and development projects in former and remaining British colonies, it swapped the legacy prefix 'Colonial' for the more politically acceptable term 'Commonwealth' in 1963. Its next big shift came between 1998 and 2000, when it reinvented itself as an equity investor. Shortly afterwards, in 2004, it spun out its general partnerships, with a number of employees transferring to the new fund manager, Actis.

Actis was given dual roles: to manage the CDC investments made to date and to as a conventional GP, able to raise new funds from the full spectrum of commercial and DFI LPs. CDC, meanwhile, was tasked to act as a limited partner, free to invest in future Actis funds but also in any other funds focused on developing countries.

The move proved controversial, for two reasons. The first is purely financial: Actis's management acquired a 60 per cent interest in the GP for £373,000 – a sum that was widely felt to be an undervalue, given that the firm had around £1.2 billion of CDC's capital under management at that point. The second was more strategic: as the territories in which CDC/Actis had focused became more developed, a proportion of the investments were made in businesses that targeted the emerging urban middle class, rather than the alleviation of poverty in rural areas – an approach that some felt was outside the spirit in which CDC was created.

It is not my role to pass judgement on the first point. The government at the time insisted the valuation was the work of external advisers from KPMG and that it would continue to benefit from a proportion of the management fees and carried interest through its remaining 40 per cent holding (which it subsequently sold to Actis's management for a further £8 million in May 2012).

The second criticism gets to the heart of the debate about what the role of private equity in emerging markets should be. Shopping centres, casual dining restaurants, telecoms companies and energy providers create jobs, many of which are taken by poor migrants from rural areas; they also drive down the cost of providing the staples of the lifestyle that people in developed countries take for granted to a point at which those things become affordable to a lot more people than hitherto. And private equity from highly regulated sources such as the UK also bring standards of environmental and social governance that avoid the extremes of conduct for which capitalism is often criticised in these environments.

At the same time, it remains the case that economic progress has been hugely uneven across much of Africa, Asia and South America, and there is a powerful case for arguing that the Western-style development model can sometimes exacerbate rather than reduce inequality. The young person who leaves a mountain village to seek work in a distant city can no longer help his or her parents on the land if they get frail; the growth of large retailers and professional supply chains can often undermine the viability of micro-enterprises, turning citizens from small business owners into employees; and, of course, following the American and European developmental paradigm entails massive increases in energy and resource consumption.

My stance on this debate is that, while all forms of development bring both costs and benefits, taken as a whole, development benefits the poor: absolute poverty is less common, and income inequality tends to be lower, where levels of development are higher. But I believe that pursuing a range of different investment strategies aimed at accelerating development in poorer countries is preferable to focusing on just one, which is why I see the recent bifurcation between the strategies of commercial and developmental LPs as a positive step.

For these reasons I welcome the fact that, in 2011, the UK government's Select Committee for International Development concluded that CDC should in future put more of its money to work in the poorest countries in sub-Saharan Africa and Asia and the most deprived regions of India, and for it to have special focuses on areas such as the promotion of small businesses, while Actis should remain free to invest as it chooses. These recommendations have largely been adopted, I believe to the benefit of the diversity of approaches that can be pursued. In particular, the existence of a large, cash-rich British DFI that has a very specific investment mandate is likely to lead to the emergence of a class of GP that meets its revised criteria, while Actis's much broader commercial remit will allow it to attract greater pools of commercial LP capital to better pursue the contrasting development model.

Being a typical Englishman, my first instincts are towards national self-deprecation, but the fact is that both CDC and Actis, which are now very different organisations, are nevertheless both extremely highly regarded internationally as exemplars of what they set out to do, so I believe that the activities of both merit examination in this book. I've begun by talking with Mark Goldsmith, Director of Environmental and Social Governance at Actis.

*   *   *

MB: How would you describe Actis today?

MG: We are a commercial private equity investor that focuses on emerging markets – Africa, Asia, Latin America. We invest in a responsible way.

We have over 100 investors, both institutional and DFIs, who are looking for commercial returns.

MB: What proportion of the funds under management are CDC's?

MG: Because private equity has quite a long time lag, there's a legacy of funds which we have continued to manage. In 2004 it was obviously 100 per cent, now it's less than 45 per cent. Going forward, for new funds it is probably going to be decreasing amounts as some of the markets we focus on are probably going to be of less interest to DFIs. Some of the Africa and infrastructure funds might still attract them – we wait to see.

MB: It seems to me that the change of emphasis from DFID [the Department For International Development, the UK government department to which CDC reports] implies that pan-Indian or pan-African funds would be difficult for CDC, because they want to focus on the poorest regions of India or countries in Africa. Does this mean that not just Actis but GPs generally will create funds that meet their investment criteria? Or will such funds not be created, in which case CDC could struggle to get money away?

MG: I think geography is not the only reason why we aren't so much on the radar for DFI money. The other big reason is that the size of investment is different. We typically invest $50 million plus, and DFI money typically wants to invest in SME [small- and medium-sized enterprise]-type businesses. They may well be sector-focused as well, there may well be specific sectors that the DFI community feels needs more support than others. So I think there definitely are opportunities for GPs who want to specifically home in on potential DFI money, and mainstream commercial funds across all the markets are going to be less likely to attract it, although maybe ones with regional side funds might be of interest.

MB: I guess there are two philosophical approaches to the relationship between private equity and development. There's one view, which I've seen in the DFID review, which says that since a high proportion of the poorest people in the world are dependent on agriculture and micro-businesses, we should help them by investing in those sectors. But there's another view that says that moving to the cities, working in factories or shops, having big corporations with efficient operations that drive down costs and an infrastructure to support these things are what take people out of poverty, so the last thing we should be doing is promoting small businesses and agriculture.

MG: As you know, we have a commercial remit on our funds, but clearly there are some investments that make a big difference to some of the countries that we invest in. You can look at Tanzania, we have an investment there that provides 20 per cent of the energy and has saved the government something like $2 billion in oil reserves or imports since it's been up and running. In Uganda we run the whole of an electrical distribution grid and we are increasing the number of customers by 30–40,000 a year. These are commercial investments, but they are making a huge impact on the countries and the people there. Although we didn't start from the standpoint of those being development impact investments, clearly they have big impact in their own right.

MB: I understand one of the biggest challenges facing the incoming management in the Ugandan investment [Umeme, the privatised electricity grid] was that only 8 per cent of customers were actually paying for their electricity; the rest just stole it. And as a consequence, the physical infrastructure was under-invested to the point that rotten electricity poles were falling on people and killing them.

MG: I think that brings one to the other point that private equity brings to companies, particularly in emerging markets: namely, governance and good business integrity.

MB: According to your website, Actis's investment strategy is about 'rising domestic consumption driven by the rapid expansion of the new consumer class and the need for sustained investment in infrastructure'. We've discussed a couple of examples of infrastructure projects in the context of energy firms; can you give some instances of investments based around the consumer theme?

MG: In the long term, domestic growth is where we want to focus. Taking China, for example, we have a budget hotel chain similar to Travelodge [7 Days], a healthy fast food chain [Xiabu Xiabu] and an investment in online education.

7 Days gives Chinese businesspeople a good, functional hotel at a reasonable price. There's also an opportunity to join a loyalty club and gain points to enable you to continue to stay at the hotels. It is basic but reasonably nice accommodation, and it has an internet link. When we acquired a minority stake [July 2008] it was the third-largest budget hotel chain in the country, with 160 hotels in 28 cities. By the end of 2011 Q2 it had expanded to 722 hotels, with another 241 under development, with 23 million members registered.

Xiabu Xiabu is a healthy fast food chain: you cook your meat and vegetables in hot water, rather than oil. It's a bit like having a fondue, and you either have one in front of you at the bar or you have a table of four and they heat it up in front of you. They specialise in making the sauces and things that you dip it in. It is a popular fast food theme and healthier than some of the fries and chicken alternatives. I wonder why they don't do it here [in the UK] in a way. We acquired a majority stake in November 2008, when it had 60 restaurants, mainly in Beijing and Tianjin; by the end of 2011 Q3 it had 211 stores.

Ambow provides online and classroom-based educational services, last year helping around 700–800,000 people. It has two main areas of focus: helping children improve their exam performance in order to get into the best high schools and colleges, and helping up-skill adults through post-graduate and mid-career training. We have a minority stake in a listed company, and it's an expansion model. In China you have almost six people supporting each child because of the single-child policy that they have had for some time: you have two sets of grandparents and one set of parents who are interested in the child's education – education being the key to going places, as it is anywhere else in the world.

MB: Returning for a moment to infrastructure, is that for Actis mainly about energy, or are there other sub-sectors?

MG: We do have an investment in a toll road, but mainly it has been energy generation and distribution. I mentioned some of our African assets, but we're also doing a lot in Central America using our platform company, Globeleq Mesoamerica. As part of this we have the oldest wind farm in Latin America, built in Costa Rica in 1996, and in Honduras we have just brought on line the largest, which is very much integrating into first-world design.

MB: Is there a distinction between your approaches with consumer-facing and infrastructure businesses, in that the former are mostly about backing and investing alongside an entrepreneur whereas the latter are privatisations or buyouts that need an influx of capital?

MG: You need to go on a case-by-case basis. For example, the electrical distribution in Uganda, 2005, was effectively a privatisation. If you look at what we have done with DEOCSA and DEORSA, the Guatemalan distribution asset, it was a non-core asset of Gas Naturale which they were looking to divest. In our energy fund that invested in this area, we have both direct investments and also investments in effectively a power generation platform called Globeleq. It holds our generating assets in Ivory Coast, Kenya and Tanzania, and a 70 per cent stake in Globeleq Mesoamerica, the Central American renewable energy platform. So we have a platform that can be used to invest in companies to manage the assets when they are up and running as well as being able to invest directly like we have done in DEOCSA and DEORSA in Guatemala.

MB: I'm interested that you are active in Central America, because it's possibly an area that doesn't receive that much attention. How do you define emerging markets, or, to put it another way, how do you decide where to invest and who your competitors are?

MG: Where we invest, which may not be the strict definition of emerging markets, is Latin America, Africa, South Asia, South-East Asia. We don't invest in Eastern Europe or the 'stans currently.

We tend to see our competitors either in a regional market, so, for instance, in Africa it could be Abraaj Capital, Citadel or Emerging Capital Partners, or to an extent the big international funds that are becoming active in our markets, the Carlyles, KKRs and 3is. But we wouldn't consider ourselves like either of these groups, because the firms such as Citadel are only really looking at a very small number of countries, while Carlyle and KKR have bigger other markets.

MB: Yours is a unique proposition: a pan-emerging markets investor that has that as its sole geographical focus because it isn't also doing things in developed economies.

MG: Yes. I think it may become less of a distinguishing feature, but what we do have is that we've got offices in a number of places that some of those big organisations don't have. That's changing, certainly in China and India, but it may take them some time to rival our coverage in Africa – we have Cairo, Lagos, Nairobi and Johannesburg.

MB: Would Actis ever consider investing in developed markets?

MG: I think we wouldn't think that would be in our skills base.

MB: How about bringing some of the emerging markets businesses you own to emerged markets such as the UK? You hinted you wondered whether Xiabu Xiabu would work in the UK . . .

MG: We have always been interested in professionalising and building family-run businesses to scale, and getting them into international markets is absolutely possible. We have also seen opportunities around non-core assets of multinationals, which may have got lost in large portfolios, where we can give them focus, management and skills.

MB: Within the pan-emerging markets approach, are there certain countries were you won't invest?

MG: There are some places that are off-limits at any point of time: for instance, Burma or Zimbabwe currently. These are the binary issues where there are dreadful human rights or sanctions problems which mean we absolutely can't invest. Then there are the classic risk-reward considerations. So sometimes there are bubbles, or considerations such as exchange rates. The entire philosophy of having a pan-emerging markets strategy is that if we see challenges in one part of the market then we have the opportunity to invest instead in another.

At the same time, there are very few countries where it is the country itself that causes the investment to fail. As an example, we invested in a rubber plantation in the Ivory Coast when it went through the last troubles in 2002 onwards; it was located in a demilitarised zone and still exited quite successfully.

MB: And how do you structure your teams and investment decisions – is it around geography, or sectors?

MG: Our investment committee likes to look for the best company in a particular sector in the emerging markets. There may be times where that
may be in Latin America, China or Africa, so we have a sector as well as
geographical structure to help us identify the best opportunities.

MB: Are your people mainly British, or locals, or some other nationality?

MG: Almost entirely locals. We employ people from the countries we invest
in, with MBAs, who have generally done some financial/investment work
in the past. Being on the ground, close to the people, is essential.

MB: How do you balance commercial returns with ESG [Environmental and
Social Governance]?

MG: We absolutely have to deliver commercial returns – we can't operate
unless we do – but I would say that so often, that and ESG are aligned.
The alignment is not necessarily in one year, when the operational costs of
ESG may be higher, but when it comes to who is going to buy the business
and what value it has, then well-run companies with good governance that
might have cost a bit to put in place, are generally worth more.

MB: There seems to be a sense that a lot of companies in emerging markets
are off the radar of the multinationals because of the lack of transparency,
whereas a private equity buyer from a developed, highly regulated market that buys a company and fixes these problems can sell it on to that
buyer because it will be clean and there would be come-back in a sound
jurisdiction if there were problems: a kind of governance arbitrage.

MG: Yes, the proof of the pudding is in the eating. The biggest private equity
exit in India in 2010 was Paras [a pharma company], which was one of
our investees. It went to the FTSE100-listed Reckitt Benckiser. We know
from the questions they asked us that they were very interested in the
governance area and that it was one of the reasons they came to the
table and that we got the good exit we did [$726 million]. Our investee
businesses come to us because they know we are going to take these
issues seriously and implement good governance systems and responsible
investments, because it is in their interest to actually make an investment
successful.

MB: How do you manage the balance between identifying and closing new
transactions on the one hand and value addition on the other?

MG: Our investment managers spend quite a bit of time finding new deals.
When they make the investment, there tends to be a team of people, and
then the partner who is in charge of that team will typically join the board,
often with one other that we have appointed, who will be a technical or a
country specialist.

   What we have done more recently is really strengthen ourselves with a
value addition group, so we now have a number of people who are more
focused on post-investment value addition, although even then they are

looking at the deals pre-investment to see what the opportunities may be post-investment. So there are now people who are mainly doing the investments but not handing over the baton completely and separate individuals on the value-creation part of the process.

MB: I suspect this is a growing trend in the industry.

MG: I think, to be fair, in emerging markets we have always had to add value to our investment companies, you can't do the financial leveraging option, whereas I suspect that was more of an option in the emerged markets. That is no longer the case, and therefore what are you going to do with these investee companies? You have got to help them on the curve of improving all the things I've talked about, all the governance, all the IT systems, all the HR, the management and things like that. Therefore, if you can have people who can help with that process, then that is obviously going to make things a lot better.

MB: Are you mainly backing the current managements, or buy-in teams, or buying businesses then going out and finding new management?

MG: Deal by deal, it varies hugely. There are certainly times when we are changing senior management. As part of our due diligence in a typical management buyout we will assess how good the management is relatively to a benchmark, and we use companies like Egon Zehnder to do that. As well as the CEO role, we consider the finance side to be absolutely critical. We also put a lot of time into getting the board structures around the management team right, and that is not just about getting the right people but also the right sub-committees.

MB: You mentioned the separate value-addition people; what else has changed about your business recently, or do you see changing in the future?

MG: We have always recognised that in our markets you have to roll your sleeves up a bit more than in emerged markets, but the recognition of having specific people who are employed to do that is a definite change.

I think the whole industry is facing transparency and regulatory changes and that we are going to see more requirements for reporting, including to wider stakeholders. I suspect some GPs may feel they do quite a lot of reporting at the moment to their LPs, but it will probably become more general. They may wonder whether this is necessary, but there are a lot of people working in private equity-backed companies, so I think it probably is right that there should be more transparency and measurement of the non-financial impact of private equity.

MB: In some emerged markets, private equity has come in for some criticism in recent years, whereas in many developing countries, where it is a much smaller part of the economies and access to capital can be a barrier to growth, it seems to me that being able to persuade governments and citizens that private equity can help drive that growth could be a good approach.

MG: Yes, the model is different in our markets, and therefore it has a real possibility of being an asset class that kick-starts investment.

I don't know how many private equity companies that are investing in emerged markets are doing the bit that the industry has been criticised for, all the asset-stripping, big reductions of staff, lots of leverage; in our markets that just doesn't tend to be the situation. We are investing in growth markets where pretty much most of our businesses will increase the number of people who work for them because there are more people they are needing to serve as part of the domestic growth story. So private equity is typically resulting in more people being employed, rather than fewer. Yes there is leverage, but it is not to the scale that there has been in the emerged markets. So the main concerns that the wider stakeholders have in Europe and North America don't tend to be as strong in our markets.

Also, I can't really speak for them, but I suspect private equity organisations have been through quite a learning curve on big leveraged buyouts, and I suspect even if it were possible to get larger leveraged deals [in emerging markets] there is a certain realism about what it could mean if there was a downturn.

MB: Is there a sense that in some of the countries you operate in, the business community is smaller so you can't easily walk away from a bad deal without it affecting future deal-flow?

MG: Yes, I'll give you an example. We talked about Umeme, the Ugandan electrical distribution network we invested in back in 2005. We knew the infrastructure had not been invested in for 20 or 30 years. There were very uncertain records of what the asset condition looked like: the percentage of people stealing, whether the public was being fatally injured on the infrastructure, that type of thing. We knew there were big issues in it, but it took us probably until 2007 or 2008 to really gather all the data, and then we realised we were in an investment where there were significant losses, the investment required a large sum to go into it to make it better. That was absolutely not a place we wanted to be in or thought we would be in.

If you had looked at it in 2007/8, there was quite a lot of pressure to come out, but we wouldn't have felt that we had done what we should have done in that circumstance. I think, in particular with a utility, you have to get it right: it has to be serving the public in the way that it should, because if you don't get that right, even if you do add good financial value to it, you would struggle to re-invest in that place, and any issues would come back to the GP. I think in the end it will be a successful financial investment, but it is critical that we've improved the infrastructure so it doesn't fall down, there's less stealing, fewer safety issues, the governance structure is right and the right people are in charge.

There's a strap-line under our logo that says, 'The positive power of capital'. You could say it is just our financial capital, but actually there is a whole pile of other things that we bring. When we did the first-ever management buyout in Egypt, for instance, we demonstrated something that can happen and then the skills and the knowledge are left behind as a legacy. So I think the positive power of capital isn't just the financial capital, it's the human capital that we bring, and that we encourage within the investee companies.

17

Rod Evison, Managing Director, Africa, CDC Group

CDC's genesis was, perhaps surprisingly, not that altruistic. Conceived in 1947, following a record-breaking harsh winter that devastated British agricultural production and forced the government to draw up plans for a famine relief programme, CDC's initial brief was to invest on a break-even basis in agricultural and commodities production in former and remaining colonies, in order to help meet basic needs in Britain and boost those nations' export incomes, reducing their reliance on financial support from the UK, which was itself saved from bankruptcy only by borrowing heavily from the USA.

From that start point, the organisation's evolution was logical: into projects such as dams that facilitate agricultural production, and from there to hydro-electric projects; and from agricultural and other raw materials into their processing and the production of consumer staples.

But it is not necessary to look far beyond the organisation's formation to see other themes developing – in particular, support for service-sector businesses and recognition of the benefits of enabling private-sector investment. As early as 1949, for instance, CDC had a Hotels Division that included operations such as the Lake Victoria Hotel, Uganda, and what is now the Radisson Fort George Hotel, Belize. The primary thesis was that a lack of comfortable hotel accommodation in many of the geographies that CDC wished to invest in represented a barrier to securing private sector investment; a secondary theme was a desire to boost tourism.

Initially largely an equity investor, in its early years CDC lost money on a number of well-intentioned but misconceived projects, as a result of which, during the 1950s, it evolved a model of providing mainly debt finance, seeking co-investment from local governments and expecting managements to risk some of their own capital in return for equity. During that decade, CDC's brief became overtly one of accelerating the pace of development in its sphere of influence: in the words of its then Chairman, Lord Reith, 'Doing good, without losing money'.

To this end, as Britain entered the 1960s – the decade in which the country shed most of its remaining colonies – CDC's emphasis began to shift. Initially, it replaced the 'Colonial' in its name with 'Commonwealth', with a remit to support projects anywhere within the latter group of nations and, later, anywhere it perceived there to be a need. And while it never deserted the basics of agriculture, commodities and energy, CDC increased its emphasis on projects intended to accelerate countries' abilities to exist as self-sufficient, mixed economies.

The next really big strategy shifts become apparent in the second half of the 1980s. In 1986 CDC was permitted for the first time to both lend and borrow in foreign currencies – a step that de-risked transactions in volatile geographies. The following year it launched its first venture capital fund, PNG Venture Finance, in Papua New Guinea. Four years later, CDC was among an IFC-led consortium of institutions that backed the management buyout of Exxon's chemicals business in Pakistan – the organisation's first MBO. A year later, in 1992, it established its first fund in which it managed third-party money, the Ghana Venture Capital Fund.

A McKinsey strategy review in 1994 led to the organisation focusing on 'pre-emerging' markets where governments had introduced reforms but which were not yet attracting private capital due to risk perceptions, and on 'additionality' – the provision of technical or management skills or bringing in private-sector co-investment – as opposed to the simple provision of capital.

It was from this point onward that CDC can reasonably be described as primarily a private equity investor. Its investment themes also began to converge with those more conventionally associated with the industry. For instance, in 1995 it began a decade-long association with a remarkable Sudanese telecoms entrepreneur called Mo Ibrahim, making a 10 per cent investment in his firm Clovergem Celtel Ltd, which had won the licence to develop Uganda's first mobile phone network. By 2005, when CDC exited, Celtel was a $3.4 billion business spanning 13 African countries.

The election of Tony Blair's Labour government in 1997 led to the announcement that CDC would become a public–private partnership and be encouraged to seek commercial LP money like any other private equity firm. While guidelines were put in place to ensure that 70 per cent of investments were in poorer countries and half were in South Asia and sub-Saharan Africa, in practice the need to generate commercial returns – CDC had been averaging 8 per cent, perhaps a third of what LPs were likely to demand – marked the organisation's managed departure from the capital-intensive, slow-burn agricultural sector.

From the formation of CDC Capital Partners in 2000, the decision was taken to focus on six core industries: minerals, oil and gas, telecoms and IT, infrastructure, FMCG [fast-moving consumer goods] and financial services. While the four core regions – Africa, South Asia, Latin America and Asia Pacific – remained, the decision was taken to put more capital to work in the larger economies, such as China, India, Nigeria and Egypt.

Attracting private money proved difficult until 2002, when CDC hit on the model of creating platform companies such as the energy roll-up business mentioned in Chapter 16, Globeleq, and seeking investment in those vehicles: in private equity terms, sector-specific funds. This resulted in the formal separation in 2004 between CDC – the governmental limited partner – and Actis, the fund manager, in order to free up the latter to offer a range of funds concentrating on different geographies and themes, the idea being that third-party investors would be more likely to come on board if they felt that the fund manager was independently managed and free from political pressures on its investment strategy. Meanwhile CDC's earlier-stage investments and those targeting countries it was gradually exiting were rolled into another vehicle, Aureos Capital, in which the Norwegian DFI Norfund became a co-investor.

The election of the Conservative-led coalition government in May 2010 led to questions being asked about whether CDC's capital was being deployed in the most effective way to alleviate poverty in the world's poorest countries. In a report titled *The Future of CDC*, published in February 2011, Parliament's International Development Committee concluded that:

> Although CDC has [...] contributed to employment and the tax base of developing countries, its development impact has been insufficient for a Government-owned company whose net investments count as Official Development Assistance. We are concerned that some of the investments CDC has made are ones the private sector would have made anyway. Over half of its investments are concentrated in four middle-income countries. Too few of its investments have been in sectors which most benefit the poor such as agriculture, infrastructure and small and medium enterprises.

It recommended that, while part of CDC's capital should continue to be invested in a range of emerging-markets GPs, on a fund-of-funds basis, more care should be taken to select projects with positive development impact as opposed to those that simply promote economic growth, and that it should also devote a proportion of its capital – subsidised by its returns from private equity – in direct investment in 'pro-poor' projects, whether by co-investing alongside private equity or providing debt, or guarantees to other lenders, to make possible high-impact projects that would otherwise not proceed. It was also tasked with doing more to facilitate the growth of small and medium-size businesses, since these tend to create the most employment and have the greatest impact on local economies.

Three months later, the Secretary of State published a business plan that broadly accepted the recommendations and provided a plan for implementation.

While CDC is not a private equity firm, it is arguably the biggest influence on development-oriented private equity investment in emerging markets, so its change in focus will be a major determinant of the evolution of emerging-markets private equity. I interviewed Rod Evison, who heads up CDC's activities in its largest market, Africa, and who was also, for the second half of 2011, CDC acting Chief Executive, to get his take on the organisation's development and its new mandate. A former commercial banker who moved into development finance with IFC in Washington, he joined CDC in 1992.

*   *   *

MB: How did you find CDC, compared with IFC?

RE: There are obvious differences in terms of the scale and the fact that it had one shareholder rather than many, but otherwise I expected it to be fairly similar, mainly providing debt, some equity, and focusing on emerging markets. But once I joined, I realised it was culturally completely different; CDC has always been much more entrepreneurial, whereas IFC was either more bureaucratic or more professional, depending on your viewpoint.

Another difference between us and other DFIs is that we are not a bank. We haven't got any debt, we have net assets of £2.7 billion, all financed by shareholders' equity. At this time about £2 billion of that is invested, about 42 per cent of it in Africa.

We are much more of an innovator, wanting to change the way we approach development. Being a DFI with a single shareholder, we are there for a purpose, which is to further the shareholder's aims in the development arena.

MB: You must have seen those aims change quite a bit in your time here.

RE: When I came, we were leaving behind an era of doing a lot of parastatal debt – CDC used to finance projects such as the Kariba Dam in Zimbabwe and Owens Falls [a hydro-electric project in Uganda] – and diversifying away from our deep history in renewable natural resources investments, such as agriculture. There was a privatisation agenda, wanting to get into privatised utilities, and of re-equipping the organisation to be able to engage more with the private sector. Between 1998 and 2000 we moved from being a debt provider to a mix of equity and debt, and from 2000 onwards it was always equity investing. Then of course there was the split with Actis in 2004.

MB: So from that date CDC was in effect a limited partner, not only in Actis's funds but in third-party ones?

RE: Exactly.

MB: What impact did that have?

RE: One of the surprises since the 2004 spin-out was that the two of us moved apart as rapidly as we did, I think for a whole number of reasons. They moved into their space much more quickly than we expected and, with influence from the shareholder, we've moved into a different space from where we were much more quickly than we expected. So even though they remain very important to us because they manage so much of our portfolio, it is more difficult now to find ways to maintain new investments with them going forward. We committed to one last year but that was a speciality fund.

In the spin-out agreement, we committed ourselves for a period of time to support their new funds. It absolutely was not a blank cheque, but there was an obligation to review and decide whether those funds worked for us or not. We thought it was going to take probably four years before we were having an active programme with a lot of other LP and GP relationships. That all happened much quicker than we expected. The reason, I think, was because of the boom that occurred, not just the developed markets but in emerging markets as well, for reasons that now we can all see. Actis, to give them their credit, saw value where it was and took money off the table where they could, so we ended up with a huge bank balance, end of 2007, at one point £1.2 billion, because Actis had been realising a lot of investments. And thank goodness they did, because that really set us up well when we went into the crisis.

We then had to very quickly start considering how to deploy that money. First of all we were informed by our investment policy: we operate under an investment policy with our shareholder. In those days, and now, geography is one of the defining features of it. In those days we had what was called the CDC Universe, and we had to only operate within the CDC Universe. In those days the Universe was quite broad, which is why we have investments in Latin America and China as well as in Africa and Asia.

Broadly, CDC was looking to develop private equity in emerging markets as a recognised asset class and to demonstrate to commercial investors it is not as scary a place to invest as they thought it might be. And we were very focused; in fact, it was one of the reasons for the split, to find ways to encourage more private capital to come into the geographies that were the focus of CDC at that time. Actis as a GP had to go out and raise investment for their funds.

And for us as an LP, we were helping other GPs to get off the ground, because we would generally be there as a first-time investor with first time funds at first close, we wanted to be a reference investor.

As at the end of 2010 we were invested in about 120 or 125 private equity funds, with around 45 managers. Actis represented about 40–45 per cent by value, for historical reasons, but that is obviously coming down each year.

We wanted to be highly professional in selecting a broad range of funds, both geographically and in terms of strategy. Even though some of the press have said that we only did one thing, in fact we invested across quite a broad range of funds with some IRR targets that were less than 10 per cent for strategies that appealed to impact investors to funds that earned more than 25 per cent, such as hard-core Chinese, Indian or Pan-African private equity funds.

MB: And I guess the ease with which some of those broader-strategy funds can now raise money suggests that CDC's capital is no longer critical.

RE: Exactly. Under the new [May 2011] business plan, we are no longer focusing on Latin America or China or parts of India. In Africa is it quite stark; we are not looking to work in the upper middle-income countries, even in North Africa, which clearly has its problems at the moment.

I would describe it as a repositioning of the type of investment – it's not that private equity will be ditched, but the geography is shrinking and it will no longer be the only thing that we do.

MB: I appreciate that the new strategy encourages you to make direct investments, which presumably means that you can work with a GP whose pan-continent funds don't meet your new objectives on individual projects that do, but isn't there something of a challenge in that there are very few funds that meet your new investment criteria?

RE: Yes; the question, though, is how do we address that challenge. For example, my colleagues who cover South Asia have been very focused in talking to the Indian GPs they have relationships with, saying things like, 'Gosh, valuations are so high in the main metropolitan areas. Why don't you look further out into some of the poorer areas? Are the valuations better there? Is there a different strategy which might not be mainstream today, but in five or 10 years' time might become so?'

We backed one initiative like that last year: Pragati. It is the first private equity fund to focus pretty much solely on small and medium-size entrepreneurial businesses in the eight poorest states within India, states like Bihar and Orissa, that frankly haven't received much private equity investment at all, whereas most of it goes to Mumbai and the other tier 1 cities.

MB: Couldn't the same argument be made for the interior and west of China? There are also hundreds of millions of people in rural China who live on $2 a day or less.

RE: Yes, one could logically make the case that there's still a major development challenge in China. But does UK public money have any role in that, given that China has, what, $3 trillion in reserves? At least, that's the conclusion our shareholder came to. You might then argue why should India be a special case. I think when you put India in the context of the Commonwealth, lots of people have views as to what the relationship between the UK and India should be.

MB: That's a controversial area – people may say, 'Why should our money go to India, when it has a space programme and a foreign aid programme and creates more new millionaires every year than we have millionaires in the whole of Britain?' There is an argument that it is for India to sort out its distribution of income and assets so it can resolve its remaining poverty.

RE: The UK has come to two different answers for China and India. I would say it is significant that DFID [the Department For International Development] still has an aid programme for India, and it is probably more of a sensitive question whether that should continue than whether it is appropriate for us to have an investment programme which is seeking to help the country but also to generate a return. The private sector is an exit strategy for aid, I would say, and trying to encourage private sector development, economic growth, more taxes, puts more money into governments and allows donor programmes to be re-oriented to the areas with the greatest need. It is absolutely what Andrew Mitchell [Secretary of State for International Development] has been doing.

MB: You cited Pragati as an Indian fund that meets CDC's new criteria. Are there other examples you can provide?

RE: I'll answer your question in the context of Africa. If Africa was a single country, there would be the same issues as in India – there are both rich and poor areas, and our focus is around the poor areas, so yes, there's the same challenge to work with good GPs with a focus on areas that scratch our itch. So far, we have been reasonably successful in negotiating excuse rights and exclusions within funds that have pan-African strategies [i.e., for CDC to have the right to have its money sit out those funds' investments that do not meet its criteria].

A GP might make exceptions for us that they might not be willing to make for others. Everything's got to be completely transparent, everybody's got to sign up to it. But it is a very important way in which we can continue to get some significant monies to work with good people but with a focus for our money into the poorer areas.

Do we ever sit on an investment committee? The answer to date has been no. We want to take a decision around selecting a GP that we have confidence in, and we want them to then carry out their investment strategy and to be responsible for the investment decisions that they make. And if they do well, they'll earn their carry, and if they do badly, they'll lose their skin of the game.

We already encourage independents to go onto investment committees – not CDC people but other skilled investors. Who knows in the future whether that will always remain the case or whether with some of the very pioneering fund managers might be open to having DFI representation, perhaps a CDC person, on their boards?

MB: Is the intention to get private money to follow your new strategy?

RE: Yes, we still want to encourage private capital to come after or alongside our money. It is a challenge in the poorer areas, as we keep moving. DFI money was very important in getting private equity up and running in Africa, and hopefully it will be similar in terms of the areas where it isn't yet so prevalent.

MB: I wonder whether that could be harder to achieve in Africa than India, because as you move into the poorer areas of Africa you're no longer in the same country, and transparency gets more difficult or you confront problems such as war or drought. I would imagine it is hard to invest in Sudan or Somalia, for instance.

RE: There's definitely a frontier beyond the frontier. For instance, a GP we invested in put money too early into South Sudan, the forestry sector. It was about improving the management of that resource and investing in a processing facility and a route to market, exploiting high-quality teak for boat-building and other purposes. Unfortunately, conflict was a problem, as was security; management felt threatened and wouldn't stay. The GP had to sell out to local partners for next to nothing because they couldn't manage the investment.

Private equity is a sophisticated product, and it works best where there is an ecosystem that supports it, and where there are other believers, the follow-on finance, co-finance, advisers, people who think the same way, so you don't have a year-long discussion about valuation with an entrepreneur who is coming from a completely different place.

In rural India or the poorer parts of Africa these ecosystems are not well developed, and it is our role to help change that. I like to think about what is an appropriate role for public money when investing in private ventures. I would say it is not to seek to be too transformational, to believe that we're clever enough to change the world, but instead to say, 'Our role is to make good things happen earlier than they would otherwise have happened.'

MB: It seems to me that CDC wants to fill a gap between what the private sector can do and probably already does on the one hand and, on the other, projects that either serve a purely political goal for Britain or cannot deliver financial returns and are hence really aid projects: areas of market failure in the provision of private capital.

RE: Yes, that's the gap.

MB: And the gap was in a different place ten years ago from where it is now, hence the change of emphasis.

RE: Yes, but there's something else we haven't touched on, which is that while money is the ultimate commodity, it can be differentiated by the hands through which it passes. We feel that the money that passes through our hands is differentiated by the standards and investment code that we ask our partners and those we invest in through them to live up to. And many GPs are now realising that, if a company is fit for purpose from an ESG [Environmental and Social Governance] viewpoint, it is attractive to a much wider range of potential acquirers than if you still have a family-owned business that still has issues that make it hard to sell it to anyone other than back to the family.

MB: What has become of the CDC Frontier proposal in the Select Committee report [a proposal that CDC be split into two parts, with one, CDC Funds, acting as a fund-of-funds investor and the other, CDC Frontier, overtly pursuing a lower-return, higher-impact remit]?

RE: The recommendation was not accepted in that form, but there is a type of CDC Frontier being built into the new business. We all wanted to have the opportunity to operate on the frontier, because that is what attracts people to come and work at CDC. Despite what you read in the press, it is not always the pay, and definitely will not be going forward. The buzz of the job comes from feeling as if you are making a difference and doing something exciting that may not have been done before. We didn't want to put that within one little unit, but instead to encourage everybody to think more about it.

But yes, we have broadened our product range so now we are not just a fund-of-fund LP within a set of GP structures. It is also direct investments, initially probably mainly as co-investments with GPs. But over time we will also address the question of how we can get money to work in places that are not ready for a traditional fund structure. I do not have the answer today, because it's still an open question, but it is likely to be through partnerships that may extend outside traditional GP/LP-type arrangements.

MB: What is the case for direct investment?

RE: First of all, the development impact we want to have. How do we measure that? Financial performance, the thing has got to be financially sustainable, *ex ante*. Economic performance is making sure that there is growth within the underlying company and not distortions by subsidies, that the taxes are being paid to governments etc. ESG performance, very important, we are taking things to an improved level. And then private-sector development, which is a broad topic but could include the four sectors that we are very focused on, certainly in Africa: new connections, taking power to more people; transportation, whether it's roads or ports or whatever to improve the efficiency of the transport system; financial services – access to finance and bank accounts, loans to SME customers; agribusiness, trying to encourage increased productivity. Those are the four measures of private sector development that we think of.

MB: And co-investment – is that about going into specific projects on softer terms than you might otherwise accept, in order to encourage a GP to support what might otherwise be too risky or too low-yielding a proposition?

RE: It could be on softer terms, or it could be on a *pari passu* basis in an investment that, *ex ante*, may even offer higher returns than they are doing elsewhere, but *ex post* could be a bit of a disaster, because it's risky. He doesn't want to put too much money in, but he's intrigued, he thinks there are some relationships that could lead to other things, so he needs some other money to come alongside him.

That would be absolutely centre-stage for us, where we are still aligned with the GP and where we would like to follow the GP and not to feel as though we have to look after our own interests all the time, so we can take a more light-touch approach to monitoring. Where we become misaligned because we're investing on different terms than the GP, along the lines that you were talking about, we would need to me more at the table to make sure that we've got the balance right and are monitoring it correctly.

MB: If you're moving from being a fund of funds to also being a co-investor and a direct investor, will that require you to create a network of investment professionals around the world, or would you still use GPs to manage the money?

RE: The old CDC had people sitting in offices all round the world that were employed to look for and manage opportunities. Maybe that works with debt, but for an equity focus it is difficult. You need to have deep networks, and there are lots of HR challenges around that. So I think it is unlikely that we will go back to having the same breadth of network. It is possible that we will open up some sub-offices over time in some of these areas, but more probably as relationship offices, not investment offices.

Relationships with whom is the question. It could be a wide range of people. It would be clearly GPs that we have invested with, and maybe GPs that we've not invested with but who are there anyway. It could be advisers that we might respect. It could be other DFIs, other international financial institutions. It could be local banks. It could be a range of different types of institutions or partnerships that we seek to get to know better and find a mutually satisfactory way of working alongside one another.

MB: What is your strategy for selecting GPs, under the new business plan?

RE: First of all, is the market that they're tackling a market that we are focused on? Secondly, is the investment strategy that they are promoting one that we think is sensible in that market? Is it a strategy that captivates us and we think is something that we want to talk about and be able to say, 'Look, we've now got this portfolio of companies.' Because we've now got 1000 companies underneath CDC. That's actually what we are really interested in. The GPs are just a way of getting to that, and it is those 1000 companies and the impact that they are having that are really the things that we are keen to elevate.

Within the strategy, we also have to ask what's the financial return that they are expecting to generate. We haven't actually said it to date, but we haven't had any money out of government for 16 years, so we have to operate in a sustainable way, and that's how we want to continue to operate in the future as well.

Thirdly, the team. Does the team that brought the proposition to us have the skills that are necessary to execute that strategy? In many instances we are backing first-time teams, there is no institutional track record that we can look at. So we are then seeking to get under the skin of the people to decide whether we feel that they are going to be cohesive as a group of people. Whether they've got a balance of skills around networking and developing interesting ideas, selecting those things that are the most promising. Closing the deal. Adding value, having a broader network, because no one individual has got the skills that a load of companies need. Having a network of people they can apply to companies when they run into the various problems they are going to have, to help them meet their business plans anyway. And, of course, in thinking about the exit strategy.

MB: I appreciate that CDC can do a lot to bring on board private LPs by doing all this due diligence and being prepared to take a punt on markets and strategies that haven't in the past attracted much capital. But with so many developed-market GPs having a tough time raising funds and the more established emerging markets delivering high growth and attracting plenty of capital, won't the next few years be a challenging time for new funds to raise capital in frontier markets?

RE: I think there's always a balance to be struck in emerging markets between too much money coming in and not enough, but received wisdom is that it will be the emerging markets that save us. And there's going to be a great opportunity for private equity within that, even if there are ups and downs along the way.

It has been a difficult fundraising environment since 2008 for emerging markets. But it has got better. We backed Helios's first fund, so it was very important to them that we gave a major commitment to the second fund in very difficult fundraising times, so we did. We made a major commitment at first close. I remember some of our board directors asked, 'How much are they looking to raise?' and we said, 'We've been told it's $600–800 million,' and they said, 'They will be lucky to raise $300 million.' And lo and behold, they eventually got to $900 million.

But I think that is the exception rather than the rule. So GPs just have to be cautious, and we always have a tough discussion with them around what the minimum size of fund it would take for the business to be sustainable. We ask them to convince us that they would be willing to work for that salary for the next five years, until they are able to raise successor funds, and if they got stuck on that size, that they would not give up and throw in the towel.

There are also issues that are hopefully short-term, such as the high inflation we've seen recently in some East African countries. Some companies will go bust, because some of these markets and their financial infrastructures are just not as robust, so that means there's more volatility in our results. There has been more volatility in our results since 2004 than before, and there will be more going forwards as well.

MB: And public markets, where they exist in developing countries, also tend to be pretty volatile, don't they? They can seize up for months or even years when you can't get new issues away, and that can take away one of your exit options.

RE: That's right, and when foreign capital leaves, as it has done, it has a big impact on prices because there just isn't that much equity within those markets.

There can also be a trend when things are going well for people to think it's easy, for many people to raise the same type of fund at the same time, teams who aren't really equipped to do that. From an LP's viewpoint, and we haven't always been good at this for various reasons, it is best to just maintain a consistent investment programme, to commit perhaps $400–500 million a year, to be there across the periods.

We are also keen to see funds targeting investment from within their own countries, encouraging an emerging investment community, the emerging middle class, and encouraging change in the regulatory systems within these countries to allow for that money to go into private equity. We're also keen to back people who have left countries in Africa and Asia to work in the City of London or New York and are returning to their own countries, setting up funds and encouraging others who have some money to invest.

18
Hurley Doddy, Co-Chief Executive Officer, Emerging Capital Partners

Africa is clearly a special case for private equity. Aggregating the data for the continent's 56 nations paints an encouraging picture: the population, at 1.02 billion, is almost as large as India's or China's, and the economy has been growing at a rate of around 6 per cent per year for the past decade. But while the urban areas of some African states contain a great deal of wealth – there are parts of Lagos, for instance, where property costs more than in much of London or New York – the continent remains home to more of the world's poor than any other.

In some cases the blame can be pinned on temporary, human factors such as civil war or corrupt or incompetent dictatorships; once these are resolved, functioning states and economies can be rebuilt, since many African nations are rich in natural resources and boast favourable demographics. In others, climate change is making it increasingly difficult for substantial populations to live self-sufficiently, and it may be that if the Sahara continues to expand and droughts become more frequent, difficult decisions must be taken between relocating large numbers of people and accepting that they could for ever require extensive humanitarian support.

Private equity potentially has a huge role to play in Africa, because the common factor in even the most affluent countries is that capital is much less widely available than it is in developed economies. But what should that role be? Without revisiting the debate highlighted in Chapter 16, should it focus its capital on urban areas in the most affluent countries – in which case, as highlighted in Chapter 17, it will increasingly have to rely on private LPs' money and need to demonstrate similar returns to GPs in developed markets – or should it take DFI money, which may increasingly come on softer terms in return for signing up to strategies that have more immediate impact in alleviating poverty among the very poorest of Africa's citizens? Which leads to the most difficult question of all – where does investment end, and aid begin?

Setting aside a handful of firms headquartered in South Africa and focused largely on that country, African private equity was a nascent industry prior to 1999, when what was then known as Emerging Markets Partnership (EMP) launched an Africa fund in which the two principal investors were AIG and IFC, with the rest of the money coming from a mix of private sector and DFI sources. Nelson Mandela headed that first fund's advisory committee.

That fund performed well, and the management team spun out, re-branding as ECP (Emerging Capital Partners). Now on its seventh fund, the firm has raised a total of $1.8 billion for deployment in Africa, which it believes makes it cumulatively the largest GP focused solely on that continent. It is among the firms that benefited from CDC's 2004 strategy shift, receiving a $47.5 million commitment to its 2005 Africa Fund II and $100 million into its 2008 Africa Fund III.

ECP has so far struck a delicate balance between appealing to DFIs and generating commercial returns that attract private-sector money. It invests in 42 of Africa's 56 countries, putting money to work in countries such as the Democratic Republic of Congo and Côte d'Ivoire, where few others are active, and pursues themes in agriculture, agribusiness, renewable natural resources and utilities that have an obvious impact on the alleviation of poverty. But it also invests in consumer discretionary businesses such as mobile telecoms and banking in some of the continent's most affluent nations, and returns an average of 2.6 times its LPs' invested capital.

ECP's co-CEO Hurley Doddy is an American, originally from Washington DC, where the firm is based. He joined in 1999, after a career in investment banking. Specifically, he has a background in risk management, which has proved helpful at ECP because it tends to do a lot of minority deals with relatively complex structures which, while they do not involve much if any debt, do include warrants and options. I was keen to understand how the firm balances economic and social returns and how Doddy sees the funding situation evolving for pan-African private equity.

*   *   *

MB: I've noticed a phrase on your website describing ECP's strategy as one of 'targeting companies that operate in business environments characterised by limited competition or in sectors where Africa has either a comparative advantage or an unmet need'. Is that a description of where ECP's strategy used to be, or where it is going, or both?

HD: It was certainly part of the original strategy and also reflects what we're looking to do now. You clearly want to go where you can make an impact because there's less competition or where there are real bottlenecks that you can have an impact on. But there's a split, though, between where

Africa has had a historical advantage and where it is going now. Clearly their natural resources have been very strong, but there are also areas where the continent lagged for decades but where there is now a chance for rapid growth. We could see what the business models were supposed to be, where what has been successful in other markets could lead to further change in Africa.

MB: It seems to me there are broadly three strategies that private equity can pursue in Africa. One is about agriculture, agribusiness and commodities, another is about infrastructure and connecting up the continent and the third is about servicing the domestic demand of the emerging middle class. Where do you sit in terms of the balance between these approaches?

HD: We aim to address all three. Telecoms and financial services have historically been our two biggest sectors, both aimed at the local consumer and business markets. On natural resources, the commodity cycle doesn't fit so easily into a private equity model, but we've had good investments in agribusiness, in rubber, sugar, fertilisers and fertiliser distribution. And we've invested successfully in infrastructure, in areas such as energy and water.

On telecoms, we were early investors in Celtel (Mo Ibrahim's mobile phone roll-out, mentioned in Chapter 17) and are investors in Orascom Telecom Algeria, a company that went from a start-up to the largest private-sector company in Algeria in about three years. On financial services we've backed Oragroup, a banking group in West Africa, and together with some of our LPs we hold a control position in Continental Reinsurance, the largest re-insurer in Nigeria. Our agribusiness investments have included SIPH, the largest rubber producer in Africa, which we put together with Michelin's Nigerian business then exited via a listing on the Paris stock exchange. And we're invested in Finagestion, which provides water and power in Senegal and Côte d'Ivoire.

MB: Given that you have both private-sector and DFI LPs, do you find there is a tension between development goals and financial returns?

HD: In general, we don't. First of all, the DFIs are looking to make profits: they make it clear that they are expecting performance. And second, I think it is important to remember the spread of countries where ECP invests. Any tension with development goals is likely to be more of an issue for some of our competitors, who, as they are getting bigger, are maybe focusing more on South Africa, Nigeria and Egypt, looking to do big deals and getting into buyouts. That starts to look less like what the DFIs are interested in.

MB: How do you expect to be affected by the changes to CDC's strategy announced in 2011?

HD: We see CDC as an important investor and long-term supporter and would like the relationship to continue in the future. We think CDC's strategy fits well with ECP's model and track record – in seeking more investments in less developed countries, ECP (with on the ground presence across the whole of Africa including Ivory Coast, Nigeria, Tunisia etc., and with less focus on South Africa than other GPs) is well suited to help find investments that fit CDC's criteria.

MB: Will you allow them excuse rights to encourage them into your next fund, or encourage them to co-invest with you in specific projects that meet their new criteria?

HD: CDC is not alone among LPs to be looking to tailor its investments. ECP continues to look for the best deals on behalf of its investors and will offer CDC co-investment opportunities when they are relevant.

I think we are committed to investing across the widest possible number of countries within Africa and across the range of sectors and themes we've discussed, because it makes for pretty good diversification by geography, currency, industry and even type of exit.

When we look at what happened to private equity in, say, the USA in 2008, we think ourselves lucky that we're not depending on the New York Stock Exchange for exits. And, in general, it's pretty hard to have an African crisis – to some extent, the people in Zambia don't care what the Algerians are doing, they're not trading with them, they're not connected, there's no shared currency. It's not like Latin America, where, if Brazil and Mexico go, all the money is going to run out of Argentina too. So the flip-side of a lack of regional integration is a lack of regional contagion.

MB: What about political risk?

HD: We avoid what we consider political deals. We've got a team of professionals who are Africans from private equity and banking backgrounds and not ex-ministers who could give us access to special deals in some way. It is important to us in our due diligence that the deals we do and any concessions or whatever that the companies have are seen to have been obtained in the correct manner.

There's a lot more democracy in Africa than there was, and there's an election in a country where we invest every two months. We don't want to spend nights worrying that our guys are going to lose and get thrown out.

I think the African direction has been towards reducing the government role as well. There's no feeling from the people, for instance, that it would be great if the government owned the phone system; it's the opposite. There are obviously risks anywhere, and things can change fundamentally, but I think we can navigate political risks pretty well.

In terms of corruption, there's a self-selection process there too. ECP is an international firm with US government money, money from the EIB [European Investment Bank] and the French African Development Bank. We don't look like the natural guys to go and talk to about any funny business, because we have a low capacity to deal with that. On the contrary, it tends to be entrepreneurs who head up growing companies who say, 'If I can bring these guys in, that's going to look good, it will help me grow and lead to bigger things with bigger investors. They'll help me get access to finance, improve my governance standards and environmental compliance so I can attract more money and be the African champion in my sector.'

MB: You mention that your team is comprised mainly of Africans. How many nationalities are represented?

HD: We've got 12 nationalities, 14 native languages, and at all levels, not just the partners but also our analysts and associates. Our analysts, for instance, typically come from Wall Street or the French investment banks, have spent a couple of years there but are interested in getting back to Africa.

MB: You said you mainly invest in entrepreneur-led businesses. Are you mainly doing minority deals, growth capital? And what do you look for in the entrepreneurs?

HD: We'd definitely categorise ourselves as growth investors. Historically we're significant minority investors about 70 per cent of the time and majority investors the rest. Usually we're backing entrepreneurs, but sometimes we're alongside multinationals: for instance, Veolia in the water and electricity distribution and waste-water treatment business in Morocco.

We typically do deals at around $50 million. Our key criteria are that we can see an exit – we've had around 20 exits, and being able to return capital to investors is critical – a sustainable competitive advantage, high growth, alignment of interest with the sponsor [the entrepreneur], his reputation and alignment in terms of what he wants to do and how he sees the role of private equity and opening up the company as a way to prosper jointly over the next few years.

MB: What types of exits do you look for? I'm conscious that some of the countries you operate in don't have developed stock markets, and there maybe aren't that many multinationals active in them.

HD: Where we are minority investors, sale back to the sponsor is certainly one option – once these companies have grown, they can access more funding, cheaper debt based on the cash-flows of the business. We've had some successful exits that way. Next is listings. These don't have to be in the market where you're operating; they can be in one of the five or six countries in the region that have stock markets – South Africa, Egypt, Morocco, Nigeria, to a lesser extent Tunisia and Kenya. That's typically a solution for profitable businesses, because dividends are very important to the local investors. Then there are the international markets – London, and to some extent, Paris, and for the resource companies, Toronto or Australia.

Another method I think is going to increase over time is trade sales. Over the decade that ECP has been investing there have been more multinationals interested in entering Africa. Then there are the trade sales within the continent, as businesses look to expand: for instance, Moroccans wanting to come down south into Senegal or into West Africa, or the Nigerians wanting to expand into Ghana and Kenya.

The Chinese typically have not been big buyers of companies in Africa, but they are starting to do so now. Just last year they bid for Anvil Mining, which we've had a position in, and the Indians – less from their government, more from their companies. And finally the Gulf investors, who have access to capital but relatively small markets, are interested in businesses in North Africa.

MB: And do you do all-equity deals?

HD: Typically our companies have leverage on their balance sheets but we don't have much in the way of acquisition financing. Often the companies are raising equity investment so they can then go on and raise more debt to finance growth. But we do have a number of structured investments, so our money does not all go in as straight equity. We have preferreds, we might have debt with warrants in order to give us downside protection while maintaining a form of equity upside.

MB: How volatile is what you do – relatively small-cap investments in African businesses?

HD: [Shows MB a pie chart breaking down the firm's exits by IRR.] About half our exits achieve IRRs in excess of 40 per cent, about 20 per cent achieve 20 to 40 per cent, around 15 per cent do less than 20 per cent, and we write off our capital in about 4 or 5 per cent of deals.

MB: How were you impacted by the financial crisis in 2008/9?

HD: Africa continued to grow, it's just that the rate came down from 6 per cent to 2. Access to finance dried up. Our companies are generally not that levered, but any businesses that ran into difficulties during that period found it very hard to raise any money, which made for a stressful time.

MB: A lot of money was raised by private equity firms for Africa last year [$1.5 billion]. Is it a bubble, or do the fundamentals justify it?

HD: We're pretty bullish, as you'd expect, but then we were bullish on African private equity in 1999 when no one had really done much. I see the same factors at work as I see in the rest of the world. We never thought Africa was different, that the people were different, that things wouldn't work.

For me, Germany pre-1989 and Korea today are examples of what happens when you have good and bad economic systems at play. The West Germans were maybe ten times richer than those in the East; the South Koreans are 20–30 times richer than those in the North. It's a similar thing in Africa. A couple of decades of bad governance was able to make things go badly, and for the past decade or more the continent has been catching up, the people are going to do it. I think there will be more competitors popping up, but in the end that shows we've been doing our job.

MB: How do you see the influx of capital changing the industry?

HD: Obviously Carlyle has announced that it's getting into private equity in Africa. I wouldn't want to comment too much on what their strategy is, but we would expect them to stay in some of the bigger markets. The big US or European shops are not going to show up with a pan-African approach, looking to do deals in Igala [a region of Nigeria] or something. The big guys are buyout guys, take-private guys, therefore we've seen them show up in South Africa, where they can do that type of business. The rest of Africa is a growth equity market, with a very local feel. I'm sure if the Blackstones of this world thought they could get a couple of billion dollars away in a strategy that made sense to them they might try it one day, but that day hasn't happened yet.

I think there could be more generational shifts, buying people's businesses because their daughters or sons don't want to take them over. In time, we could see public to privates, but it could be a decade before getting funding from, say, Nigerian banks to buy Nigerian companies off the exchange is a major part of the business, in part because there are not enough companies on the stock exchanges of Africa and it would be hard to get control of any of them, and in part because there's still a fair amount to do on the growth side.

I think there's a huge potential market in real estate private equity in Africa that's pretty much untouched. When you look in the developed markets, those fund sizes are comparable to the whole of private equity in Africa. And African real estate is still very hard to finance, so I think there's good money to be made there.

Clearly there's also the question of how long private equity on the continent stays pan-African. Does it go sub-Saharan, does it go regional? I there'll be room for that, that's going to be more important. Ten years from now there will be East African funds. But there will still probably be room for pan-African and sub-Saharan African business plans and therefore funds to fund those businesses. And there will be industry-specific funds.

MB: And how about the changing role of DFIs?

HD: There's always the risk for the industry that the DFIs pull back too early, that they don't recognise the importance of what they're doing in terms of building private equity funds in Africa. There's also, I think, a risk of importing some of the rules and terms that are relevant for developed markets into developing markets. For instance, there's the idea that the GP should put up 3 or 5 per cent of the money. That's not the reality of who the new GPs are, they're not going to be in a position to put $3 million into their first $100 million fund.

There are also regulatory risks that could make it tough to raise money in Europe. One problem we have is that we have a fundamentally higher cost structure, our model is based on having offices all over the place and we have to fly around a lot. To have to have a European nexus before we could go fundraising would risk slowing the whole thing down.

MB: How do you see ECP evolving over the next five or ten years?

HD: In five years' time we'll hopefully be investing our Africa fund IV, and I think we'll have a similar team, perhaps a little bit bigger, raising a fifth fund that's maybe a little larger. We will probably have an office in Nairobi. [The firm is currently in Washington DC, Johannesburg, Douala (Cameroon), Paris, Abidjan (Côte d'Ivoire), Tunis, Lagos and Casablanca.]

The past ten years has gone by fast. I think the next ten will as well. So I think our strategy is going to last for ten more years, but I think there is a question when you get to that length of time of whether there is a role for independent firms as the market matures.

MB: So ECP could at some point be picked up by one of the big groups?

HD: Yes, exactly, once this is institution-sized, they've got the relationships and they can raise the money more easily, and I suspect that they will. Certain firms at some point will buy. They are already buying Brazilian firms; that means five years from now they will be looking to buy African firms too.

MB: So that could be your exit?

HD: I'm not sure it would mean an exit, typically they want you to stay around and actually do the work. But yes, I think it's a possibility.

Another factor is that local investors will start to be big. The other question is how long does it take before the GPs can have enough size that they can invest hundreds of millions of dollars per transaction and will there be a bubble in Africa? It'd be nice for me to be around still investing when the bubble happens. It's going to be a lot of fun when people are throwing money at us. It hasn't quite happened yet, but when I look at Brazil I see they're getting a lot of money...

MB: It seems to me there's a tipping point in any given emerging market where people come to accept that the place is fundamentally capable of generating returns on a par with the developed world, then capital flows in quite quickly.

HD: If that happened, it would be good for Africa. When we were just starting our fundraising in '99, I remember *The Economist* ran a front cover which said something like, 'Africa: The Hopeless Continent.' It was a picture of some ten-year-old kid with an RPG. I thought, 'Great, this is going to be a tough fundraising.'

That kind of story is not in the news much these days, but I'd like the story of modern Africa to get more of a hearing. It's entrepreneurial and it's fast-growing. That's why I'm excited about investments such as Wananchi Group, East Africa's first triple-play TV, telecoms and broadband company, or Lilas, a female entrepreneur who makes diapers and feminine hygiene products in Tunisia, which we invested in to help expand production into Algeria. I think if Wananchi works it's going to be a heck of a deal. And Lilas is a great company.

19

Mustafa Abdel-Wadood, Chief Executive Officer, Abraaj Capital Ltd, and Tom Speechley, Chief Executive Officer, Riyada Enterprise Development

If private equity in emerging markets is about balancing strategies that benefit from the increasing participation of its peoples in the mass affluence taken for granted in the developed world with targeting capital towards those countries and populations currently held back by a lack of finance, I believe that few firms better combine the two approaches than Dubai-based Abraaj Capital.

On the one hand, the MENASA [Middle East, North Africa and South Asia] investor possesses many of the characteristics of a mature, developed-market fund manager. It is now two years into investing its fourth fund, a $2 billion buyout vehicle, having already returned more than $3 billion to investors; it is a multi-asset manager, having also a $2 billion growth and infrastructure fund and a (Sharia-compliant) property vehicle; its corporate governance code is more extensive than that followed by many publicly quoted UK companies; and it operates a stakeholder engagement programme that is among the most far-sighted of any private equity firm, anywhere in the world. It is also a firm that generates proven returns, with its first two funds having delivered IRRs of 67 and 70 per cent.

On the other hand, Abraaj is also among the region's largest investors in SMEs, initially through its 2009 vintage, $650 million Riyada Enterprise Development (RED) fund, which puts to work sums as small as $500,000 (less in some territories) to pump-prime the growth of SMEs in the Middle East and North Africa and subsequently through its 2011 acquisition of Kantara, a $161 million SME fund active in the Maghreb countries of Morocco, Algeria, Tunisia and Egypt. And in early 2012, the firm acquired the ex-CDC Aureos Capital fund manager. Integrating the 153 portfolio companies in Africa, Asia and Latin America, representing $1.3 billion under management, has made Abraaj almost certainly the world's largest investor in emerging-market SMEs.

Abraaj's mainline funds pursue strategies based unashamedly on the pursuit of commercial returns. Many of its investments are made in relatively affluent countries such as Jordan and Turkey and its native United Arab Emirates and in sectors targeting the wealthy, such as luxury yacht construction and maintenance, private schooling and medical services. So it is unsurprising that its investors are private-sector ones, rather than DFIs. In contrast, around half the capital managed by RED and Kantara is from DFIs, though it is heartening that a number of mainstream Abraaj investors also participate in those funds. And with the firm boasting a total of 12 offices in as many countries, even before the Aureos acquisition, there is a sense that the more philanthropic SME funds are made possible by their ability to piggy-back on the infrastructure created for the larger buyout and growth ones.

Given the range of funds and approaches, I felt it appropriate to interview two representatives of the firm: Mustafa Abdel-Wadood, Chief Executive of Abraaj Capital, and Tom Speechley, Chief Executive of RED and the man overseeing the recently acquired Kantara fund. Before joining Abraaj, Abdel-Wadood worked for EFG-Hermes, the Egyptian investment bank, whose alumni are widely distributed within the region's private equity industry. He also co-founded Sigma Capital, a corporate finance and investment banking group, and prior to that was responsible for development and investments at Egypt's Orascom Group. Speechley's background is quite different: a UK-born corporate lawyer who has written two books on acquisition finance, he worked on the legals of private equity transactions, including a number of Abraaj deals, before being invited to join the team as a Senior Partner in 2006.

*   *   *

MB: You started with mainly regional LPs. Are these family offices in the Gulf?

MA-W: Yes, primarily high-net-worth individuals and family offices and a few institutions in the Gulf. These were people who invested with Abraaj in the early days or had historically invested with Arif Naqvi, the founder of Abraaj, on a deal-by-deal basis prior to Abraaj. Following that, the investor base grew to encompass a much broader group of institutional investors, especially as fund size grew and as the opportunity became more obvious to a broader group of investors on the back of our track record. By the time we had launched our third fund, the interest in the region and the opportunities presented by the region was broader than just regional investors. Today approximately 20 per cent is from outside the region.

MB: Is there a tendency for sovereign wealth in the region to want to either invest directly or to co-invest, rather than to invest as LPs?

MA-W: Different investors have different profiles. Some of them actually look for active co-investment opportunities, and that's part of the thinking behind investing in the fund. Others are pure fund investors. Depending on which institution you talk to, some SWFs [sovereign wealth funds] do have pockets for direct investments and will do deals directly.

MB: Your first two fully realised funds achieved IRRs of 67 and 70 per cent. How did you achieve those numbers?

MA-W: It's a combination of things. As with most emerging markets, most of the value creation comes from the actual growth of these businesses in terms of EBITDA over a period of time, so that's been the core driver of value creation. We have rarely seen leverage play any significant role in terms of value we're creating.

I think it's largely two things that make a difference when you invest in private equity. There's the selection process around the companies you invest in. We have a very strict selection process where we focus primarily on proprietary deals, not the deals being shopped around but the deals that we want to do. Historically around 70 per cent of our deals are proprietary. The second part is the value-creation process. These are primarily high-growth businesses to start with. We work with them to see how we can accelerate these growth plans through a combination of capital and the strategic support we provide and working on the different aspects we mentioned in terms of the governance and other value-creation levers.

MB: You said 70 per cent of your deals are off-market. So how do you source them?

MA-W: We have a number of senior people in our organisation; it's a very senior-skewed business. They know the region and have strong track records in it. We have 12 local offices on the ground; we don't rely on just sitting in our Dubai office and looking for deals. We spend time with businesses, and we leverage our networks, including our own investors. We engage and a lot of times deals don't happen at that point in time, but they come back at a later date and the pieces fall into place, but by that point they know us, we know them, they see us as a reliable counter-party.

I think one of the key factors that allows us to pre-empt auction processes and differentiates us is that when we talk to people they recognise that we've done it before. There's a number of companies in the past that we've backed that have been successful, so people acknowledge that we have had a positive contribution to a number of portfolio companies. The second thing is it's all about alignment and finding the right partner and investing in growth businesses. You can contrast that with the model that was adopted in Western markets prior to the crisis: the focus was on buy-outs and auction processes. Prices are a major determinant when you are looking at growth-capital-type transactions, obviously, but it's not the only one because in a lot of cases the founder or owner of the business is stay-ing on, believes in the growth opportunity so wants the right partner, as opposed to the partner who will simply pay the most. They look at you as someone they are going to work with.

MB: I see a lot of your deals are minority shareholdings.

MA-W: We have active minority shareholdings in some cases; we have con-trol stakes in some cases; we have equal control stakes in others. The core thing we look for is the ability to actively influence the outcome. In many ways we structure that into the deal, but they're not all majority deals. So for example, with GEMS [a UAE-based private school provider) we only have 25 per cent. The founder has 75 per cent. He was not willing to give up more than that, given his belief in the growth of the business, but he did want a partner to help him take it to the next level and that's how we came in.

MB: When you come on board as a shareholder, is your money going solely onto the balance sheet of the company or is some also going to the owner?

MA-W: Primarily onto the balance sheet. There are sometimes occasions when there may be some owners who are unrelated to the business who are effectively not involved and maybe disruptive or unaligned, so you want them out. The focus, generally speaking, is on money in the busi-ness to help support the growth of those businesses as opposed to cashing people out.

MB: Some of the companies you are dealing with are quite sizeable. Could the public markets be an option for them?

MA-W: We bridge the gap between being founder-/family-owned and being ready for the public markets or a trade sale. At a stage where they still have a large enough growth profile to justify the PE returns we seek. They need a bit of work before they're ready for the public markets or trade sale, and usually the work is around scaling up because scale is relevant in terms of public markets exits. It also involves establishing the things we discussed earlier, corporate governance and the framework of how to operate when dealing with outside shareholders. It's a very different model, and I think there's a bit of a learning curve before the mindset of the entrepreneur or principal is accustomed to having, or being accountable to, more than one shareholder.

MB: Are your exits mainly to trade, or public markets?

MA-W: Historically they've mostly been trade sales, but we've also backed a number of successful IPO exits.

MB: Are your trade sales to companies in the region, or multinationals?

MA-W: It used to be multinationals looking for entry points in the region; now it's a combination because now you have regional players that are consolidators themselves, national champions in their industries, looking for further growth in the region.

The regional players are more aggressive on consolidating the region today than are the multinationals. Ten years ago, when the mobile licences were being offered in the Arab world, it would be the Vodafones and the France Telecoms of this world bidding. Now it's the Zains and Orascom Telecoms. They're the ones who see the value and understand these markets and now have more appetite in terms of risk as far as these markets are concerned.

MB: Returning to deal-flow, what are your teams looking for?

MA-W: We think thematically first, so there's a screen around what makes sense in terms of investment themes over our investment cycle for each fund. In a lot of these markets there are some factors that weigh in their favour: demographics, for example. These are young, fast-growing populations with fast-growing economies, so increasingly these are domestic consumption stories. If you look at just the Arab world, that's 300 million people or more. If you look at the broader region, including Turkey, it's a much bigger number. If you include South Asia, then it becomes a huge number.

The demographics of the region make the story around increasing consumerism and themes around that consumer story work. So whether it's food, whether it's retail, whether it's consumer finance or banking, there is enormous upside. Banking is a great proxy on the growth on some of these economies.

The other theme is one around areas where the region is naturally competitive. If you look at some of the GCC [Gulf Co-operation Council] countries specifically and take the hydrocarbon resources for example, there's some investment ideas around that. We look at areas where the region is naturally strong. Take the fertiliser industry, for example: the region is a natural location for it. The reason is cheap energy, location works well for all the key markets, so it would make sense to look at an industry like fertiliser and consolidate it.

You look at areas where's there structural demand built into these under-invested economies. You look at healthcare, education – again the demographics and pent-up demand support investing in these sectors. That's generally how we screen.

Now specifically, because in a lot of these deals we are in partnership with people, we look for alignment. That's an easy word to just throw around, but you want to make sure that your counter-party wants the same outcome or understands the outcome that you want, that you want a business to grow to a certain level, that at some point you'll need to be exiting and that in order to get it to that level certain things need to be done, and these involve issues around operational efficiencies, governance, understanding that there are other owners. It's not about just taking the cheque and you get on with life; in reality, there's a responsibility that comes with taking that cheque.

You can do all the documentation in the world, but if you can't get comfortable around alignment, then you have an issue because the minute you have to pull that documentation out of a drawer you know that something's already gone wrong. So we structure deals very carefully to protect ourselves, but we also spend a lot of time with our partners, discussing where the business is going to go. It will never play out to an exact script, but at least you have a view as to how you would like it to go and then you have an adaptive process from there.

When we are conducting due diligence, we're also identifying where the gaps are, and that feeds back into what we call the value-creation plan and we spend time with the people saying OK, this is where we see the business, this is where we feel we could add value, this is where we feel there's value for both of us to contribute. That's another filter. We like to see good management: at least a core team that we can build on. You'll rarely have a management team in these growth businesses that's perfect across the board. Often you'll find the finance function or some other area is not up to par or has not grown fast enough to support the business growth. You'll often find someone who's been an entrepreneur and grown the business but in other organisational areas the business could probably be cracking at the seams, so there is a need to augment the management team.

MB: You mentioned alignment; one criticism that is levelled at emerging markets is that sometimes the legal systems don't work well in dealing with civil disputes.

MA-W: If you have to rely on the legal system to sort out your disputes in any market, you are already in a very disruptive situation. So which market the dispute is in almost a secondary issue. I would think that if you have to go down that route in the UK, the USA or Germany for that matter, you already have a bit of a challenge on your hands.

Having said that, we at least know what works and what doesn't work in the various jurisdictions we operate in, so we structure the deals in a local context. Our agreements are typically English law, and a lot of it is structured offshore so we do what can be done in terms of the legal agreements, and they're very strong *per se*, but I don't see agreements as a substitute for investing in a good businesses.

MB: Going back to your IRR figures, what are your typical hold periods?

MA-W: Typical hold period is a function of the cycles. We typically invest looking at a five-year horizon. Granted, if you're in a positive cycle you may achieve the growth and the returns ahead of time, and in order to optimise you may exit early, and hence that may somewhat explain those IRRs where you've had some fairly rapid exits. What we're trying to do is balance IRR with MOC [multiple on capital or cost]. Increasingly as we get more institutional investors who are more geared towards getting MOC as opposed to just driven purely by IRR, we target a balance of the two metrics for our returns.

MB: Your fund size has also increased in recent years: could this lead to the pursuit of different strategies, or to lower returns?

MA-W: The strategy has been consistent in that it's buy and build, playing on the growth dynamics of the region. We've always looked for businesses that can leverage their core strengths to have a stronger regional presence through a combination of organic growth and M&A. As fund sizes grew, we've looked at larger businesses with that same approach. The management in these larger businesses tends to be largely professional. You can argue that these larger businesses have a slightly lower growth profile, but we're still able to see substantial growth from regional expansion, and we also see less execution risk in terms of their growth plans and eventual exit.

MB: Over time has there also been an evolution in terms of geography, in that your roots are perhaps more in the Arab world and the recent expansion has been in North Africa and South Asia.

MA-W: We've historically focused on the Middle East, North Africa and bits of South Asia. About five or six years ago we added Turkey through a physical presence and a full Turkish team, and we have made a number of solid investments there. North Africa with exception of Egypt has always been part of our geography but historically was not a core focus. We didn't have a physical presence. We've now established one through acquiring a team with an established fund [Kantara] covering the Maghreb countries and are thus able to do it the justice it deserves.

Recently we've set up an office in Singapore with a team on the ground that looks for opportunities around South-East Asia. These are fairly similar markets in terms of characteristics and in terms of the investment opportunity, contiguous markets. We have experience in those markets through some of our portfolio companies expanding into them, and that's usually how we stretch our boundaries. We will continue to grow and expand our geography into other emerging markets, leveraging our networks and our expertise.

MB: I'm interested that you've invested in Turkey. It seems to me to have very attractive macro-economics, and yet there isn't that much private equity money going in.

MA-W: I think it is at a crossroads in terms of attracting Middle East and European capital. It falls somewhere in-between. A lot of Turkish corporates, especially in the past few years, have been looking east and south for growth, so we have significant value-add and a major selling point when we approach these businesses. They find that extremely attractive that we can open up markets that they see as fast-growing relative to Europe. We have found Turkish companies to be good operators in an emerging markets' environment, and they have the emerging markets' DNA so understand how to grow outside their markets. Turkey has attracted a lot of capital in terms of multinationals choosing to operate in there, and I think Turkish conglomerates themselves have evolved and now are key players. In terms of financial sponsors covering the Turkish market, we would be one of the largest. There's a handful of players still, despite the opportunity.

MB: And what is the thinking behind the office in Singapore? Isn't that a mature market? And there's a lot of capital there, not least the sovereign wealth fund Temasek that buys anything that looks attractive.

MA-W: We're there because it's the gateway to South-East Asia, just as Dubai is the gateway to the Arabian Gulf, though we would also like to invest in Singapore itself. Indonesia and Malaysia are sizeable countries with favourable demographics. There are quite a few markets around South-East Asia that are attractive from a PE perspective. If you look at most of the large emerging markets such as Turkey or Indonesia, the perception is that there's a lot of PE activity, whereas in fact they are under-invested. The demographics are attractive, the private sector is taking a much more active role, and there's the emergence of strong local businesses that are looking for capital to help them pursue that growth. Our model tends to work well in such markets.

MB: Will your strategy stay the same in South-East Asia? Some people would look at Malaysia and, especially, Indonesia as big growth areas for outsourcing as China experiences upward pressure on labour costs.

MA-W: You could play the outsourcing and export story, but ultimately that's not the big theme for most of these emerging markets. The long-term story is about domestic consumption.

MB: How about political concerns?

MA-W: Political concerns have always been a consideration when it comes to emerging markets. I think one thing that we can probably do better than most is strip out reality from perception. There is obviously a reality around that political risk, and it's just one of those things that you have to build into your thinking, but in today's world you get that volatility in different forms everywhere. In today's volatile world, all markets have their risks. Europe has its risks. The USA has its risks. Some of the biggest risk recently came from the developed markets.

Even in the areas where we've had regime changes, such as Egypt, we look at businesses we've invested in there, and life goes on. Obviously you have to constantly reassess things in the context of new policies of the regimes. What is the impact? What is the growth? You've got to look at that, but if you believe in the overall macro and you take a long-term view they remain good investments. Those are issues you do have to deal with and they are real. It's a combination of taking that right view there and diversification across a number of these markets.

MB: Where do you draw the line in terms of the risk factors?

MA-W: Iran is not somewhere we invest in, due to current sanctions and restrictions. Syria is also a challenge. So what do we look for? Large markets, such as Turkey, Indonesia, Egypt, Saudi Arabia. Underlying economic growth. Countries with relatively developed capital markets and a history of M&A activity. A regulatory framework that's relatively conducive. A level playing field is also a key element if you are investing long-term. The more a country has a level playing field, the more attractive it is from a PE perspective and also in terms of SME investing.

Some markets that don't have all these characteristics can be accessed indirectly via expanding the geographic activities of the portfolio companies, thereby capturing the market opportunity with less direct exposure, or by SME investing. In some countries, big business does not operate on a level playing field, and that is a negative as it can cut both ways. The SME space is below the radar screen, and accordingly it's a much more level playing field.

I think one of the positives of the Arab Spring is that you're creating more accountable governments and accordingly a more level playing field, and even if as a result of these developments you have muted growth for a year or two, ultimately that combination of more accountable governments and a more level playing field can only be a good thing and will result in a more inclusive economic growth model.

MB: This is the patronage theme, the idea that some business environments favour certain incumbent firms?

MA-W: It's also not an environment that is conducive to entrepreneurship *per se* because people only take risks if they feel they'll pay off. If they don't, then they just don't even bother. So the minute they feel entrepreneurial efforts will be rewarded, you'll find that the level of entrepreneurial activity in these countries just shoots up dramatically. If the system is clogged and distorted because of patronage or rent-based economies, there's a massive challenge.

MB: So is this part of the strategy in also having SME funds, that it enables you to go into markets where the big companies don't face a level playing field or where there isn't a mature M&A market?

MA-W: It's a bit of that; also, a lot of the opportunities that we see are SMEs, and when we started out, as our initial fund was relatively small, by definition we did small and mid-market deals. We did well in that space and continue to see very solid opportunities, so it is also opportunity-driven.

MB: Tom, what is your perspective on that opportunity?

TS: On the one hand you've got all the macro factors that make private equity investing in the region solid, but also SMEs have been overlooked by finance for years and so there's not much competing capital. Secondly, because of the nature of the markets that we operate in, which are relatively fragmented, there's not been a great deal of consolidation, you don't have lots of multinational corporates. SMEs are still fighting for serious market share in a lot of traditional industries, and they pretty much dominate in new industries, so you have an opportunity, right now, to get companies that are in market-leading positions but that are SMEs. SMEs are also a vital part of the solution for job creation in the region. So investing in them makes sense for the local economies too.

MB: It's interesting that your LPs are around a 50:50 mix of DFIs and private money. Is there any conflict between the development goals and economic returns?

TS: I don't think so. We definitely put return as our main target. But because of the way we're investing, we will end up creating a positive developmental impact as it is about long-term, economically sustainable investing. It's the opposite of the grant mentality. If we invest well, people will come back to us with more money to invest – in effect, to re-invest the profits we made for them – so it becomes self-sustaining and the second [target] is that if we invest in the right way we create jobs and economic growth. And by 'right way', I mean investing for growth, specifically growth equity in SMEs.

MB: Are there geographical conflicts? For instance, the UAE might offer safer returns than parts of Africa.

TS: Our SME funds are mostly investing outside of the GCC. But even within the GCC, SMEs have been neglected and under-funded, and by investing in SMEs you contribute to wealth trickle-down, which has not necessarily happened even in the wealthy states.

MB: Are you generally backing existing entrepreneurs, or are there any buy-ins?

TS: We don't do buy-ins; we're looking at companies where there's an existing management solution. In almost every case they're founder-led.

MB: What financial returns are you targeting?

TS: If you look at the fund prospectuses, you will see 30 per cent and 3x return. However, because of the types of investment we typically make, I would say the businesses we aspire to invest in tend to generate significantly more than 30 per cent.

MB: I see that you are targeting around 100 relatively small investments.

TS: Yes. It's a function of the structure that we have, which is a master fund for the broader MENA [Middle East and North Africa] region, then country funds. We will end up investing in, on average, ten companies per country team, either directly through the master fund or through the country funds. When you put that all together, it adds up to investing in about 100 companies, which in our view is unusual and frankly ground-breaking, but it is also efficient and manageable, given the structure that we have put in place. We've hired about 30 investment professionals, aiming to have two or three in each country and a central resource base out of Dubai supporting them.

MB: I'm keen to understand the differences between these firms and those that Abraaj might invest in. Can you give me an example of a typical RED or Kantara deal?

TS: Let me talk about one in Palestine. It's a company called Thimar, and it illustrates the impact you can have through investing in SMEs. It's run by a gentleman called Imad Nusseibah, who grows herbs in the Jericho Valley and sells them into the USA. They are some of the most expensive herbs in the world. Part of the reason is that the Jordan Valley, just outside Jericho, where his land is, is a long way below sea-level, so the ultra-violet radiation is lower and the temperature is more temperate. That benefits his growing patterns and the quality of the product. In addition, the water comes up through artesian wells that are sunk into the Jericho Valley, and they create a very strong flavour for these herbs.

Everything he produces is sold. Yet no bank would give him a loan to finance growth, partly because he's in agriculture and partly because his was a relatively informal business at this stage. We came along and our investment enabled Imad to acquire additional land and water, so that almost overnight he was able to treble his capacity. In the space of three months he more than doubled his workforce and employed a lot more women from the local area. With RED's assistance, he is also building a packing house where he can oversee the packaging himself and brand the products as his own, something he wasn't able to do before.

What does he achieve with this? He achieves greater quality control over his brand, which inherently is value-creative, and he moves up the value chain with his products. You can do all of this with around $2.5 million of investment. So an entrepreneur has increased his production three-fold and our investment benefited commensurately. Obviously there's more to do, we've got to realise that investment at some point, but we think that food's a sector that will consolidate.

We've got a similar business in Egypt that produces artichokes which are also sold to the USA and Europe – a similar story in the sense that the founder started off by cutting and trading fresh artichokes, and he realised that by canning them he could augment the value of his product. We're helping him with additional facilities, acquisition of land and all the other aspects of institutionalising the business, financial reporting, and setting in place better governance.

MB: Taking the Palestinian example, what stake do you hold, and are you concerned about the prospects for an exit?

TS: We hold just less than 50 per cent. It's true that the Palestinian market is not especially liquid, but our view is that there will be consolidation because SMEs still have significant market share as there have not been the multinationals there to do the consolidating. It doesn't matter whether you are the big fish that eats up all the small fish or the small fish that gets eaten up by the big fish; you'll still find your liquidity event.

MB: So could the next stage be for you to provide development capital so some of these agribusinesses can buy out their competitors?

TS: If we invest in 100 companies, is it possible that ten will be in agriculture and food production? Yes. Then you start to get options, because first the regional consolidators start to look at you, then the internationals for footprint market share.

MB: So by pursuing a regional rather than national investment strategy by sector, even if there aren't natural buyers within a country, you may be able to access a regional or multinational one?

TS: Exactly.

MB: This could also represent quite an attractive valuation arbitrage, because you're buying into SMEs in a country where capital is constrained with the intention of rolling them up and selling them to consolidators at international prices.

TS: Yes, but you'd never assume in an investment thesis that we're going to make returns from multiple expansion.

MB: I see you are mainly acquiring minority stakes. Why not go for control?

TS: I'd almost go as far as to say that we positively do not want controlling majority positions in SMEs. Why? Because we want the founder entrepreneurs to continue to believe that these are their businesses and that they are working first for themselves, and only second for us. That's the essence of entrepreneur-led businesses, I think. We prefer to take around a 30 per cent stake. We ensure that everybody signs up to an agreed business plan; there are board discussions around anything outside of that, with reserved matters. We use preferred equity as our main instrument because there are certain rights that you want to have as the institutional investor including rights around exit, but also preferences in a liquidation scenario, for example.

MB: How enforceable are contracts in these markets?

TS: Compared to the BRICs I think we probably have favourable legal systems or favourable ability to enforce contracts, actually. It's one of the great ironies that the BRIC countries that take the lion's share of the emerging market private equity commitments have some of the worst levels of corruption and enforceability of contracts.

MB: Are you looking for the same things as Abraaj in a deal?

TS: We're looking for three things. One, the entrepreneur needs to be a winner. Two, the quality of the earnings and the projected growth is strong. And three, that it's the right place and time for that business.

MB: It seems to me the balance between supply and demand for capital is very different in the markets where you're investing from some other emerging markets.

TS: That's a big part of the opportunity. In India and China there are so many fund managers chasing the deals that the entrepreneurs drive the deals and not the investors, in a sense. We won't go into a competitive process. For us, it is all about the quality of the conversation we're having with the entrepreneur. On the one hand, it's a relationship that we've maybe built up over years and they'll say they're opening up the capital of their company and would we like to come in as their partner. On the other hand, it's about maximising price: the highest bidder wins.

MB: What about the value-creation strategy?

TS: Everyone signs up to a Value Creation Plan before we invest. It isn't just about money, it's also helping them hire people. SMEs that we back can hire people they wouldn't otherwise have been able to attract. It happens all the time that I'll pick up the phone to the person we want to hire – a CFO, for example – and say we're coming into a company, we really want them in there. They become part of the Abraaj family as a result, and people find that attractive. And third, we upgrade their internal financial reporting considerably. We have an IT solution that's almost proprietary that creates an interface between us and the company. The company provides the monthly management report, but they also use it for business intelligence, so for the first time they get a powerful tool that can enable them to look at the working capital position, customer acquisition, you name it, on a monthly basis.

MB: How do you see SME growth capital investment developing in your region over the next few years?

TS: Dearth of capital is one of the themes we will continue to see. You will also see dual-track growth shaped by companies that can gain access to capital, as opposed to those that can't. I also see the macro fundamentals and demographics continuing to support a regional growth story; but ultimately it is also a function of how much capital comes into this space.

MB: Economic theorists would say that if you deliver good returns, other capital will come into the space as they see you earning an economic rent.

TS: We hope it does, to be honest. It validates what we're doing. We've scratched the tip of the iceberg. We've looked at 450 companies in the last 12 months; we could probably have invested in a lot more than we did.

There's a real entrepreneurship rejuvenation going on in the region. It's a bit like the democratic or political self-determination that's gone on: people have also decided on economic self-determination. There aren't the jobs out there, so people are saying, right, I'm going to take it into my own hands, I'm going to create a business.

MB: And Mustafa, how are you seeing the future, for Abraaj, and for private equity in the region?

MA-W: The most significant event in recent financial history, the fall-out from global financial crisis, has had a major implication on PE globally and to a certain extent regionally. In the region pre-crisis you had announcements of perhaps 40 or 50 funds. It was mostly home-grown stories, first-time fund managers and teams coming together because money was flying around, deciding to launch, and then the reality is, that never lasted long enough for anything to happen.

The market has now contracted to one where only the serious established players with track records and solid teams have survived. Those that were disciplined and differentiated did emerge stronger – you didn't have to be the biggest, you had to be among the best – and I think you now have a much more disciplined industry as a result. I think people have gone back to basics. LPs differentiate based on track record and what they believe teams can deliver. That was important, we had to go through that.

Increasingly investee companies are starting to understand the role that private equity can play. They understand that they need to select the right partner, as opposed to simply playing off firms against each other in order to maximise valuation. There is also an increased understanding of the danger of excessive leverage and a better appreciation for a growth-based investing model focused on active investing.

I think one of the challenges that remains is less of a regional issue and more of a global challenge, which is what's happening with equity markets worldwide and that affects exits. However, those are cycles you go through, and we're still seeing that, for the right assets, you're seeing interest.

MB: How about the risk that the big US mega-funds will turn up in your region, as they have in India?

MA-W: The active investment model has shown that you need to be there on the ground. If it's a major commitment for them and they are willing to have the staying power and the commitment and it's not a fringe strategy, then, yes, there's room. I think ultimately this needs to be a core business for anybody in order for it to succeed.

MB: Do you think there are things that private equity in developed markets can learn or adopt from what works in your region?

MA-W: I think it's something they knew but perhaps forgot as leverage became easy, which is that the role that private equity plays is to bridge a specific period in the life-cycle of the business. That role often involves active support around the growth strategies of that business, it's not purely about financial engineering. I think it's not a lesson they don't know; it's something they know but conveniently forgot.

20

Hisham El-Khazindar, Co-Founder and Managing Director, Citadel Capital Ltd

It is striking that while GPs and LPs alike have spoken of the 'two-plus-20' model coming under pressure at the margins, the fundamental structure of private equity – a closed-end, ten-year fund, extendable by up to four years, with investment decisions made by a professional general partner and capital provided by limited partners – remains largely unchallenged. I wanted to finish the main body of this book by interviewing the co-founder of one of the few firms that has successfully operated within a profoundly different format, to establish whether it could provide a useful model for other firms.

The manager in question is Egypt-based Citadel Capital. Founded in April 2004, the structure (see Figure 20.1) consists of four types of entity:

1. Citadel Capital itself, the general partner. This is listed on the Cairo stock exchange and is majority-owned by management and staff. It generates revenues from three sources: dividends and capital gains generated by investing in portfolio companies as a limited partner (Citadel Capital generally provides 10 to 20 per cent of the capital deployed in its transactions); management fees and carried interest earned as a general partner; and, finally, advisory fees charged to investee businesses for strategic input, M&A activity and recruitment;

2. Two Joint Investment Funds (JIFs), one focusing on the Middle East and North Africa and the other purely on Africa, which contain mainly money from DFIs such as the International Finance Corporation (IFC), the African Development Bank (AfDB), the Netherlands Development Finance Company (FMO), the Société de Promotion et de Participation Pour la Coopération Economique (Proparco), Deutsche Investitions und Entwicklungsgesellschaft mbH (DEG) and the European Investment Bank (EIB), which collectively will invest $2 for every $1 provided by Citadel in the kinds of projects that appeal to DFIs;

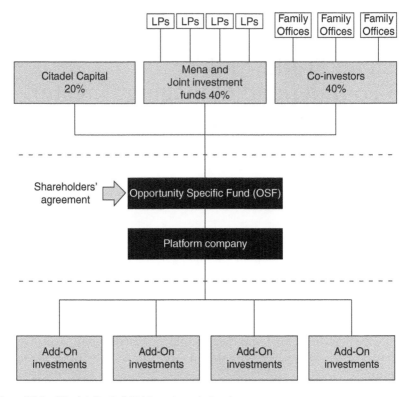

Figure 20.1   Citadel Capital Ltd investment structure

3. Co-investors, mainly sovereign wealth funds and family offices from the region, which collectively provide the greater part of the capital for most of the firm's transactions;

4. Opportunity-specific funds (OSFs). These sit at the heart of what makes Citadel different from other private equity firms, and go a long way towards explaining why other aspects of the structure differ from the norm.

An OSF is a holding or platform company created by Citadel as a vehicle for managing a series of related companies that together are expected to become a single, synergistic entity. In most cases these businesses are acquired; sometimes they are created from scratch. There are currently 19 OSFs, spanning sectors such as cement, mining, energy, food, transportation and logistics and metallurgy. The approach is to acquire a national champion and then build around it, expanding up and down the supply chain or geographically within the region.

To illustrate the vertical expansion model, consider the example of agriculture and consumer food brands. In August 2007 Citadel established an

OSF for the sector, Gozour Holding, funded 20 per cent from its own balance sheet and 80 per cent from co-investors. Its first transaction was the acquisition of Dina Farms, Egypt's largest privately owned farm and the country's leading producer of fresh milk. The firm subsequently added Elmisrieen, a leading cheese brand, and Enjoy, the country's second-largest milk and juice drink brand. Both FMCG brands received significant management attention and investment on joining the portfolio, with the former beginning its first TV advertising campaign for a decade and the latter benefiting from upgrades to its production facilities. Together with other acquisitions, a portfolio of eight businesses has been brought together in a single consumer-facing entity, the strategy being to capture the entire value chain from early stages of cultivation/ production to the end consumer in what is otherwise a highly fragmented market.

Perhaps Citadel's most ambitious project to date, and certainly the most impressive demonstration of use of OSFs to pursue geographical expansion, is its project to put together an integrated logistics and transportation network along the eastern side of North Africa. The project had its roots in the observation that, prior to 2007, 96 per cent of goods and raw materials were transported within Egypt by truck, an unusual situation brought about by subsidies to fuel prices. Citadel took the view that, with oil prices rising and the subsidy likely to be removed, there would be a growth in rail and river transportation.

Egypt's rail network is state-owned, and the government was unlikely to privatise it or enter into a commercial partnership, so Citadel instead created a holding company, Nile Logistics, initially to buy and refurbish existing barges (it has since constructed a fleet of new, environmentally friendly vessels) and to develop and refurbish river tunnels, in order to make the transportation of goods by river an attractive alternative. At the other end of the network, in northern Sudan, river transportation is the dominant player due to the road and rail alternatives being unreliable, so Nile Logistics acquired a control stake in the existing business that moves freight between Khartoum and Juba on the water and invested in trucking firms that could shift loads between river ports and their sources or destinations.

Citadel created a second platform company, Africa Railways, to acquire a control stake in a concession to operate the Rift Valley Railway, which consists principally of century-old tracks laid down by British and French colonists. The firm is not only refurbishing the line and introducing operational improvements but, crucially, is also extending it so that, in conjunction with Nile Logistics, it offers an integrated transportation solution between Egypt's Mediterranean ports (Cairo and Alexandria) and other African sea ports at Port Sudan and Mombasa, on the Indian Ocean. In time, it hopes to link up this rail network with rivers that lead to a number of other ports across Southern and Eastern Africa to create a pan-African integrated logistics business.

Prior to the Arab Spring, 84 per cent of Citadel's investments were based in Egypt; while the demographics of the country and its physical location may be positives, the events of the past two years have demonstrated that heavy dependence on one nation within an emerging market carries risks. Citadel's share price has suffered as political turbulence in its home country impacted on trading in portfolio businesses and delayed expected exits. The firm had to raise additional capital in late 2011 through a rights issue and announced a change of strategy: a renewed focus on operational improvements and exits, with further investments unlikely until 2013, from which point it expects only 40 per cent of capital to be put to work in Egypt, with increased allocations to other countries in Africa and the Middle East.

Citadel's co-founders Ahmed Heikal (Chairman) and Hisham El-Khazindar (Managing Director), the latter of whom I interviewed, worked together at EFG Hermes, with Heikal in particular having been instrumental in the early 1990s in driving its growth from a financial consultancy boutique into its role as the region's leading investment bank. There they helped the national champion telecoms firm, Orascom, to leverage the mobile phone licence it held in Egypt to acquire licences elsewhere in the region, subsequently taking it to IPO. It is perhaps no coincidence that Abraaj's Mustafa Abdel-Wadood too is an alumnus of both of these companies, an illustration of the fact that liberalisation in financial and professional services and consumer businesses in emerging markets not only creates jobs and wealth in those firms but also provides a platform for the personal development of the next generation of entrepreneurs and investment professionals for the region.

*   *   *

MB: What's the background to the two of you setting up Citadel?

HE-K: Around the time that we did the IPO of Orascom Telecom in 2000, EFG had started developing a private equity business of its own, whereby it would syndicate opportunities on a deal-by-deal basis, with EFG as a minority investor, but not within a formal fund structure with EFG acting as a GP; it was more consortiums of investors for each project doing minority growth capital investing.

Some of these deals did very well. In the telecom space EFG invested alongside Vodafone in the second GSM [Global System for Mobile communications] licence in Egypt and that did very well. Others, such as an investment in media, turned out quite badly, and Ahmed left EFG in 2000 to focus full-time on trying to turn around these investments because he felt a sense of responsibility to the other investors.

These experiences, where we had been acting as *de facto* advisers, fundraisers and executors of transactions on behalf of large corporates and where we had seen EFG as minority private equity investors do well on some deals, but less well on several other transactions, informed our decision in mid-2003 to establish a pure-play investment firm that would not have other financial service activity, that would be a hands-on control investor rather than as a passive financial investor, and would essentially do for itself and for its investors what we had been doing as advisers to some of the other corporates: go and look at industries where we saw opportunities for consolidation, for buy-and-build in the regions we knew, which for us were really North Africa and parts of East Africa. Ahmed had been going to Algeria since 1996, when no one would go there, and I'd been going with him to Ethiopia since 1997, so there was a breadth of relations and understanding of some of these markets that we had developed. We viewed Egypt as a good centre of gravity for North and East Africa, the way South Africa is a good centre of gravity for the southern part of Africa.

MB: How much private equity was there in the region at that time?

HE-K: EFG was the key player within Egypt, but 'key' doesn't say much because it was an underdeveloped industry. Elsewhere on the Middle East side you had some firms starting to do what they called private equity but which was really pre-IPO investing, where they would take positions in large companies as minority investors ahead of these companies being IPO-ed, and then on the African side, other than a few South African-focused players (and South Africa really has a dynamic of its own), there were virtually no African-based private equity firms doing private equity in sub-Saharan Africa, just a few US- and London-based old hands, such as Tom Barry at Zephyr. So we started at a very interesting point in time.

MB: You said you wanted to focus on control deals leading to consolidation and buy-and-builds. Why is that?

HE-K: If you look at emerging markets' private equity in general, I think you'll find it falling into two broad categories. You've got the more traditional players doing primarily minority growth capital: coming in to mid- to large-size companies, gaining a 20–30 per cent stake and trying to ride the growth of those businesses.

Our approach was a little bit different. It's probably closer to that of guys like GP Investimentos in Brazil, who we hadn't heard of at the time. But as we grew and developed, we realised that there were some other specialist firms doing exactly the same as us, which is not to think of ourselves as financial investors, but rather to think of ourselves as entrepreneurs or industrialists who use financial tools as they pursue opportunities. Our goal was to buy control of existing companies and in some cases establish companies from scratch when we saw gaps within certain sectors and bring together a certain vision, capital and the right management team, whether it's local or international. We wanted to end up being very hands-on owners of businesses who could act almost as strategics while we owned them, but at the same time to be financially sophisticated in the way we would fund these opportunities and in our willingness, unlike a family conglomerate, to sell a business at the right time when we'd be getting the value for it.

This was our driving philosophy from the beginning, and the first deal that we did was really the deal of a lifetime. We got extremely fortunate on that deal, but it was very representative of our strategy. In early 2004 we identified a highly distressed Egyptian group focused on cement and construction. That group was and is called ASEC. It was historically a cement technical services business that in 2000 had expanded in cement production through the acquisition of a state-owned cement play. It had funded that acquisition through leverage and had gotten unlucky, making the acquisition just at the point where, post-Asian financial crisis, post-internet bubble burst, post-September 11, we had the global slowdown, including a slowdown in the Middle East/North Africa and a drop in cement consumption and demand. So they hit a wall essentially, and when we started looking at that business it was technically bankrupt and the principal owner of the company was ailing – he had cancer – and was looking at potentially divesting the business. His daughters lived in Switzerland; they had no interest in taking over.

We started looking at that business and spent approximately eight months diligencing it, putting a plan together and lining up a management team to take over the firm. In the interim the owner passed away, and we went back almost to square one and started negotiating with his heirs. They appointed UBS as financial advisers, and they ran an auction, but a lot of the parties that were interested such as the global cement companies didn't have the benefit of having done all the work we'd done, so we were able to step in and put an offer to buy that business for $50 million. It owned a 4.5 million tonne cement plant and really was the school in Egypt as far as cement expertise is concerned but had huge debts, and therefore the equity ticket was very little.

Our offer was actually not the highest offer: Lafarge had put in an offer slightly higher than ours, but theirs had a lot of conditions associated with it, so the heirs and their advisers decided that our offer had a greater chance of being closed. We funded the transaction by borrowing $38 million from Barclays Capital as acquisition finance and raised $12 million of equity from friends and family, and some of that was money that we borrowed and put into the transaction, so we started the firm with £2 million Egyptian, at the time around $400,000 of our own capital.

We had an A–Z plan of how to turn it around and really got very lucky because the timing coincided with a recovery in the Egyptian economy, and cement prices and demand moved up a lot faster than we had anticipated, so the three-year turnaround plan ended up taking place in a year, and this company that was losing approximately £2 million Egyptian on a consolidated basis when we bought it, ended up making £150 million Egyptian of profit the next year.

All the global players that initially had looked at ASEC but had shied away because of the risks started approaching us to acquire the company, and we opted at the time not to exit the entire group but instead to sell its core asset, which was a cement-producing plant south of Cairo, and to retain the rest of the group and the expertise and develop it into regional cement play. We sold the cement plant for $560 million to Italcementi and obviously repaid the acquisition finance. Our investors made three or four times their money, and all of a sudden this firm, which we had started with $400,000 of capital, had $100 million of capital to invest, even after recapitalising ASEC for it to be able to pursue this expansion project and paying ourselves a nice dividend. This allowed us from that point on to continue to be able to be not just a fund manager but instead a principal investor that brought alongside us other third-party investors, but where we were always the lead. We have a lot of our own money at stake in the deals that we do, which makes for a different mindset, and investors recognise that.

MB: I can see that this was the start of the first part of the difference between Citadel and many other firms, in that you are able to put meaningful capital of your own into transactions. But how about the other aspects to your structure?

HE-K: Our heritage and the heritage of private equity in the region was that investment was typically raised on a per-project basis, and there remain some investors that prefer to pick which deals they participate in and which they don't. Investors in the Gulf, for example, which historically was the primary source of capital for us, are typically family offices or high-net-worth individuals who don't think of themselves as passive LPs, who are happy to pay the GP management fees and the carried interest, but want to pick which deals they get exposure to and typically want to have some form of representation on the boards of these companies.

But there was also a sub-set of investors, particularly Western institutional investors and development finance institutions which are backbone investors in the markets we invest in, that prefer traditional fund structures. That's why a couple of years ago we started raising two conventional funds, a MENA fund and an Africa fund, that would invest alongside us and alongside those investors that prefer to invest on a deal-by-deal basis.

So if you look at the structure today, we've got three pots. When we're doing a deal, you'll have us typically as the largest single investor. You'll have the MENA fund and Africa fund investing alongside us on a fixed ratio and then co-investors who like that particular deal.

The challenge of our model is that you need to stay very close to both your public market investors through analyst calls etc. and to your long-term co-investors, some of whom in the Gulf want to be very close to these investments and others, such as DFIs, who have requirements from an environmental and social perspective that you need to be able to meet. I think we've adapted over time to be able to address that, but Ahmed probably spends two-thirds of his time on the road, divided roughly equally between meeting with investors of the different types and looking at our different investments. I spend probably 40 to 50 per cent of my time on the road, and most of that is spent meeting with investors rather than visiting our subsidiaries or platform companies.

MB: And what about the fourth aspect of your structure, the platform companies or OSFs?

HE-K: Typically, when we're raising money, it isn't just for a specific acquisition or project but for a theme, so for instance if we're raising money for an investment in food processing, it won't just be for one deal but to use it as a base for multiple other acquisitions to create a regional play in that industry.

Just to put some numbers on that: as you know, we own a platform called Gozour in that sector. It started with the acquisition of the largest dairy farm in Egypt. We first had to put in a deposit of our own money of approximately $10 million to lock in that transaction. The price we had negotiated was approximately $80 million, but in fact we raised approximately $250 million of commitments, of which the first $80 million would be disbursed immediately to do the first acquisition. We wanted the expectation to be set among the investors that we were each putting in approximately a third initially of the sum we expected to draw down over the next three years.

MB: When you asked for $250 million, did you already have follow-on deals lined up for the remaining $170 million?

HE-K: No, it was an expectation, as opposed to anything else.

MB: It seems to me an interesting model. Have you thought about taking it to developed markets, doing the reverse of what the big fund managers do and hiring some Americans or Brits or Germans and investing in the USA or Europe using this model?

HE-K: We think of our strength as being that we understand the markets we invest in. Unlike a passive financial investor or an asset manager that might want to have a global footprint from a diversification point of view, we think of ourselves as industrialists and entrepreneurs who understand a number of markets very well and believe that we can generate disproportionate returns and have done so.

Even as we expanded from Egypt to North Africa, then to East Africa, it's been a very cautious, very slow process. When three years ago we bought the railway monopoly in Kenya and Uganda, which was really the flagship deal we've done in sub-Saharan Africa so far, that was after having spent three years in Kenya, Ethiopia, Uganda and Tanzania looking at a variety of opportunities there, either re-igniting or developing relationships. I fundamentally think of private equity and certainly of long-term investing – which is how we see what we do – as a local business. It's not a business that lends itself to global funds.

MB: Some of the big asset managers as they now call themselves are moving into Africa. What are your thoughts on that?

HE-K: The difference between a Citadel Capital and, say, a Carlyle is that Carlyle fundamentally is a fee-generating machine. The partners of Carlyle make most of their income out of management fees that they get on how much assets under management they have and therefore the incentive from their perspective is to expand globally, raise new funds and expand that fundraising machine. The principals might and do have some money in their funds, but the key source of revenues from their perspective is management fees and, to a lesser extent, carried interest.

Because of our structure, the key source of income for us is capital gains. So I'm more interested in focusing my capital on a relatively smaller number of opportunities, in a relatively focused geographic area that I understand very well, rather than stretching that capital and maximising third-party fees.

We have done 19 deals [OSFs] so far. We have not seen competition on any of them. This is a place where around a billion people live, and there is plenty of infrastructure and social development that needs to happen. I don't think one can talk about there being a great deal of competition within the next ten years or until another $20 billion or $30 billion of private equity has come into the market. Given where the world is at this point in time, people will be risk-averse for some while, and that will impact the amount of capital flowing into the region, and that will affect asset prices. So I don't think asset prices are in danger of over-heating within the next three or four years. And I am unable to see beyond that time-frame.

We did the Rift Valley Railway transaction originally for $50 million, and then we increased the capital. The same week, or maybe two weeks later, Berkshire Hathaway bought CSX [a railroad operating along the East Coast of North America] for $50 billion. The two are almost equivalent in terms of length of tracks.

MB: Do you think your structure could work in a developed market, if implemented by a GP that really knew that territory?

HE-K: Not a chance. Our model requires you to be able to do fundraising on a very quick scale that is more based on trust than on due diligence and information. Institutions in the West would rather make their due diligence once to invest in a fund, and that fund would then invest in 15, 18, 20 investments, whatever the number is. But in order for us to have this model, it is really premised on the fact that we can raise money fairly quickly and at a very fast pace. So if you want to do 15 investments, you are raising money not once, like the traditional fund structure is, but you are raising it 15 times.

MB: I understand that some of the sovereign wealth investors from Asia and the Middle East and also one or two of the North American pension funds are now focusing much more on co-investment. So wouldn't the deal-by-deal way of working that you have established work well for them?

HE-K: They are doing it, for a small number of large transactions. But they don't have the capability of doing due diligence on 20 or 30 investments at a time. It is harder to replicate what we do in an institutional setting. Our co-investors are mainly high-net-worth individuals and family offices that we know and who know us. Sometimes they have just 72 hours or a week maximum to wire the money to us. Who can do due diligence in that time? This is a system that is built on a trust relationship that is created over a long period of time. For institutions in the West to replicate the same model, they would have to employ 15 different teams to look at all the opportunities.

MB: So you see your strengths as being based around knowing the territories in which you operate and having relationships with non-institutional investors who trust you so will co-invest swiftly, without the need for their own due diligence?

HE-K: Our strength is we intermediate capital with opportunities in the Middle East and Africa. We have people who are able to play that role efficiently between the Gulf and the DFIs. We are able to tap a lot of pools of capital, and that capital is both equity and debt, and we are able to intermediate where there is a lot of development and growth that can take place in those places.

I fundamentally think that the term 'private equity' refers to very different things in different parts of the world. I know you're writing a book about the future of private equity, but to me, frankly, the future of private equity is different things that won't necessarily all be called private equity. I've said I think of what we do as long-term capital, not necessarily private equity, because what we do is fundamentally different than what is called private equity in the USA or in Europe.

There you've got fundamentally mature markets where the opportunity is in financially optimising mature companies that have existing cash-flows. What we do is really entrepreneurship and long-term investments on a large scale and behaving not so differently from the way a family-owned business would, except that we're financially more sophisticated, and, unlike traditional emerging market conglomerates, we don't feel the need to pass on businesses from father to son. We're willing to sell those businesses at the right time and if you look at how we've evolved – and that evolution is not complete – I think as time goes on, we're actually getting closer to an investment holding or a conglomerates model than to a US-style PE model.

We are having a strategic debate now internally about whether, over the next couple of years, we want to start focusing not just on the four or five core themes we're already focusing on, but within these themes, whether we should reduce the number of industries we have exposure to or be willing to take an even longer view, instead of five to seven years, potentially ten to 15 years and really act not just as a *de facto* strategic, but as an aggressive emerging market strategic across these industries. We're thinking carefully as to what that would mean for our co-investors and as to whether, perhaps, it might make sense to swap some of these investors into Citadel Capital so as to provide them with the liquidity that they need because they would own the listed stock and then instead of us owning 20 or 30 per cent of these businesses, owning a majority or 100 per cent of some of these businesses and that way shifting even closer to an investment holding model than to a US or a European PE model.

And the sense we're getting is that, perhaps, given some of the challenges presented by the markets we invest in, and the opportunities as well, that this might actually be a better model, that you don't want to find yourself having to exit after five years. That sometimes, you really want to take a longer view on deals.

If we're consolidating a small number of industries, and the ones we're thinking of are agriculture, mining, logistics and energy, increasingly people will look at us and apply a multiple to our cash-flows rather than to look at our NAV, because like most listed private equity we currently trade at a discount to NAV.

MB: Have you looked at Warren Buffett's vehicle, Berkshire Hathaway, as a model? Is that the kind of thing you would consider doing?

HE-K: They are probably a bit more passive than we are. Maybe we would like to think of ourselves more towards a GE model than a Berkshire Hathaway one. Not necessarily synergistic or fully integrated like a Unilever, but where you are deeply entrenched in the strategic direction of those companies. Were we to move in this direction, it would change our DNA. We would need to bring more operational people on board. Most of us at this time are transactional people. If we want to change this, we will have to admit a little bias towards stronger operational performance, and in order to do that, we would need to bring more operational people on board.

I think if I had to predict how Citadel would look at some future date, it may be that we would split into a conglomerate-type investment firm and a traditional private equity business, because there could be scope to pursue both strategies.

As I've mentioned, I've come to think of what we do as more long-term capital than private equity – if you're going by the Western markets definition of private equity, that is. What we do is really entrepreneurship and long-term investments on a large scale, and, unlike family conglomerates, we're willing to sell those businesses at the right time. In this sense, transformation into an investment company-type model may be a natural evolution for private equity players in our part of the world who are willing – as we are – to be aggressive strategic emerging markets players across high-potential industries.

MB: Could you follow the US model and also get into investment banking?

HE-K: I would imagine that it is a recipe for conflict, especially in the scope of the investment banking business. Maybe you could split them totally and they don't have anything to do with each other or split the management, but I don't see the two sitting together easily.

MB: Are there any themes that interest you that your current OSFs are not exploiting?

HE-K: Healthcare and education are a couple of areas that you could easily think of, and more or less, those are the two areas where we want to make investments but we have not; but at this point in time we are going to focus on making sure that the performance of our existing investments is top-notch as opposed to adding more. We have a vast array of fantastic investments. We need to get them working together and working properly before we think about making additional investments. We have plenty of investment opportunities within our existing platform companies, and the risk-return is very favourable because those are investments that you know: you have diligenced them and you have been working with them for the last three or four years, so why make an investment in a new industry when you have plenty of fantastic investments that you can do within existing platforms?

MB: How were you affected by the Arab Spring and its aftermath?

HE-K: It added an additional layer of uncertainty. Historically, when people came to talk to us about investing in Egypt, they were talking only about the opportunities. Almost nobody talked about politics, and if they did, they wanted reinforcement that Gamal Mubarak was coming after his father. And of course, in the short term the macro-economic environment in Egypt has deteriorated.

But otherwise, the impact on private equity has not been as great as expected for two reasons. One is that we did not have any investments in Syria, Yemen or Libya, the three other countries that had the most serious impacts from the Arab Spring. Two, financing is probably more available now than prior to the revolution, because the DFIs want to help the countries, so you find more commitments to investing in our part of the world. So actually, they have stepped up to that commitment and they have made a serious difference in making financing available for a lot of our projects.

The area which was impacted the most was our own balance sheet, because we were relying on either exits which are not going to be forthcoming or on dividends that were going to come from companies we invested in that have experienced short-term trading challenges. We had to strengthen our own balance sheet by doing three things. The first was a $175 million rights issue. The second was that one of the DFIs worked with us to achieve a further $150 million debt facility. And the third is that we've made some minor divestments.

MB: I understand that liquidity of all kinds can be quite volatile in many emerging markets; I assume that's why your expected exits have not taken place over the past couple of years.

HE-K: In order to have exits, even if your exits are trade sales, you need to have equity markets buoyant, because that provides the comps [comparators] that you are exiting relative to, and you need to have very strong commercial debt markets in order to give your buyer the acquisition finance at the level they need. When the two systems come back, there will be good exits, but when that will be I don't know.

MB: I guess this links in to your strategic discussions about whether to become an investment holding company, at least in part. Taking the Rift Valley Railway and Nile Logistics as an example, in due course you could sell them to someone like Deutsche Bahn, or you could keep them and be valued on a multiple of free cash-flows; but if you are operating in a relatively volatile market, there's a risk that the time when the business is strategically ready to be sold may not coincide with when the market is right for such a sale, resulting in capital being tied up unproductively while you miss out on other opportunities – which may point toward the latter having merits.

HE-K: Yes, because even for multinationals, it's difficult to get an exit if the local comps are weak.

Conclusion

An observation cropped up in my interview with CDC's Managing Director for Africa, Rod Evison, that merits revisiting: 'While money is the ultimate commodity, it can be differentiated by the hands through which it passes.' Evison made this comment in the context of his organisation's impact on environmental and social governance, but I believe that there are a number of other ways in which money can be affected by the identity and actions of its provider. Together, they go to the heart of why private equity in the developed world lost its way in the middle of the last decade, but also why the industry holds the potential to enjoy a bright future in terms of both economic returns and its contribution to society.

Many of my interviewees were publicly critical of the US and European buyout mega-funds; some were even more forthright off the record. If I had to identify the two most commonly occurring complaints, they would be these: first, that there's no skill in buying an 'on-market' business by being the top bidder in an auction process and then relying on high leverage and a rising market to generate returns greater than those of the public markets; and second, that these funds not only sowed the seeds of their own under-performance in the downturn, but because they are so large, their dismal returns since 2008 have resulted in the industry as a whole being stigmatised.

In essence, the mega-buyout funds stand accused of failing to differentiate their capital. However, that accusation could equally be directed towards much of the rest of the industry. I doubt anyone could read the interviews in this book and not conclude that the best private equity firms add value to their capital and hence to investee businesses by the pursuit of differentiated strategies and operational capabilities. But does the public, and do governments and regulators, understand and appreciate this distinction? In other words, is the better firms' capital differentiated in the eyes of wider stakeholders, as opposed to the managements of their portfolio businesses and the more active and engaged of their limited partners?

The industry has so far fought shy of openly distancing itself from the worst excesses of the handful of big firms. Wol Kolade, who chaired the BVCA when the then Labour government very publicly accused private equity of asset-stripping and shedding jobs and getting rich on the proceeds, described the dilemma thus:

> I could honestly say, 'I don't recognise what you are saying, it's not like that in my day job. And I'm a private equity guy. You're tarring us all with the same brush.' The trouble is, you can't just say to them that they should just be talking about a small group of people such as Blackstone, that they shouldn't be using the words private equity to describe the actions of the big buyout firms, because it means they'll just go and have an argument with them separately...
>
> For a while the industry as a whole did very well and it seemed as if private equity was magic, but actually it was a combination of a lot of hard graft and the fact that a lot of people, particularly at the top end, were using a lot of debt. But when debt doesn't work, it really takes you to the cleaners.

Kolade's firm, ISIS Equity Partners, has among the most meticulously thought-through and best-resourced approaches to identifying and approaching potential investment opportunities and creating value in portfolio companies of any of the firms I've covered, and it does not use a lot of debt. I would argue that its performance not only illustrates its founder's point about long-run returns coming from hard graft but also demonstrates that it is dependent on other factors present in his business but which he is perhaps too modest to highlight: strategic, operational and inter-personal insights that result in the creation of genuine enterprise value.

But in the developed world, in recent years, this emphasis on value creation by private equity has been in the background, except in the niches where high leverage is unavailable or inappropriate (or both): growth, where Kolade operates, and turnaround, where the alternative to rescue by a specialist private equity firm is normally the closure of the business. The challenge for the industry is that, while it can and should highlight success stories in these niches, there are many examples of profitable exits having been achieved without significant value creation at the level of the portfolio company, through financial engineering, and plenty more where that tool has led to bad outcomes.

So while differentiation through PR and stakeholder communications by those managers that create genuine value would doubtless help them attract capital and deal-flow – and, in the case of a handful of managers, such as Steve Klinsky's New Mountain Capital, to make the moral case for the firm's contribution to society – it may be difficult for the industry in its totality to reposition itself until the controversial deals have either exited or fallen apart and, if the latter, enough time has passed for memories to fade. And if interest rates remain low for as long as I suspect they might, and with banks continuing to restructure debt in 'extend and pretend' exercises, the threat of big buyout insolvencies could be hanging over the industry for some while.

The trouble is, as central banks in the developed world have created additional liquidity to recapitalise their banks and sovereigns, there must be lingering doubts about whether in time this liquidity will feed through into the real economy in a spectacular fashion and lead to the creation of the next bubble. Before that happens, there may be merit in Jon Moulton's suggestion that government should limit the amount of debt interest that can be expensed pre-tax. As things stand, the fiscal policies of most countries provide a perverse incentive to favour debt over equity financing and to downplay the importance of dividends as recompense to investors for providing the latter.

Should legislation not be forthcoming – and change is unlikely, since it would be difficult for any one country to introduce such a rule unilaterally – I wonder whether the private equity industry should consider introducing a voluntary code of conduct to which reputable firms might sign up and which LPs might encourage those firms to adhere to as a condition of receiving investment. Such a package need not limit the amount of leverage in acquisition structures, provided managers undertake to provide further equity money should it subsequently be required. Similarly, in the absence of legislation, a code of conduct or tighter legislation limiting claims for treatment as capital gains to only those forms of income that represent a genuine return on a partner's invested and risked capital, would help rehabilitate the industry's public image.

In emerging markets, where debt is much harder to secure, but where economic growth is generally higher (if more volatile), private equity investment is premised on active engagement with exceptional businesses that offer the potential, with the provision of the right expertise and/or capital, to grow even faster, and be less volatile, than the market. And while businesses in high-growth countries can be very fully priced, the best fund managers successfully differentiate themselves and their capital, and are hence able to buy in at sensible valuations.

As I wrote the last two paragraphs, I wondered whether it is any longer appropriate to talk about the developed and developing worlds as binary concepts. Are Shanghai, Mumbai, São Paulo or Lagos less developed than Athens, Detroit, Hull or Belfast? In terms of infrastructure and a social safety net, which arguably reflect a nation's historic rather than current or future affluence, perhaps; but measured by growth prospects, diversification and income per capita on a purchasing power parity basis, I'd argue the fundamentals of the most successful parts of so-called emerging economies are either ahead of the more challenged areas in the supposedly developed countries or are set to surpass them very soon.

Just as entrepreneurs in high-growth countries are keen to pick up insights gained in Western business schools or through experience working in the West – factors commonplace among private equity professionals in those markets – so, I believe, developed-market private equity can learn from and adapt the experiences of practitioners in the parts of the world where the industry is relatively new and has developed new approaches. If nothing else, with the banks in much of the western world currently trying to strengthen their balance sheets, the ability for private equity to deploy large amounts of debt, or the willingness of corporates to do so, may be impaired for some time, so there has to be merit in listening to those who have operated in places where it has never been on the table in large quantities, and indeed where equity capital also has been harder to come by.

I'll provide a (contentious) example. The mega-funds have been criticised for their management fees and for making rash investment decisions. In the short term, they will continue to invest the $1 trillion or thereabouts of 'dry powder' committed in the boom. Even with extension periods, those commitments will start to fall away pretty sharply in 2013 and will largely have expired two years later. Given the managers' performances over the preceding decade, it will be hard for them to raise new funds on anything like the same scale, not just because of concerns over returns but also because most of the big North American LPs are over-exposed to the sector and many of those working for them are wary of being seen as advocates for such funds, given the pay-to-play scandals, and because solvency regulations are making it hard for many other types of investor to increase their commitments.

But opportunities to do large buyouts will continue to present themselves. The obvious solution is to fund them much as Citadel Capital does in Egypt, on a per-project basis, with LPs as co-investors, or even for LPs to put together their own deals. The big Canadian pension funds are already progressing along this route, with OMERS targeting internal management of 90 per cent of its capital by the end of 2012. While it is legitimate to question whether public bodies are willing to provide sufficient remuneration and alignment of economic incentives to hire and retain people capable of making such decisions or to resource themselves adequately to due-diligence such transactions, even imperfect management of such direct investments could perhaps be preferable to signing up to a 10–14-year commitment to a closed-end fund when there are reservations about how the capital may be deployed, succession planning within the fund's management or the fee structure and the incentives it creates.

Hisham El-Khazindar's observation that he can fund a platform company – which can entail a commitment of $250 million, a typical deal size for a mid-market buyout in Europe or the equity cheque for a larger, leveraged one in the USA – in 72 hours to a week, based on personal relationships, points up another difference between the developing world's private equity firms and many of those in mature economies: 'A system that is built on a trust relationship that is created over a long period of time', is how he describes it. And the same can be said of deal-flow and of deciding which entrepreneurs to back. Here's Warburg Pincus's Niten Malhan on relationships with managements:

> As minority investors, we spend a lot of time with the entrepreneur to really understand what is the ultimate objective of the guy, not just in relation to the exit, but, ultimately, to governance. That doesn't mean we will not have disagreements along the way, but we must have enough conviction to say that the thought process of the individual is rational, is based on facts and taking account of the reality on the ground and that history has been somewhat consistent in getting us some comfort that he has behaved in a certain way. I think that's the element of art, in addition to the business analysis, of a potential investment in India [...]
>
> This applies on the other side as well because, from the perspective of an entrepreneur who is selling a portion of his business, if he is smart and if he is thinking about it the right way, his criteria for evaluating investors ought therefore to be not simply the price that he can get for his asset or for a portion of his asset, but also who it is that he's inviting into his company. And I think that over time, as more investors play for longer in India, the conduct of different investors will be clearer. There will be differentiation and entrepreneurs will be asking, 'OK, so who are the investors that have truly been good partners to companies? And who are investors that have essentially not been good partners, because their conduct has not been fair or because they've panicked when things have not gone well or even though for all their talk about being long-term investors, they haven't behaved in that manner?'

Malhan's observations could be dismissed as being relevant solely to minority deals in countries where the legal systems are stigmatised as being slow and bureaucratic. But as a number of emerging-market GPs have said, it doesn't matter how good the courts are: the minute you have to rely on them to assert your position as an investor, the deal has gone bad. So even in the most efficient jurisdictions, and with control transactions, there is much that GPs could adapt from the ways in which their peers in developing countries reach out and establish relationships with management teams and make assessments of their motivations and capabilities based on establishing relationships over a period of time, prior to transacting.

Where auction processes are run by corporate finance houses and a management buyout is one of a number of possible outcomes, advisers to vendors traditionally try to keep managements apart from potential backers. This seems to me a short-sighted approach, because, although there may be times when a deeper understanding of management by private equity may lead to a negative assessment and hence a low-ball or no offer – in the current, cautious climate that is all too often financial buyers' default position, in any case – so co-operating with management and their advisers to facilitate relationships with private equity ought to serve the interests of enlightened vendors by helping build confidence in financial buyers to achieve attractive transaction prices.

Alignment of interests, both economic and non-economic, are what private equity, at its best, does well. I believe it is the most fundamental reason for believing that the industry will recover in developed markets and continue to grow in emerging ones. After all, what are the alternatives? Ownership by founders and their descendants is the only model in which management and shareholders are perfectly aligned, since they are one and the same. But it has its flaws: such firms must choose between low growth or dependence on debt finance, which entails risk and can be hard to obtain; and there can be suc-cession challenges, as many of the much-envied German *Mittelstand* firms have discovered in recent years. And owner management can be a poor servant of the interests of other stakeholders, not least employees and society, because illiquid shareholders may favour high dividends and low growth over the longer-term creation of enterprise value, which in the long run brings with it additional employment and tax revenues.

But it is the dominant model of large business ownership in developed mar-kets that I think warrants the closest comparison with private equity. Over the past two decades, I would argue, there has been a de-coupling of economic alignment between the owners of public companies and their managements. Certainly, share prices have stagnated since the Millennium, a period during which executive compensation has soared.

A number of factors have contributed to this. First, there has been a rise in, initially, professional fund management and, subsequently, its electronic equiv-alent, exchange-traded funds (ETFs); these create a barrier between the ultimate beneficial owner of a share and the management engaged to act on its behalf. The remaining private direct investors now trade mainly through online plat-forms that hold shares in nominee accounts, which have the effect of depriving the investor of the opportunity to attend AGMs and vote on board resolutions.

Second, the growth in hedge funds and algorithmic trading means that the typical holding period of a share has plummeted. Robust data are impossi-ble to obtain, but I've been told that more than half the shares traded on the London Stock Exchange are transacted electronically, with the figure for New York being closer to 90 per cent, and that the average hold periods are now around nine and six months respectively. Few shares, and even fewer quoted companies, therefore have long-term owners who are interested in engaging with management about future strategies or taking a short-term hit in earnings or dividends in return for long-term value creation. Indeed, with the growth in short positions, at any given time a substantial proportion of the people that have an economic interest in a firm would prefer it to do badly than to prosper – a perverse situation from society's perspective.

Third, even active fund managers are increasingly reluctant to engage: when asked how he would respond if he reached the conclusion, ahead of the market, that a management team was flawed, a highly respected investor, interviewed off the record for this book, responded that he would sell his holding and consider re-investing after market sentiment had caught up. He was not averse to challenging the management, but he saw his, and his investors', economic interests being best served by taking a capital gain (or avoiding a loss) rather than doing a lot of work with no certainty of a return and with others gaining a 'free ride' from his efforts.

Finally, given the transience of managements and of shareholders, the best mechanics yet developed to align interests are relatively short-term, potentially jeopardising long-run value creation and opening up the possibility of being 'gamed' by managements. In particular, while such incentives reward executives for value creation when things are going well, their interests are misaligned with shareholders in difficult times, when only the latter suffer real capital losses. If share options are under water and bonuses unlikely to be triggered, it is in management's interests to suck in as much bad news as possible and manage earnings and the share price down as low as they are able, in order to re-base the incentivisation plans for the next period.

Of course, this Anglo-American, shareholder-based model is not the only one applicable to public companies: there's also the (essentially Germanic) stakeholder one, in which the executive board reports to a supervisory committee that represents not only shareholders but also other interested parties, such as workers and local or even national government. While this adds a longer-term perspective, it seems to me to introduce a additional layer of agency costs in that it empowers a group of people who are not providers of long-term capital but who seek the furtherance of their interests by influencing management to act in their interests rather than serving the equity providers. In theory, a supervisory board comprising major shareholders and answerable to investors might be a preferable governance model, but of course it would face the challenge that much of the shareholder base of quoted companies – at least in developed markets – is transient, and those that are long-term are largely disenfranchised.

In contrast, ownership by private equity provides a company with a highly concentrated and motivated shareholder that has a relatively narrow range of other investments, deep business expertise and significant legal and relational influence. In most instances, the economic interests of the individual investment professionals exercising that influence are relatively well aligned with those of the ultimate providers of the capital, in that they want to achieve the highest possible internal rate of return on the equity component of the deal between two fixed events: the dates of the buy-in (or buyout) and the subsequent divestment. And, perhaps as important as all of the foregoing, management incentivisation is typically also aligned with the ultimate capital providers' IRRs.

I am not suggesting that the private equity model is perfect. Some hard-to-justify sweeteners crept into the terms of partnership agreements when the balance of power swung in GPs' favour in the boom, such as transaction fees and deal-by-deal carry on closed-end funds. And there remain structural imperfections, such as the relative lack of power of LPs, who are by their nature geographically dispersed and disparate in nature, interests and skills, to challenge GPs in areas such as the extension of investing and realisation periods – which has led to the creation of the so-called 'zombie funds' – or in their investment decisions.

But outside the industry, it is the total amount of GPs' remuneration that courts controversy, rather than the partnership structure or the detail of partnership agreements. I'm referring, of course, to the famous – or infamous – 'two and 20' model.

Many, if not all, of the funds I've featured in this book take very proactive approaches to the identification of acquisition or investment targets, often building up relationships long before they deploy capital, or have to kiss a lot of frogs to find their princes or princesses. They also tend to be very hands-on in the value-creation activities of those companies, in some cases seconding their own people to those firms, temporarily or even permanently, and in others hiring separate operational improvement teams – a growing trend – in additional to their deal-sourcing and executional people. These are all additional costs, and together suggest that the 'two' – the 2 per cent annual management fee – may be fully justified and may well represent the true running costs of their businesses (and, indeed, some provide audited financials to substantiate this).

But there are plenty of firms for which this is not the case, for which management fees are a source of significant personal enrichment and a drag on investors' returns. The big buyout firms are an easy target here: while their management fees are typically 1 or 1.5 per cent per annum, in recognition of the larger amounts of capital deployed, over ten to 14 years on a $20 billion fund this represents a total of between $2 billion and $4.2 billion. And of course, such firms run multiple funds, each of which generates its own set of fees, despite senior management, back office and some investment professionals being split across several funds. It is difficult to accept that this reflects the true cost of running such a firm, a view that is strengthened by the fact that the general partners in such businesses have been quick to monetise expected future cash-flows through the public markets.

Even a mid-market European buyout house would appear to do rather well on management fees: a typical £1 billion fund with a 2 per cent annual charge generates £20 million a year from this source; a firm that raises a ten-year fund every three years would have more than three times that sum at its disposal each year to pay and accommodate perhaps ten partners and a further ten to 20 salaried analysts and support staff and pay fees on aborted deals to those professional advisors not working on contingency-based agreements.

In practice, few partners draw the kinds of annual profit shares that these numbers might suggest, not least because many sacrifice much of the potential current income for enhanced economics in their funds. While this reassures LPs, by increasing the incentive for GPs to deliver high IRRs for investors, paradoxically it also makes it harder for them to do so by increasing the total proportion of the total returns that go to the GP rather than LPs. In an environment in which raising new funds in developed markets remains difficult, I am surprised there aren't experienced teams who have done well enough on past carry to have achieved financial freedom that are offering to manage investors' capital solely for the carried interest on new funds. This would not only improve the IRR for the benefit of both LPs and the GP but would also eliminate the 'zombie fund' misalignment of interests.

It would be heartening, too, to see LPs be more accepting of the formation of funds by people new to the industry. No matter how much due diligence is done into a fund's management, past performance is an imperfect guide to the future, and an over-emphasis on giving wide discretion to proven managers rather than working with potentially capable newcomers on a tighter rein does a disservice to the ultimate providers and beneficiaries of the capital – mostly current and future pensioners on modest incomes – because it acts as a barrier to market entry and thus reduces the downward pressure on fees that ought to be accompanying a period in which capital has become scarce and returns depressed.

Carry, too, is an area in which there can be some misalignment of interests. Typically the threshold above which the GP starts participating is 8 per cent; as Endless LLP's founder Garry Wilson argued, this figure has not reduced, despite the fact that much of the world now inhabits an environment in which the cost of capital has slumped since that number was arrived at, and is expected to remain low for an extended period. I think his view that the share of carried interest that GPs receive should be layered depending on the levels of return is an interesting one. Combined with the first part of his suggestion, it has the attraction of retaining an economic incentive for GPs to achieve a positive level of return for investors at a point at which they could currently, recognising they were unlikely to hit the hurdle rate, either walk away or defer exits to live on the management fees, while also reserving the opportunity for the truly exceptional value-creators to make the super returns that they deserve and which will hopefully encourage them to remain in the industry rather than taking their talents elsewhere.

There are other, more detailed, areas in which the model may be imperfect. For instance, several investment professionals and limited partner representatives that I spoke to in the course of researching the book raised, off the record, disquiet about how economic interest in a fund, and management authority, is dispersed within a general partnership. Many GPs are started by one charismatic, high-profile individual. The smartest of these recognise that everyone has shortcomings and so surround themselves with people with complementary skills, providing their teams with sufficient economic interest to remain loyal and incentivised and giving them, collectively, sufficient governance power to ensure that the strategic direction of the partnership and its investment decisions are not driven by one person.

While LP advisory committees are now fairly widespread, their terms of reference are narrow (seldom do they go much beyond consultations on potential waivers of provisions in partnership agreements), and it may be that with the shift in the balance of power between LPs and GPs, the former will in due course become more assertive – a move that is probably in the best interests of those on whose behalf they manage capital.

Some of the best practice in corporate governance from GPs currently is demonstrated by firms such as Abraaj and Actis that specialise in emerging markets – both because it is demanded by DFIs and, as several of my interviewees have explained, because in countries where governance standards are customarily fairly low, there exists the potential for what I call 'governance arbitrage': namely, buying companies that multinationals would not touch because of ESG concerns and then implementing world-class governance standards, thereby opening up the possibility of exiting to a category of well-funded buyer that had previously shied away.

While the influence of DFIs on governance, both at the GP level and in portfolio companies in emerging markets, is overwhelmingly positive, I detected reservations – especially off the record – from some GPs about CDC's revised geographical and developmental focus, and concern that it might spread to other DFIs. However, good GPs continue to be able to raise capital from private LPs for other emerging-market strategies, and there would still appear to be a gap between those strategies and areas in which commercial returns may well be achievable while also achieving significant social benefits in communities where there is an absence of capital from other sources. This leads me to think that CDC's new approach, while controversial, may well achieve the desired goals. But I hope the organisation will monitor closely the impact of the changes: Africa, in particular, receives a tiny proportion of the capital committed to private equity globally but arguably has the greatest need of capital, and any suggestion that any restrictions in the availability of DFI money was resulting in private investment being withheld should, in my view, be met with flexibility.

In developed markets, the big picture will, of course, for some time be dominated by the fate of the mega buyouts completed near the peak of the market. While those firms' diversification is a well-established trend, it will be interesting to see how the mid-market buyout firms respond. Many in the USA are doing well, as corporations de-leverage by selling off non-core business units at historically attractive prices. There has been less of that in Europe – so far, at least – and there are currently, on the face of it, more firms of that size – in London especially – than can easily be supported by the likely deal-flow, and many will not raise new funds. Already a number are in zombie mode or have themselves become targets secondary funds; my guess is that, as the market thins, the best will prosper, perhaps up-weighting their emphasis on growth and the provision of development capital.

While it seems likely that private equity in the developed world may never again achieve the scale that it reached in 2007/8, I think there's an argument for saying that this is a good thing, that capital is like food: too much of it, especially of the wrong kind, can be as harmful as too little. With hindsight, too much money was poured into the industry in the USA and Europe as part of the great global disequilibrium in capital flows brought about by the global trade and currency imbalances of that time, and in particular, debt was too widely available, with in many cases little oversight or caution exercised by lenders, and as a result was deployed incautiously.

Today we're at the opposite end of the spectrum, with the two positive notes being that more capital is flowing into some, if not yet all, emerging markets, where its social impact is incalculable, and that the economic imperative to generate returns without use of high leverage is handing a competitive advantage to the developed-market firms that have been honing that approach all along, while forcing the rest of the industry to adapt quickly.

In this context it seems appropriate to close with a quotation from Mustafa Abdel-Wadood from Abraaj. In response to my question about what GPs in emerged economies could learn from those in developing ones, he said the following:

> I think it's something they knew but perhaps forgot as leverage became easy, which is that the role that private equity plays is to bridge a specific period in the life-cycle of the business. That role often involves active support around the growth strategies of that business; it's not purely about financial engineering. I think it's not a lesson they don't know; it's something they know but conveniently forgot.